AF505491

MARY OBERING

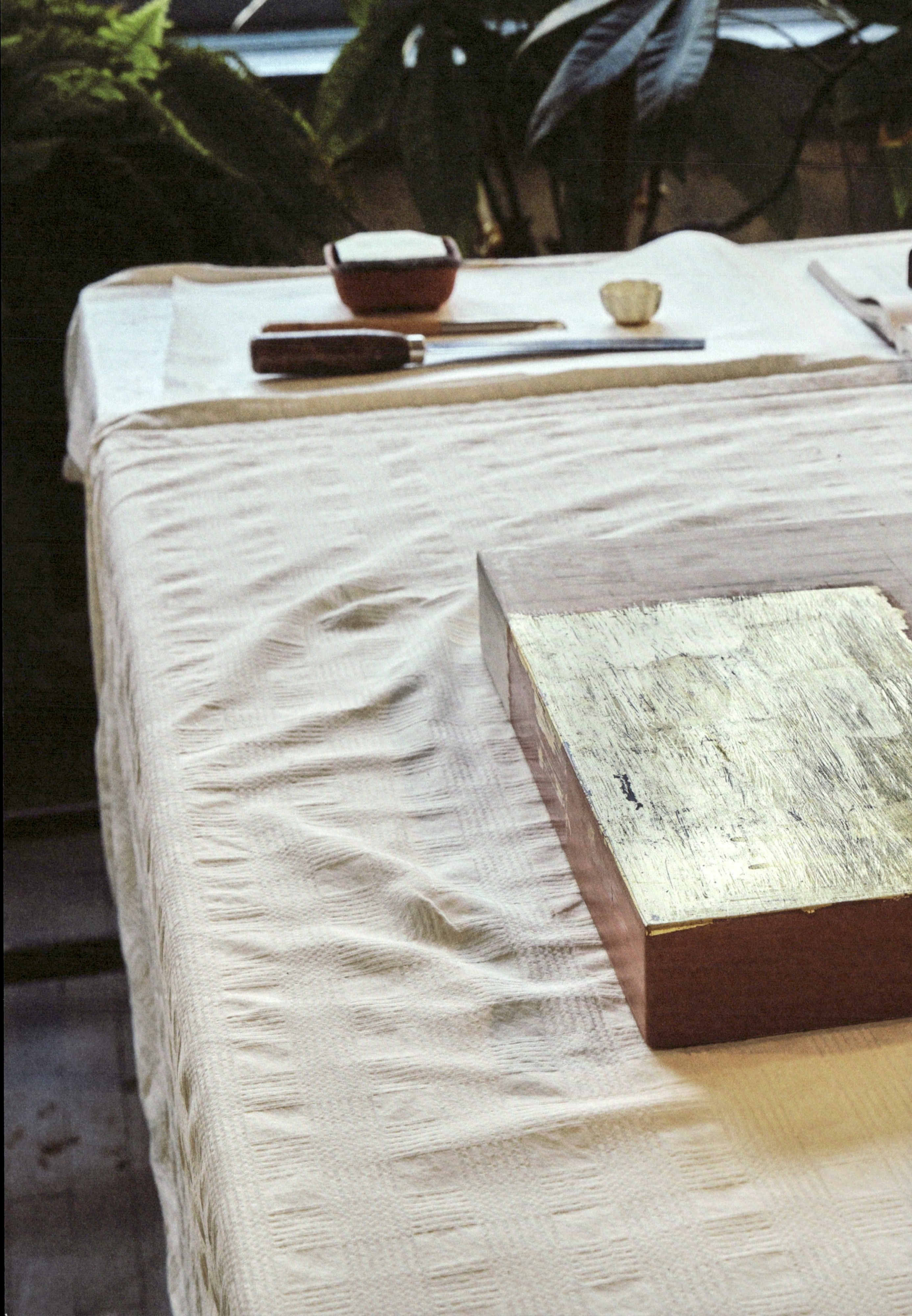

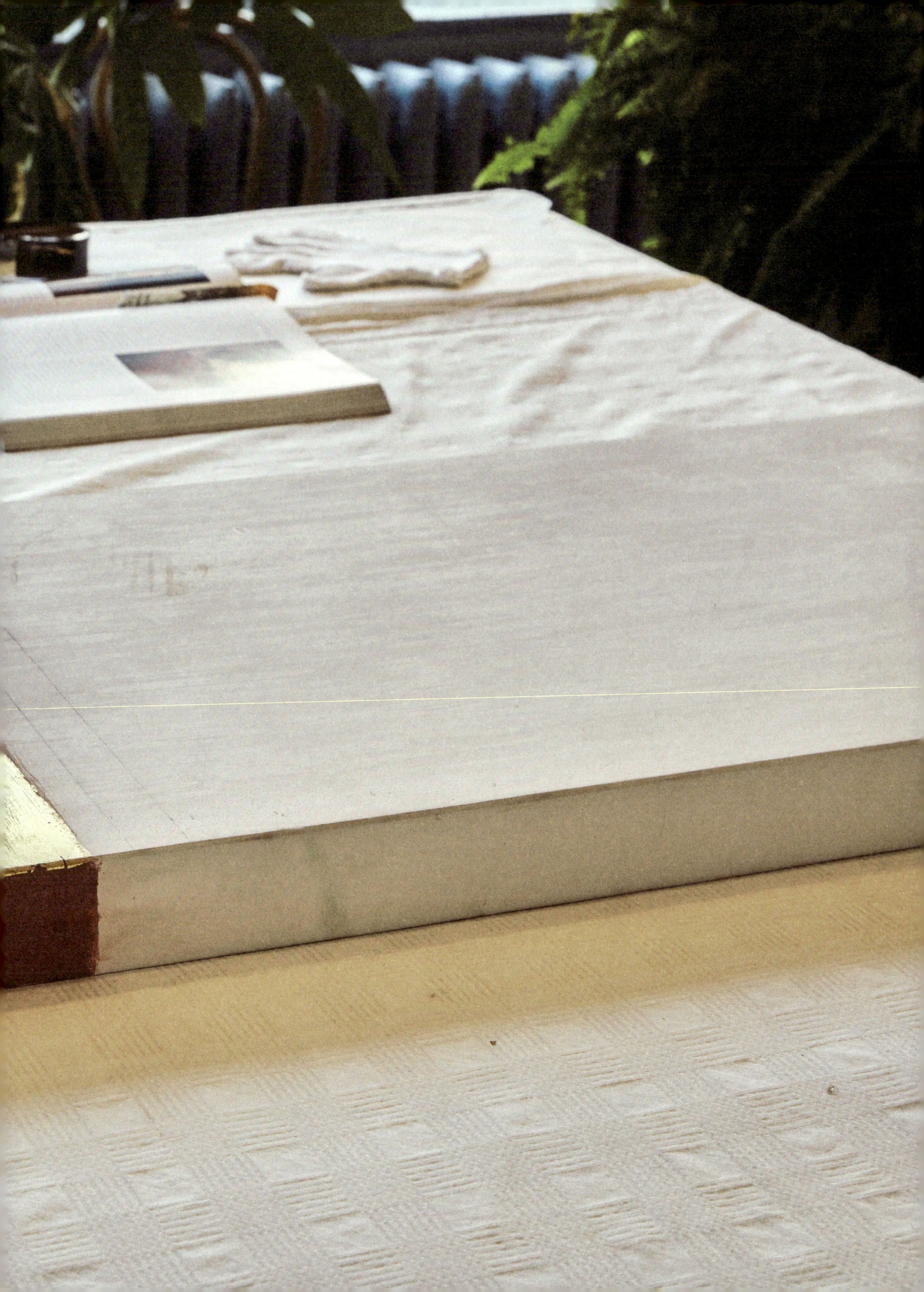

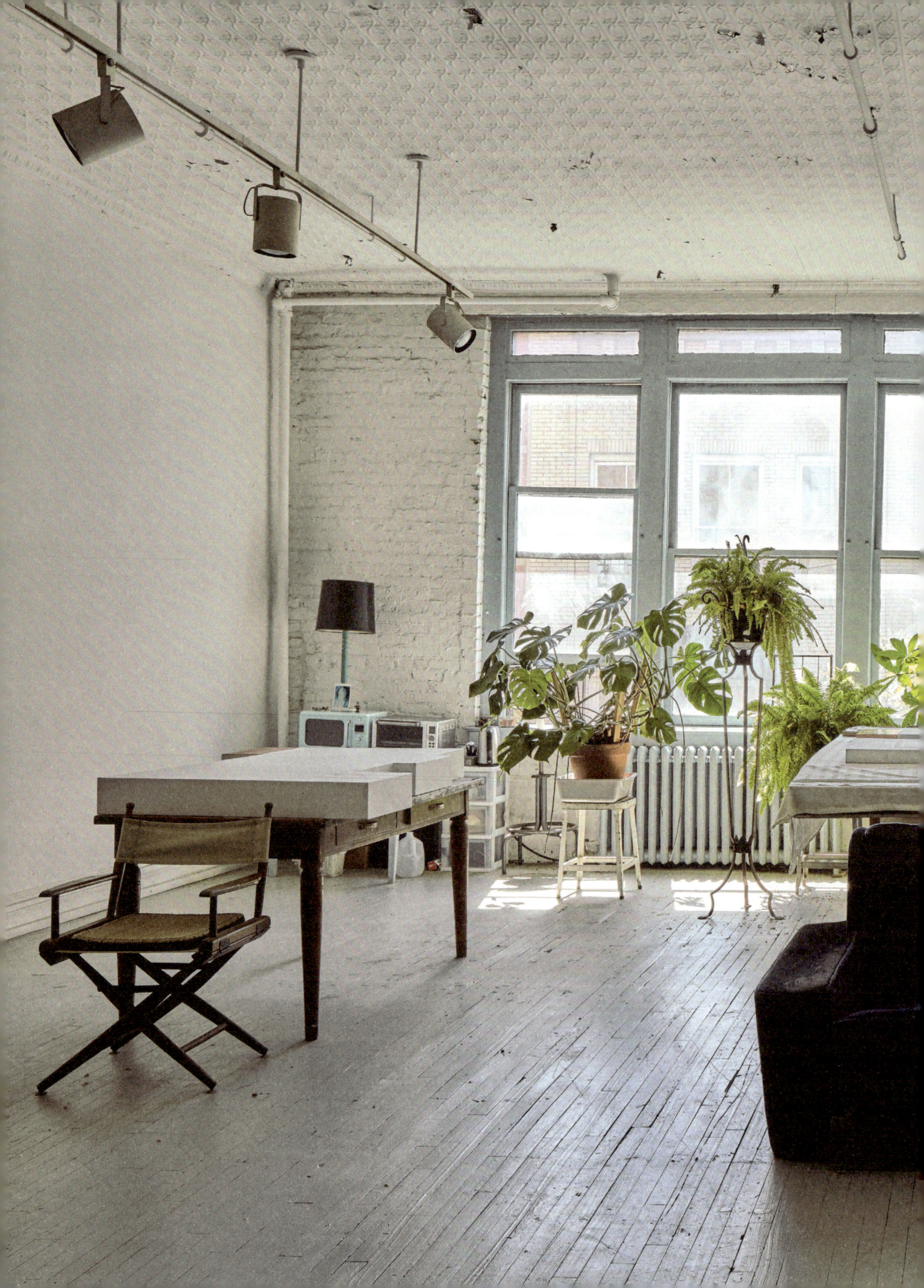

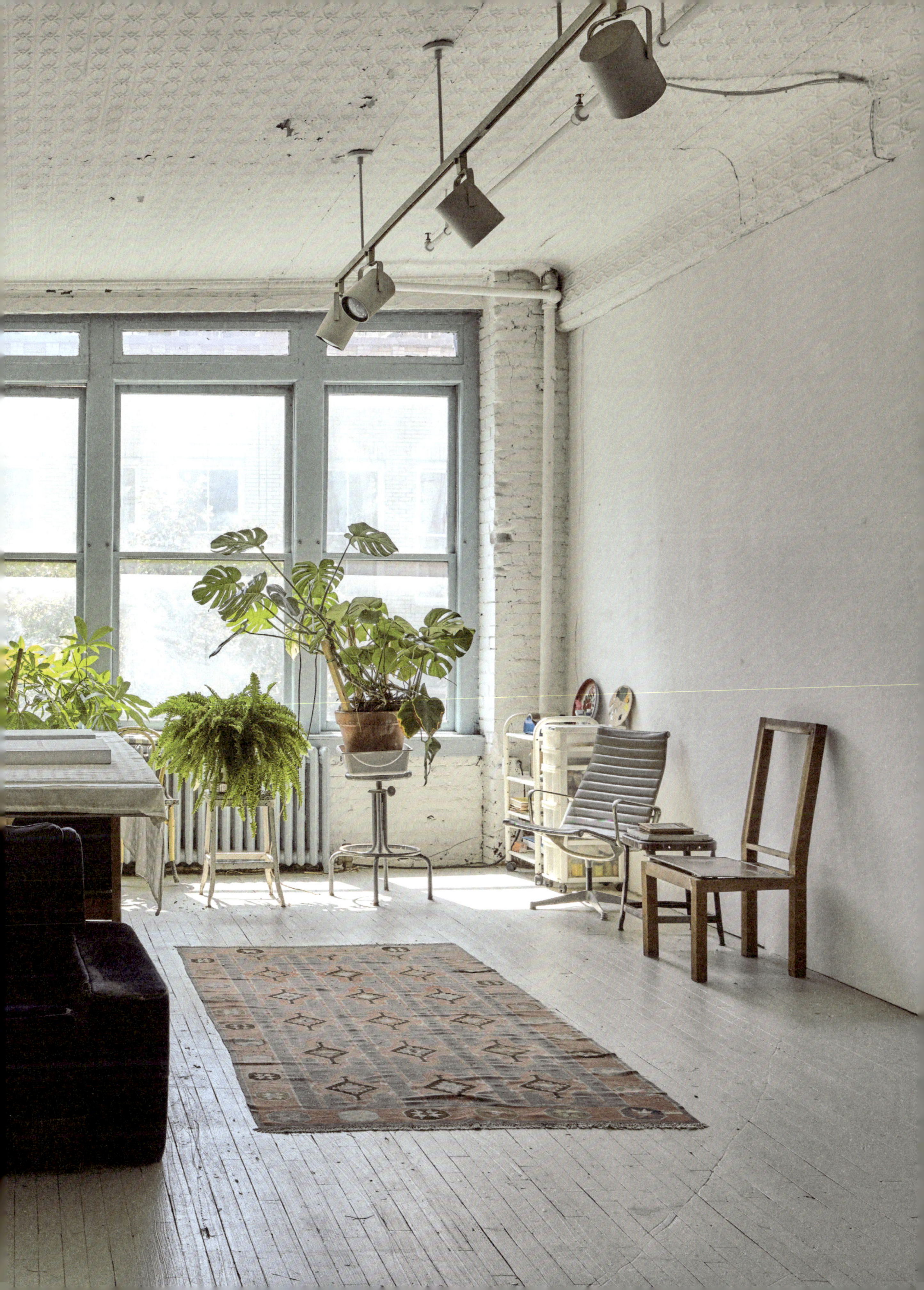

INVENTORY PRESS   **BORTOLAMI**   Kayne Griffin

MARY OBERING

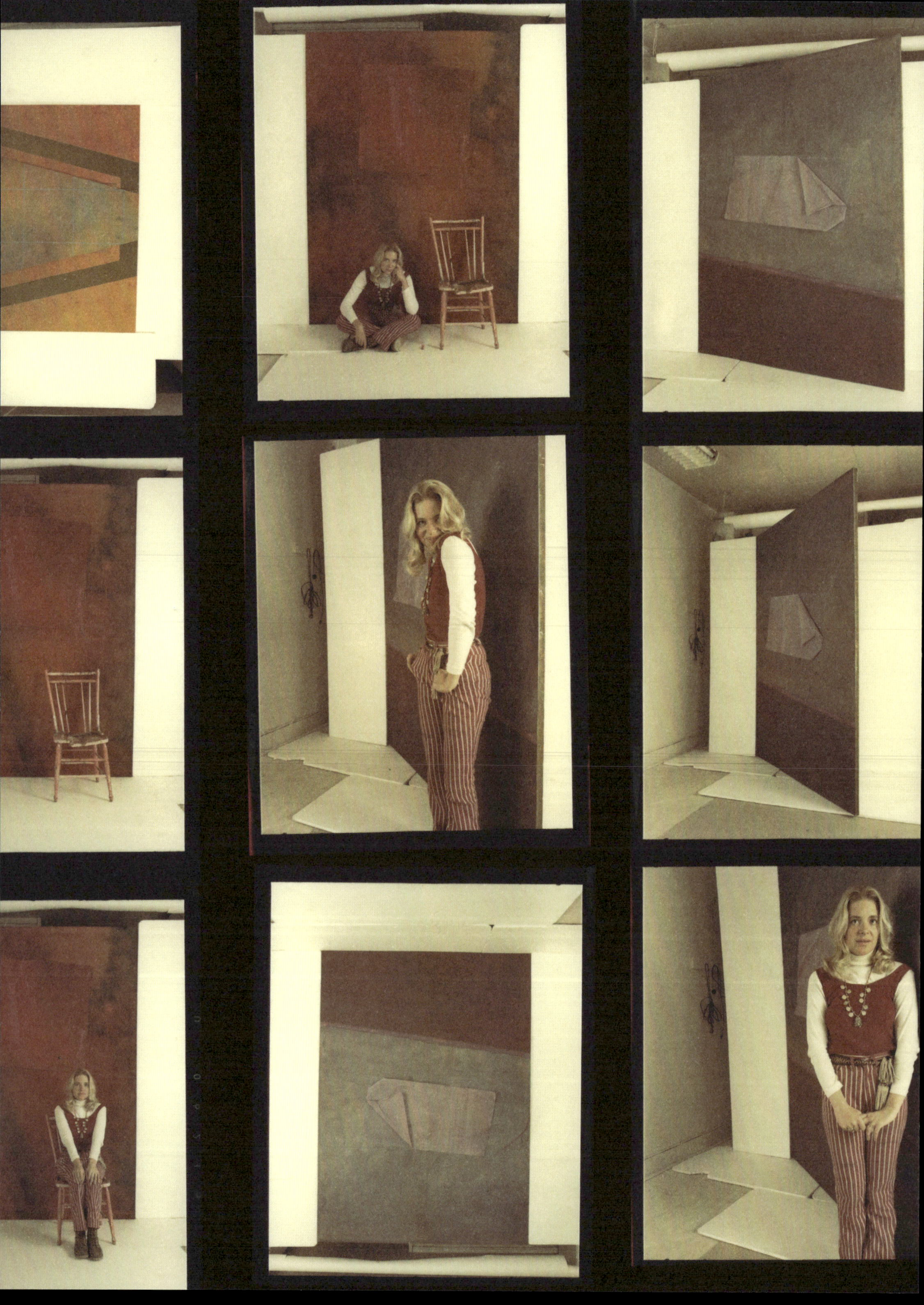

FOREWORD

LYNN ZELEVANSKY

Born in 1937 in Shreveport, Louisiana, Mary Obering arrived in New York City in 1971, settling in Soho, the center of vanguard art at the time. She had graduated from Hollins College in Virginia in three years, majoring in experimental psychology, and had studied with B. F. Skinner at Radcliffe (then the women's college associated with all-male Harvard), before realizing that she was an artist. She attended art school at Denver University in Colorado and left for New York soon after graduation, bringing her young daughter with her.

There she was surrounded by a community that shared her interests and values, including friends Carl Andre, Sol LeWitt, Donald Judd, and Marcia Haffif, as well as her fellow Louisianan, the well-connected curator, art advisor, and collector, Janie C. Lee. Obering was an active member of the community, and she showed with gallerists whose programs were central to contemporary art discourse at the time, including John Weber, Annina Nosei, and Julian Pretto. She exhibited in Europe as well, but major recognition eluded her. Happily, she is now receiving renewed attention.

From the beginning, Obering was a painter of geometric abstractions. Her graduate school thesis shows her to be sophisticated, and many of her concerns of that time remained central to her art. Her initial influences included Henri Matisse and Marc Rothko because of their use of color. She became an original colorist, able to work with hues such as dull browns that in other contexts would be lifeless, but in her hands were surprisingly complex. The influence of early Minimalism is evident from her thesis. She wrote that she didn't want to make a statement about her work: "I think my art can stand or fall on its own," she noted. Its "meaning or lack thereof (depending on the viewer) comes from the only place it can—the art object."[1] Like the strategies of repetition, modularity, and geometric form, which play an important role in Obering's art, the notion that all meaning resides in the work itself and not in any external associations to it was also integral to Minimalism. The same is true of the idea that the viewer completes the artwork, giving it meaning, which Obering expresses in the parenthetical comment above. Although the first Minimalists were half a generation older than she was and had come to prominence years before she appeared on the scene, they would become the colleagues to whom she related most.

Obering was a presence in the New York art world, but it was her practice rather than her career that sustained her.[2] This may have had something to do with why, active though she was, lasting

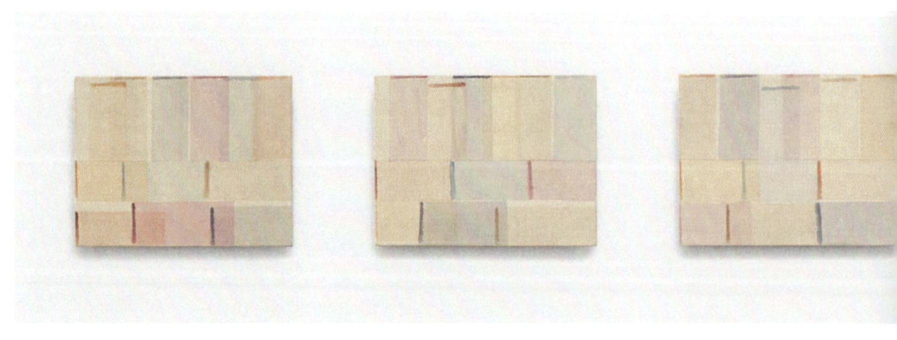

1 Mary McLean Obering, *Untitled,* MFA thesis, University of Denver, June 1971.

2 Katherine Driscoll, Studio Director at Mary Obering Studio, in conversation with Obering's daughter Amanda Obering, July 6, 2021.

3 Author interview with Carolee Schneeman, Los Angeles, March 14, 1996. Quoted in Lynn Zelevansky, "Driving Image: Yayoi Kusama in New York," in *Love Forever: Yayoi Kusama*, exh. cat. (Los Angeles: Los Angeles County Museum of Art, 1998), 24.

4 Driscoll and Obering, 2021.

recognition eluded her. And, although second wave feminism was burgeoning in the early 1970s, it was just the beginning of a serious struggle, and bias against women artists was still profound. Carolee Schneeman, a pioneer of performance art, recalled that just a short time before Obering arrived in New York, women artists often felt the need to affiliate with interesting men to get attention and even then, the attention wasn't the most desirable kind: "You could be an artist, but you were [really] a kind of … mascot. You had to be good looking."[3] It would take decades for women artists to make real headway.

Feminism brought with it AIR, the first female artist-run gallery in the United States, located in Soho. In 1982 and '83, Obering participated in group shows there, yet she did not consider herself a feminist. Like a number of women who had achieved a degree success at that time, she wanted to be seen as an "artist" not as a "female artist."[4]

Obering was not a joiner and her interests never aligned with the most current art trends or ideologies. While hard-edge painting and Minimalism still had great currency in the 1970s and '80s, by the time that she arrived in New York, they were no longer new. Various forms of post-Minimalism and Conceptual art had taken their place, and they brought serious attention to a few women, among them Yayoi Kusama, Eva Hesse, and Linda Benglis, who made art that focused on the body, was sensual and sometimes overtly sexual, and was experimental with mediums and genres; very different from Obering's work. She was a painter in the 1970s, when painting was said to be dead.

She knew that she had to go her own way and, in the middle of that decade, her work took an unexpected turn. Her love of Italian Renaissance and Baroque art led her to experiment with materials used by artists from those periods. She painted on Masonite panels cradled on the back to prevent warping, mimicking the wood panels used by the old masters, and in 1977 she completed her first work in the ancient medium of egg tempera. She created *For Morandi* in 1978. Named for the modern Italian master of modest still lifes, it is a serial work consisting of six twelve-by-sixteen-inch panels, each with a similar grid painted in pastels with shorter lines in bolder colors indicating where her brush rested before starting each brushstroke. She also learned to use gold leaf, and from 1978 that material appears in nearly all her works. Hard-edge painting combined with gold leaf, though difficult to categorize, produced inventive art.

Art history is a funnel. In the beginning all the artists are swimming around at the top, but very quickly it becomes a trickle, as we remember only the most prominent artists, and sometimes not even them. That Obering, a woman when few women were taken seriously as artists, was never in sync with the most prominent art tendencies as they emerged, further diminished her chances of becoming part of the trickle—until now. Today pluralism holds sway in the art world, and together with the long overdue recognition of artists of color, there is strong interest in women artists who have never gotten their due. Obering, persistent in her commitment to her art, in many ways daring and unique, deserves consideration.

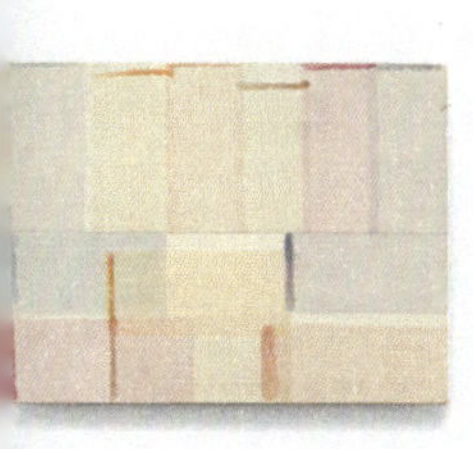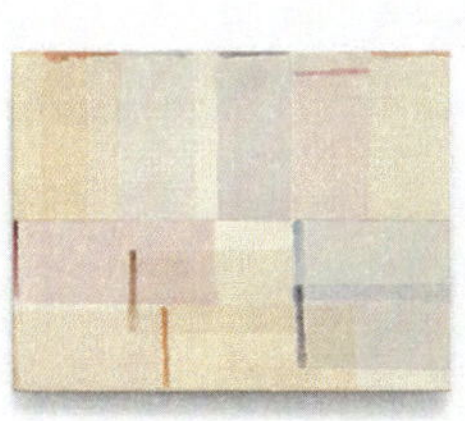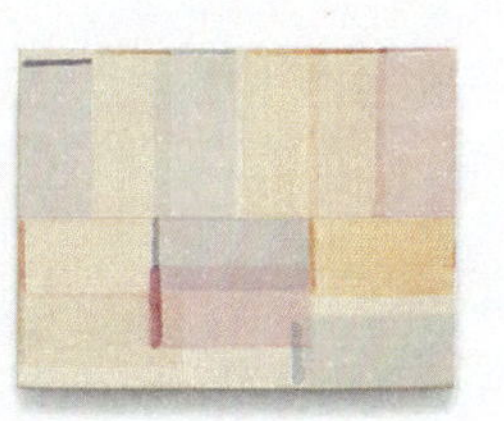

For Morandi, 1978
Egg tempera on Masonite
6 panels, 12×16 in. each
(30.48×40.64 cm)

PROVINCES, KINGS, MOUNTAINS

MATTHEW L. LEVY

The stories we tell about abstract painting often adhere to the extremes of the genre's structuring binaries: gesture and geometry; reference and non-objectivity; literal materiality and pictorial illusion. The most canonical abstract painters tend to be those who elevate one of these terms to some new height while suppressing its antipode. Think, for example, of the unbridled gesturalism of Jackson Pollock or the fastidious grids of Piet Mondrian. The painters who operate in the spaces between these poles, however, confound pat art historical narratives and consequently often slip through the cracks of historical memory. Such is the case of Mary Obering. Over the course of her more than fifty-year career, she has created paintings that refuse subject matter yet invoke a host of diverse references, including Renaissance altar painting, particle physics, landscape, and the human figure. While her geometric compositions have aligned her with Minimalist peers, such as Carl Andre and Donald Judd, her paintings' sumptuous brushwork and complex color relationships evince a sensualism at odds with a movement known for its cool detachment. Obering's work resists both easy categorization and tidy summation. Painting has served her as an arena for exploration and discovery, always evolving to reflect her observations and insights about art, history, and the world around her.

When Obering relocated to New York City in 1971 shortly after earning her MFA from the University of Denver, she had already arrived at a practice that demonstrated a sophisticated understanding of current trends in advanced American art. Working with diluted acrylic paints, she stained unprimed canvas in a manner similar to Color Field painters such as Helen Frankenthaler and Kenneth Noland. Prominent critics, including Clement Greenberg and Michael Fried, had upheld this staining technique as a means by which painting abrogated tactility, thus rendering color purely "optical." Yet where Frankenthaler and Noland's color appealed to "eyesight alone," to use Greenberg's coinage, Obering introduced an undeniably tactile element to these works by affixing stained pieces of canvas to the painting's surface, creating layers of literal depth. This practice was encouraged by Carl Andre, with whom she became friendly during a trip to Italy in 1970. In key respects, Andre's work diametrically opposed that of the Color Field painters. Where they advanced radiant expanses of seemingly dematerialized hue, Andre centered the viewing experience on the physical encounter with materials in time and space.

Already demonstrating her predilection for mediating antitheses, Obering's early paintings triangulated between these positions to create a hybrid entity.[1] In a painting like *After the Dance* (1972), overlapping pieces of canvas create a striped zone in which chromatic and spatial relationships stand in tension with one another. Whereas the bands of color enact their own optical dance of push and pull, these relationships are distinct from the literal spatial recession established by their physical overlap. Obering added an additional level of complexity to this tactic in her Window series of paintings, which were exhibited at Andre's invitation in an artists' selection exhibition at the legendary independent gallery Artists Space in 1973. Long vertical canvas strips create a framing motif that evokes the Renaissance conception of painting as a window onto an illusion, an effect enhanced by oblique bottom edges that invite a perspectival reading. Yet where the framed old master painting opens onto a cohesive illusion of recessive space, Obering's overlapping sheets of canvas assert the real space of the viewer.

With the Window series, Obering had arrived at a novel entry into a crowded artistic milieu marked by competing camps associated with Color Field painting,

1   Alex Bacon describes this state of hybridity as Obering's "ambiguity." Alex Bacon, "Mary Obering: The Appeal of Ambiguity," in *Mary Obering*, exh. cat. (Los Angeles: Kayne Griffin Corcoran, 2018), n.p.

2   Obering had early exposure to this tendency toward novel materials in the work of her University of Denver professor, Roger Kotoske, who was a pioneer in the use of fiberglass and cast resin in sculpture. Besides Obering, the other important example of an artist from this generation taking material inspiration from the Old Masters was David Novros, who, beginning in 1970 with a wall in Donald Judd's Soho residence, used the true fresco technique to create abstract murals.

Minimalism, Post-Minimalism, and Conceptual art. One would forgive a young painter for lingering on this new-found territory—particularly after one of her Drop series paintings, a subsequent and related group—was exhibited in the 1975 Whitney Biennial. But within only a few years, Obering would move on, preferring risk and experimentation to the comforts of the familiar.

The introduction of egg tempera to her practice in the mid-1970s precipitated a significant change in style. Her interest in this medium stemmed from her admiration for early Renaissance painting that dated back to her travels in Italy as a teenager. In tempera, ground pigment is suspended in diluted egg yolk to produce a quick-drying, durable film of vivid color. Unlike her earlier work with acrylic, in which paint soaked into unprimed canvas, tempera is applied over a smooth layer of gesso so that the paint rests on top of the support. Visible brushstrokes, heretofore absent from her paintings, thus entered her work. In her Sets series, one finds a painter delighting in the process of mastering a new medium. Each panel features an irregular grid composed of stacked horizontal drags of the brush. The series foregrounds the act of making in a manner reminiscent of the process-oriented paintings of Robert Ryman. With each stroke, one can imagine Obering acquiring a feel for tempera's unique fluidity as the brush passed from its loaded to discharged state. But where Ryman worked with white monochrome to isolate the materiality and movement of the individual brushstroke, Obering embraced a glittering array of jewel tones, showcasing the chromatic potential of her new medium.

Working with tempera sparked an even deeper investigation into the materials of the early Renaissance, and by the late seventies, Obering would learn the process of gilding from a professional gilder. Tempera and gold leaf, the materials of Renaissance altar painting, would be her mediums of choice for the remainder of her career. Video footage of Obering gilding a painting in her studio in Puglia reveals her to have been faithful to the details of the historical process. On a wooden panel primed with smoothed gesso, Obering applied a layer of bole, a liquid suspension of red clay and animal hide glue that served as an adhesive for the gold and imparted it with a rich, warm tone. She then laid sheets of gold foil, pounded so thin as to be semi-opaque, on a leather pad and cut them to the desired size before laying them down on the moistened bole with a special animal-hair brush. Lastly, she polished the gold with an agate-tipped burnisher until it was smooth and gleaming.

Obering's choice of materials might seem peculiar for an artist of a generation renowned for its desire to unburden itself from the weight of art history. Her peers were more likely to work with the latest advances in polyester resins or automotive paints than revive vaunted artistic traditions.[2] However, there is a peculiar historical logic to her practice. In his 1961 essay, "Byzantine Parallels," Clement Greenberg observed formal echoes between modernist painting and the art of Byzantium, a phenomenon he attributed to their shared disavowal of illusionistic pictorial space. Here it must be noted that the early Renaissance altarpieces that Obering so admired derived from the tradition of Byzantine icons, and they shared the same material practice and theological understanding of gilded panel painting. Historical panel painters eschewed illusionistic backgrounds for their divine figures in favor of flat expanses of gold leaf to signify their transcendent status—the reflective gold surface evoking an aura of heavenly light. Obering's paintings, however, strip this material of these theological connotations, leaving the viewer solely to contemplate its literal perceptual effects, realizing the historical convergence described by Greenberg:

> The Byzantines dematerialized firsthand reality by invoking a transcendent one. We seem to be doing something similar in our science as well as art, insofar as we invoke the material against itself by insisting on its all-encompassing reality. The Byzantines excluded appeals to literal experience against the transcendent, whereas we seem to

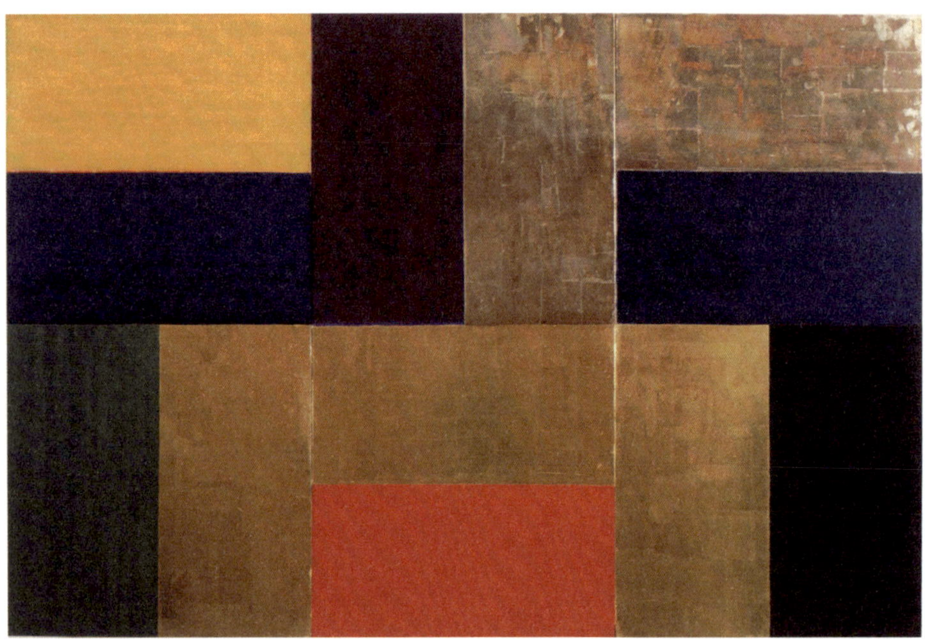

3 Clement Greenberg, "Byzantine Parallels," in *Art and Culture: Critical Essays* (Boston: Beacon Press, 1961), 167–71. For more on the historiography of Greenberg's essay, see Jessamine Batario, "What could have been and never was: the intellectual context of Clement Greenberg's 'Byzantine Parallels,'" *Journal of Art Historiography* 18 (June 2018): 1–20.

4 Quoted in Mary Obering, "Statement by the Artist," 1988, unpublished, Mary Obering studio archives.

exclude appeals to anything but the literal … A radically transcendental and a radically positivist exclusiveness both arrive at anti-illusionist, or rather counter-illusionist, art. Once again, extremes meet.[3]

Obering's paintings enact this meeting of extremes, as she invoked the materials and techniques of a bygone age to suit the aesthetic criteria of her own time.

Over the ensuing decades, Obering would adapt this material vocabulary to a variety of ends. She was never doctrinaire in her approach to abstraction, viewing it instead as a means of testing material and formal possibilities and giving physical expression to her observations of nature and understanding of the world around her. Beginning in the late 1970s, she configured geometric forms into loosely figurative arrangements, as in *Montezuma* (1980), in which the gilded surface reverses its historical function as background to assume the role of a bipedal figure against a painted ground. Perhaps sensing the threat this path posed to her modernist commitments, she followed this series with more rigorously abstract paintings on shaped panels that were inspired by her fascination with particle physics and astronomy. Commenting on these works,

she quoted the philosopher A. J. Ayer, who, in a text on Wittgenstein, wrote that physics could be "felicitously compared with a net which is thrown over phenomena, and the possibility is allowed of the use of nets with different meshes to describe the world. Laws … are said to be about the net and not about what the net describes."[4] This passage appealed to Obering because it characterized science as an abstraction—a construct that, like abstract painting, can correspond to nature without being purely illustrative of it.

This interest in drawing her art closer to nature prompted Obering to create paintings that foregrounded their material construction. The Slip paintings, begun in 1986, isolated each step of the gilding process. In *Blue Border*, for example, a thin blue band of tempera frames concentric squares of gold foil, bole, and gesso, exposing preparatory materials that remain invisible in a conventional panel painting and asserting them as objects of aesthetic interest. The concentric pattern in this particular work creates a corridor-like illusion of spatial recession that parallels the stepwise exfoliation of panel painting's material layers—an updating of the play between optical and literal depth found in her early canvas paintings.

Upholding the materials of panel painting as being worthy of aesthetic

Montezuma, 1980
Egg tempera, gold leaf, and silver leaf on gessoed panel
48 × 75 in.
(121.9 × 190.5 cm)

5   Donald Judd, "Specific Objects," reprinted in *Complete Writings 1959–75: Gallery Reviews, Book Reviews, Articles, Letters to the Editor, Reports, Statements, Complaints* (Halifax: The Press of the Nova Scotia College of Art and Design; New York: New York University Press, 1975), 181.

6   The Sala series draws on patterns in the tile floor of the Musei Capitolini, while the PA series references mosaic border ornament in the Piazza Armerina's Villa Romana del Casale.

7   Quoted in Obering, "Statement by the Artist," 1988.

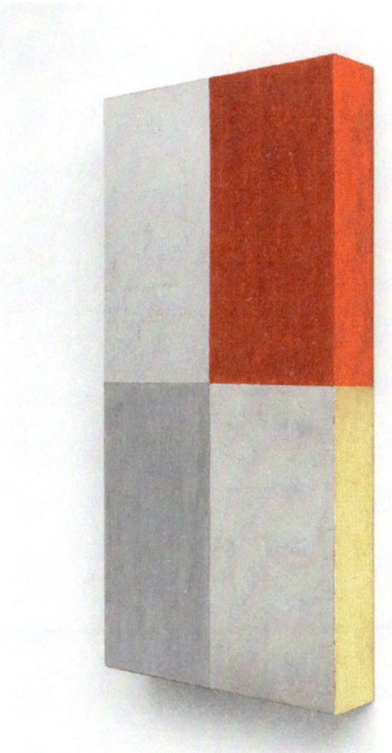

PD, 1994
Egg tempera, copper leaf, and white gold leaf on gessoed panel
48×24 in.
(121.9×61 cm)

contemplation demanded a simultaneous reckoning with the physical construction of her panels. Put another way, her work needed to succeed in both painterly and sculptural terms. She began working with increasingly thick panels, extending the painted and gilded surface to include the edges. In the right lighting, the gilded edges cast a seemingly magical aura on the wall, a canny reimagining of this material's historical function as a signifier of heavenly light. The deeper panels brought Obering's work into the realm of relief, denying painting's exclusively frontal mode of spectatorship and opening the work up to a full 180-degree arc of vision. This move aligned her with the thinking of her friend, Donald Judd, whose essay "Specific Objects" of 1965 proposed just such a state of inter-medium hybridity with its famed opening line, "Half or more of the best new work has been neither painting nor sculpture," which is to say, it existed in a space between the two.[5] Obering would later pay tribute to Judd with her Shudder, Stutter, Sputter… series, made shortly before his passing. The lateral array of concentric white, black, and gold rectangles creates an illusionistic play of projection and recession that echoes the oscillation between void and volume found in her friend's art.

Obering would continue to experiment with new materials and approaches to composition, producing a body of work as varied as it is utterly singular. The Sala (1990) and PA (2003) series applied a strategy of quotation, deriving their forms from Roman and Sicilian historical ornament respectively,[6] while her work from the late '90s and early '00s asserted a blunt materiality, incorporating slabs of cut stone sourced near her studio in Puglia. Her work has refer-enced the landscape—as in the Arch (1975–76) paintings' repeated evocation of the horizon line—or expressed personal loss—as in the elegiac Greek crosses of *Stations of the Stone* (1997), made in memory of the victims of the AIDS crisis (including her longtime gallerist Julian Pretto). While not expressive in the conventional sense (they possess none of the emotional gesturalism of the first-generation New York School painters), her paintings are nonetheless a reflection of the life's journey of their maker. Obering herself shared this understanding of the personal nature of her practice, as revealed in a passage from Jorge Luis Borges' final interview, which she cited in an unpublished artist statement: "Through the years a man peoples a space with images of provinces, kings, mountains, bays, ships, islands, fishes, rooms, tools, stars, horses, and people. Shortly before his death, he discovers that the patient labyrinth of lines traces the image of his own face."[7] Looking back at the totality of Obering's five-decade career, such a portrait of the artist comes into view.

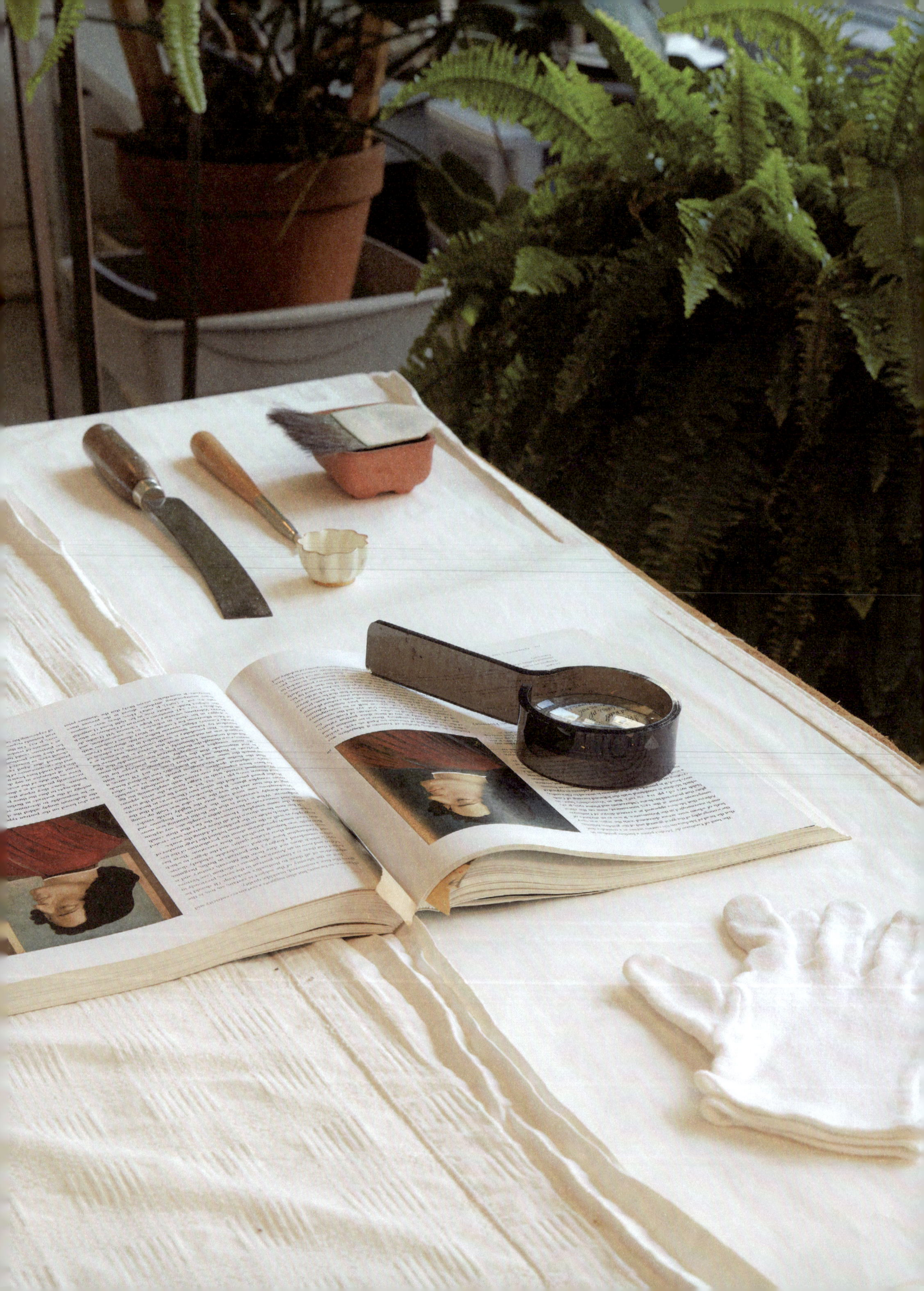

WORKS

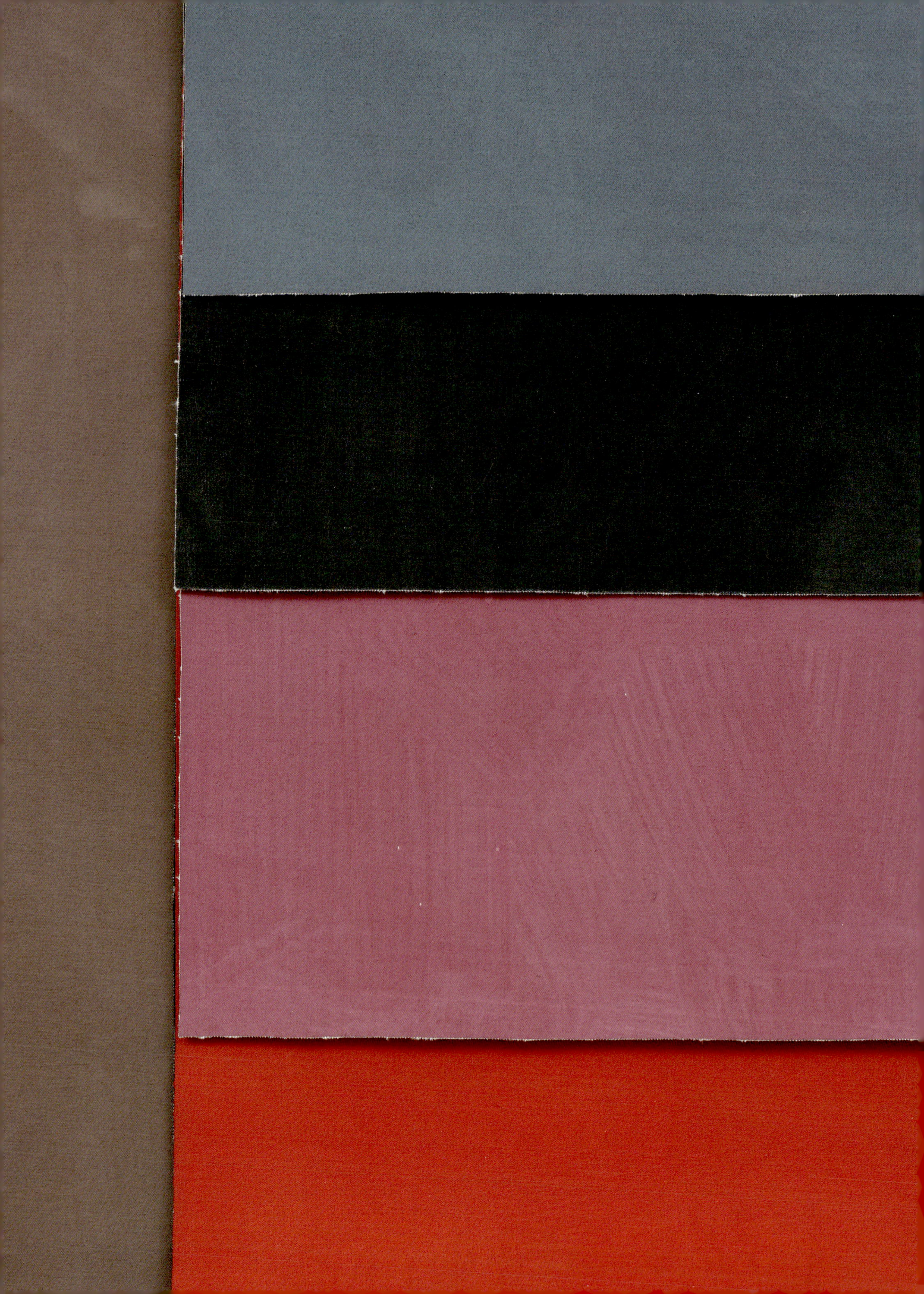

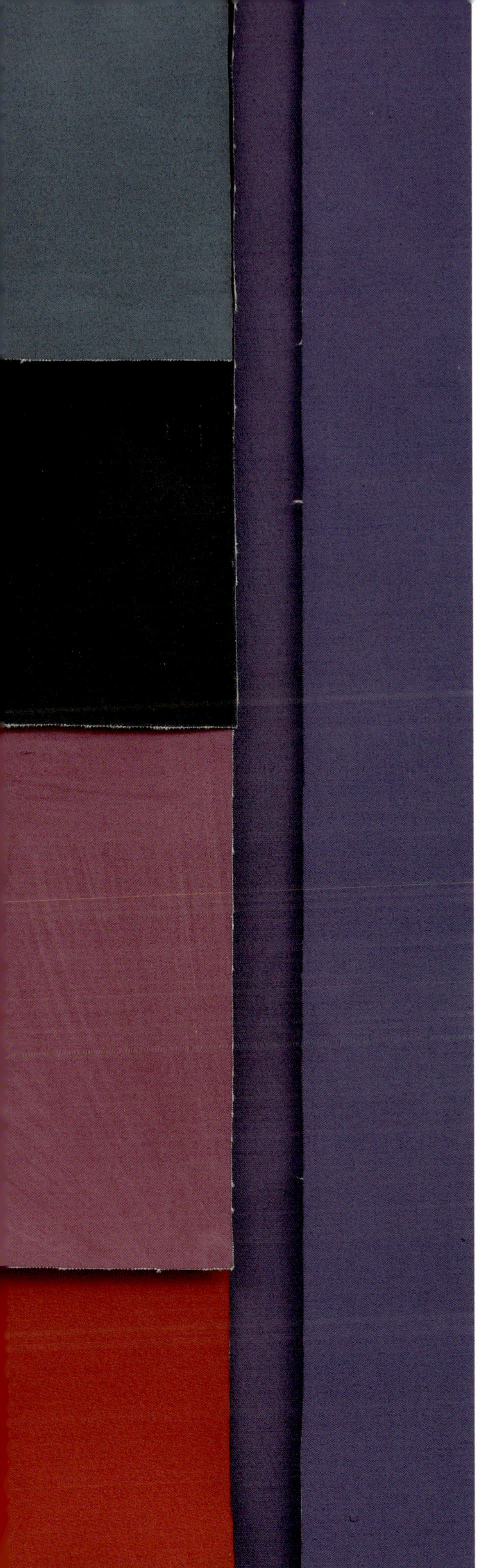

DROP SERIES

CHINESE SERIES
WINDOW SERIES
DIAGONAL SERIES
SY SERIES

In the Drop series, begun in the early 1970s, draped vertical strips of canvas, produced with fluttering brushstrokes, are laid on stretched monochrome canvases. Tacked with finishing nails and hung from the top of the stretched canvas, the layered paintings suggest entryways, like portals, into a minimalist scene of the artist's imagining. The Chinese series works are identical in composition, differing only in color combinations, suggesting particular seasons and landscapes, from snowy mountains to a spring rain shower, and titularly referring to Tang Dynasty poetry. Whereas, the Window series, first presented together as a group in 1973, is a succession of jewel-toned abstraction that playfully calls to mind Leon Battista Alberti's Renaissance notion of the framed painting as a window onto the world. Both the Diagonal series and SY series allude to the painting's arena as a liminal screen, adorned with drapery.

Window Series #2, 1973
Acrylic on canvas
96×96 in.
(243.8×243.8 cm)

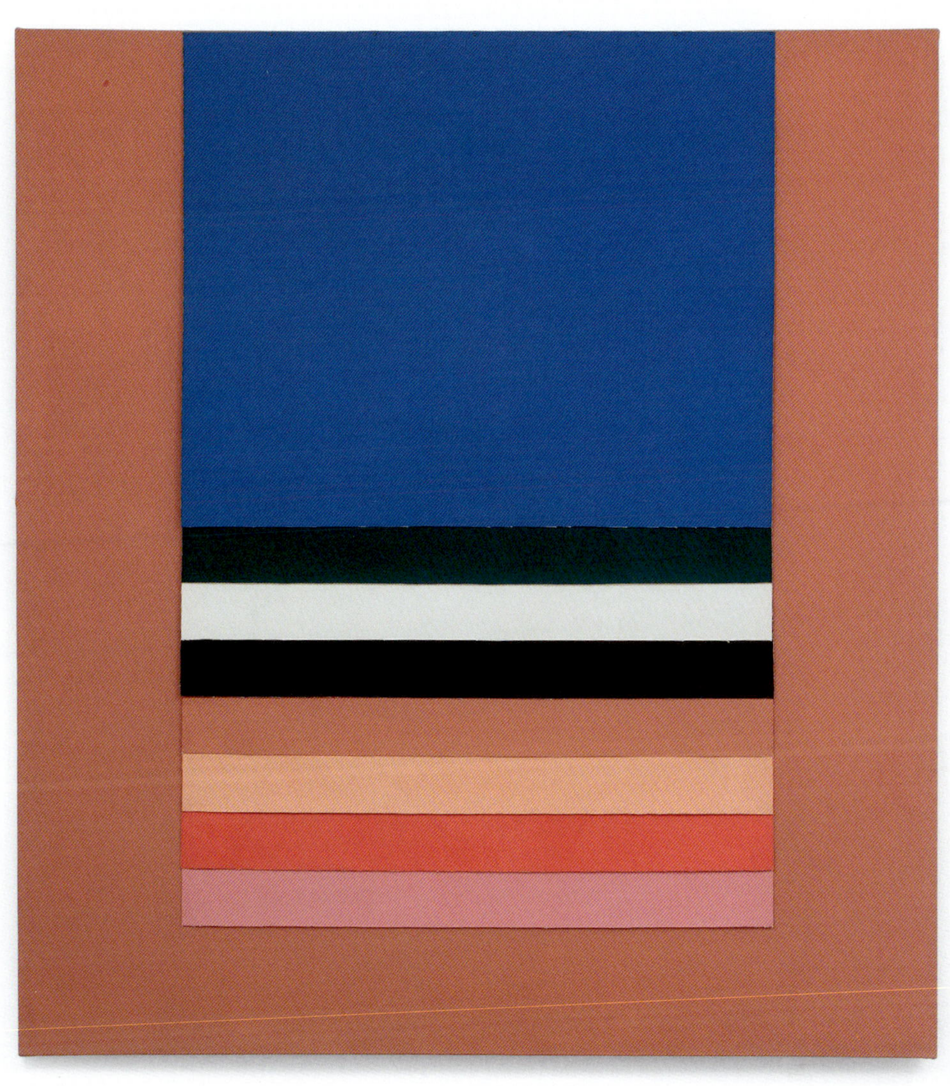

After the Dance, 1972
Acrylic on canvas
72 × 66 in.
(182.9 × 167.6 cm)

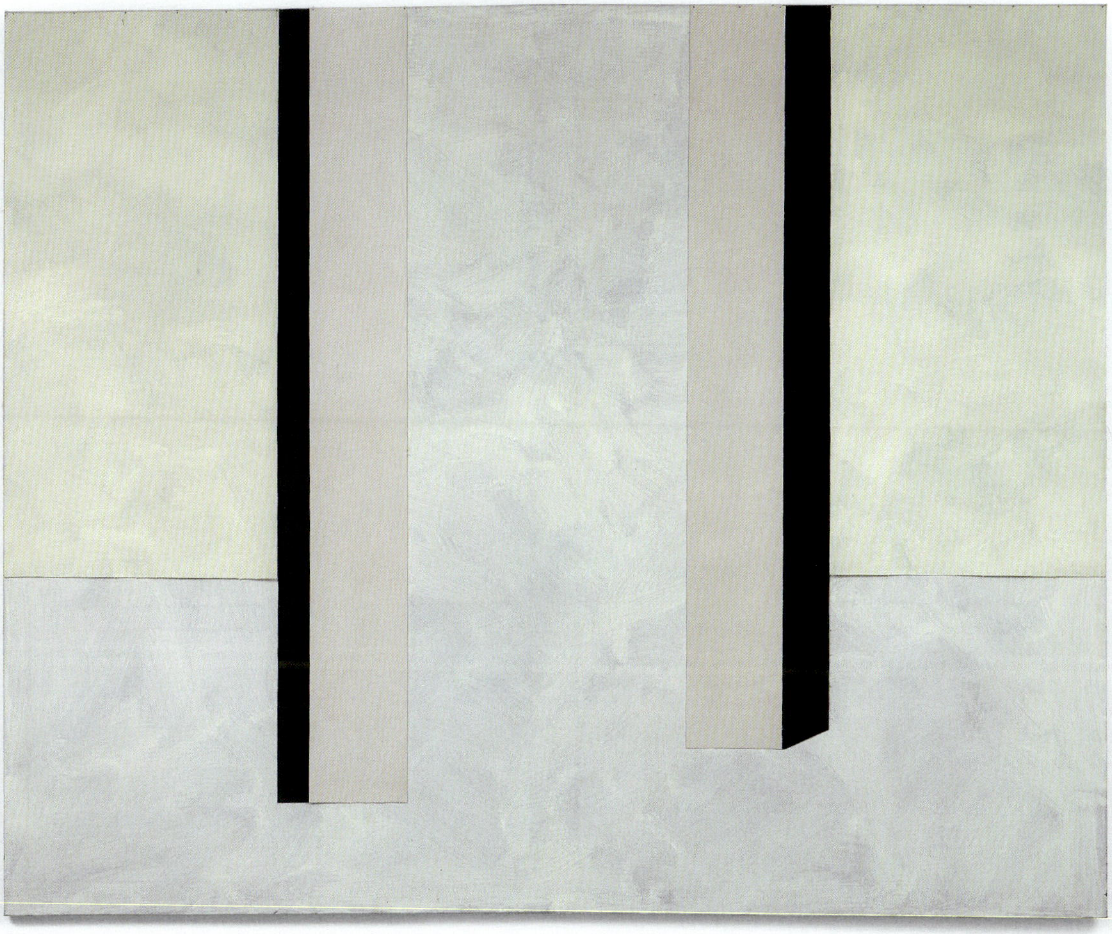

Through Snowy
Mountains at Dawn, 1973
Acrylic on canvas
96 × 120 in.
(243.84 × 304.8 cm)

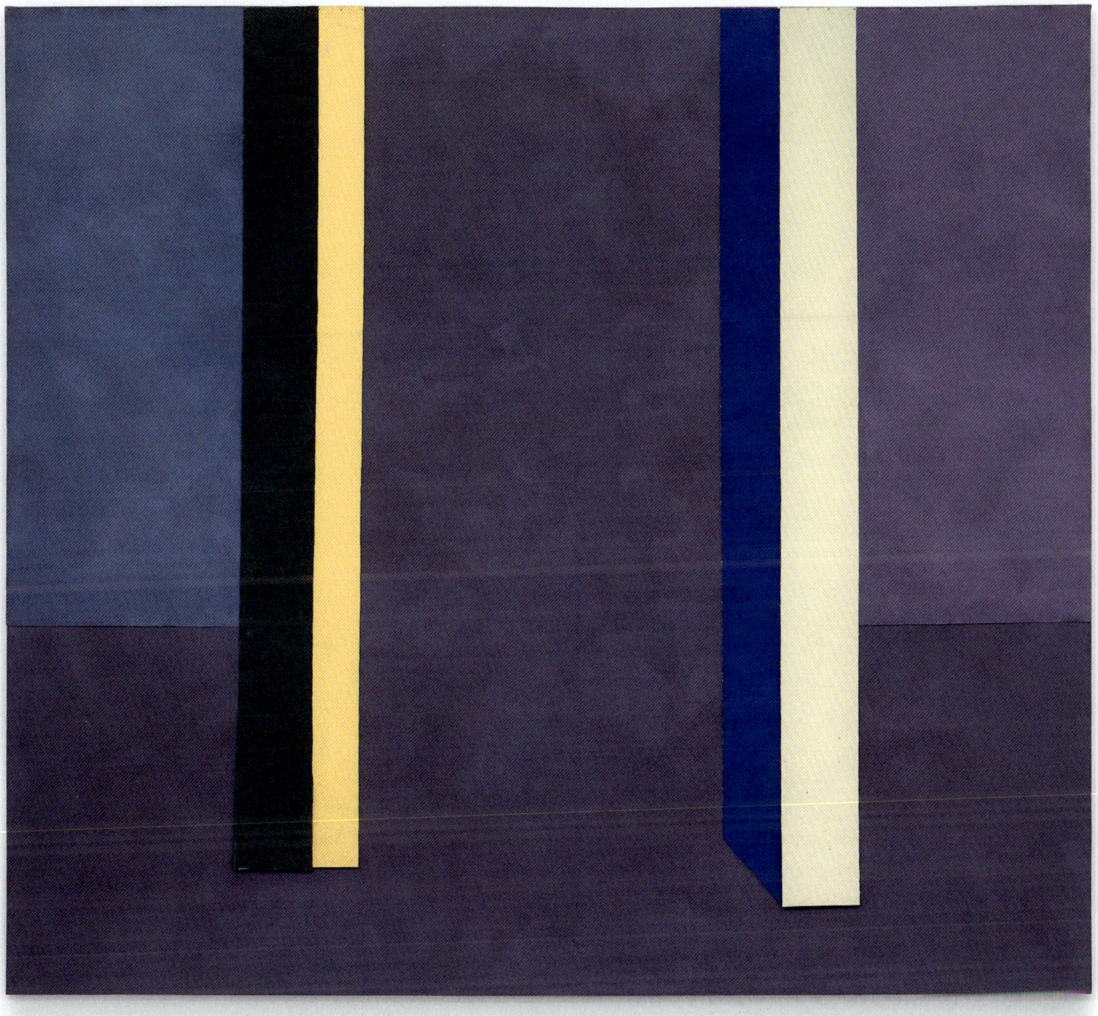

Colorful Spring Rain, 1973
Acrylic on canvas
96×108×1⅜ in.
(243.8×274.3×3.5 cm)

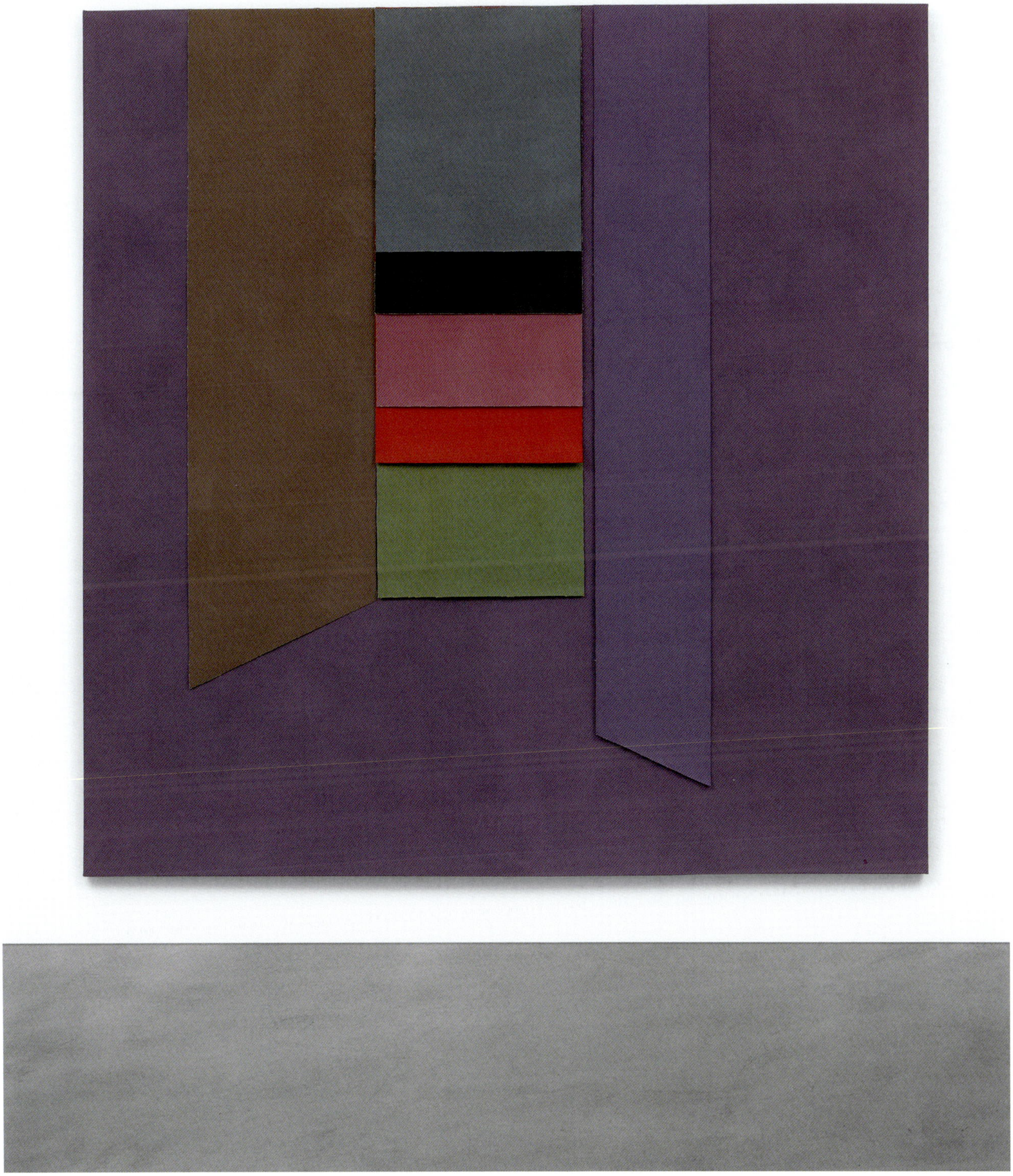

Window Series #2, 1973
Acrylic on canvas
96 × 96 in.
(243.8 × 243.8 cm)

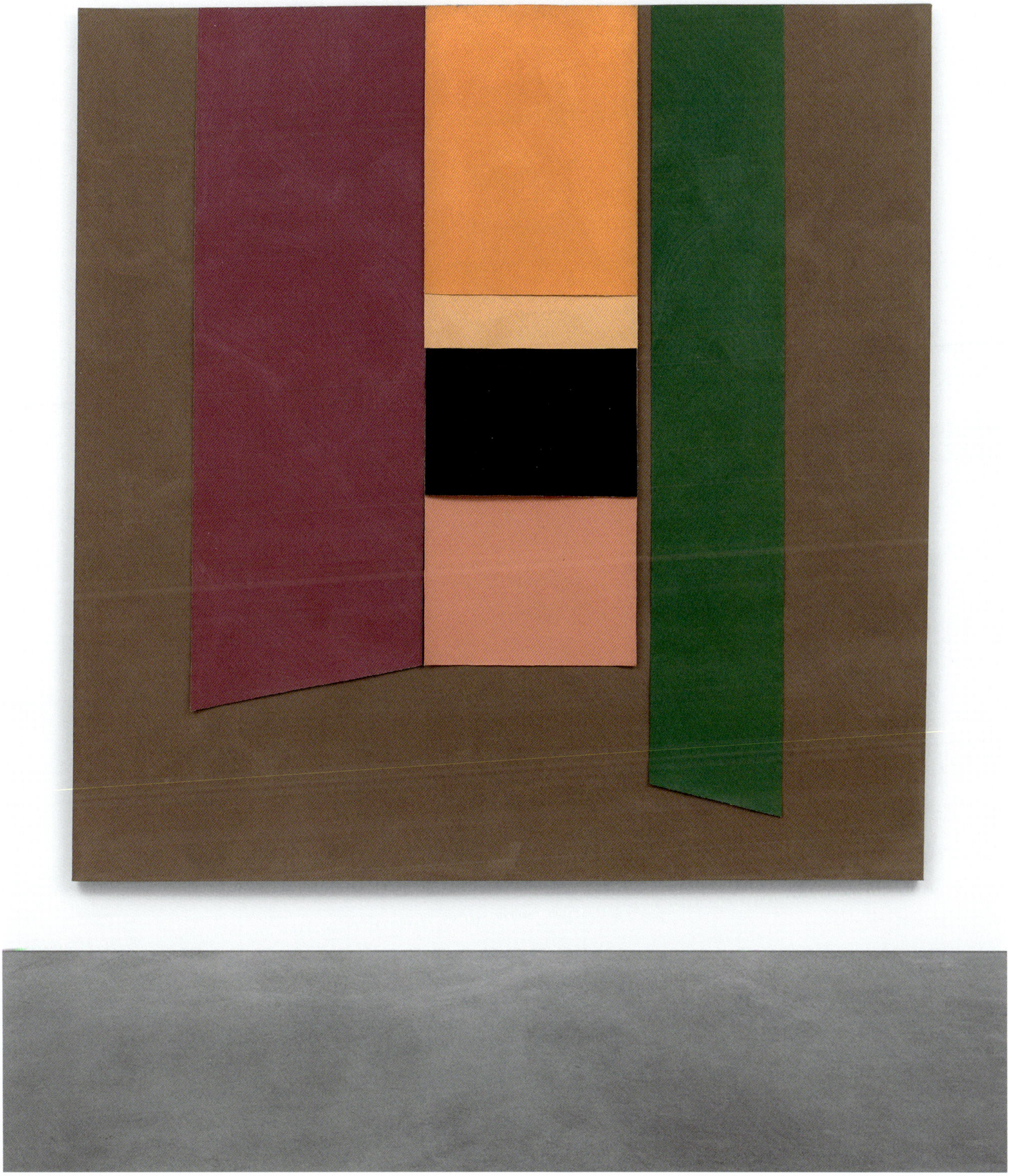

Window Series #3, 1973
Acrylic on canvas
96 × 96 in.
(243.8 × 243.8 cm)

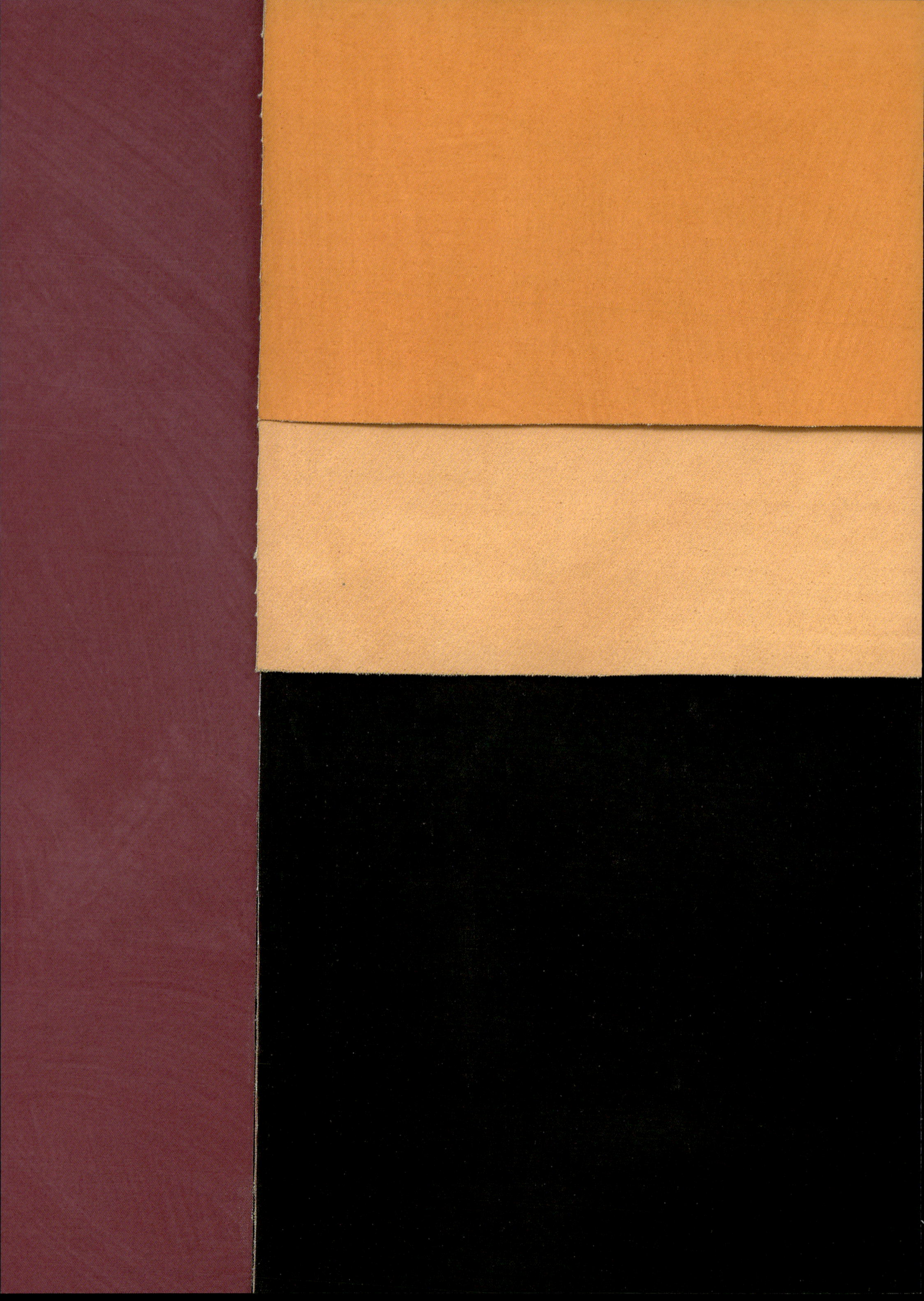

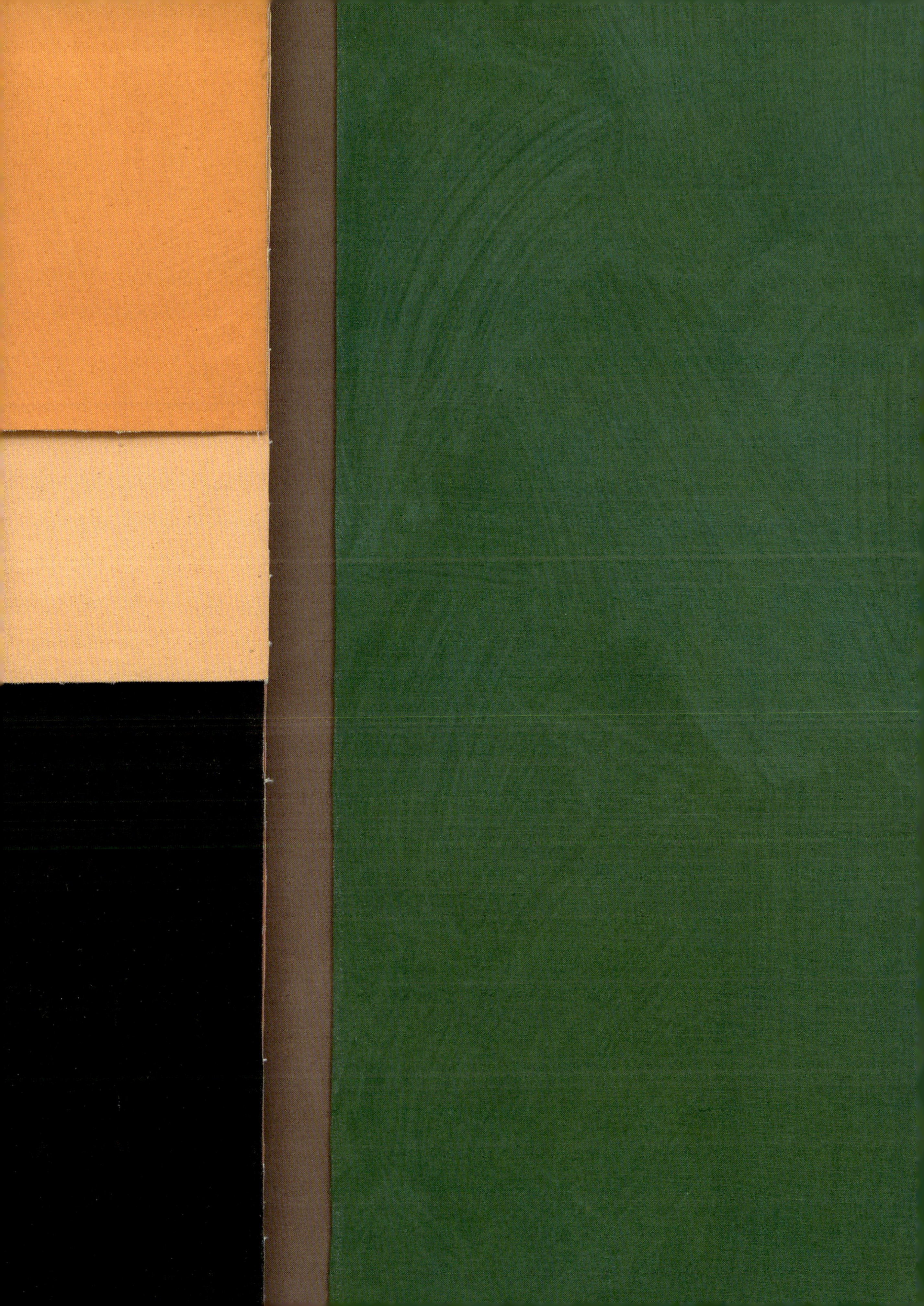

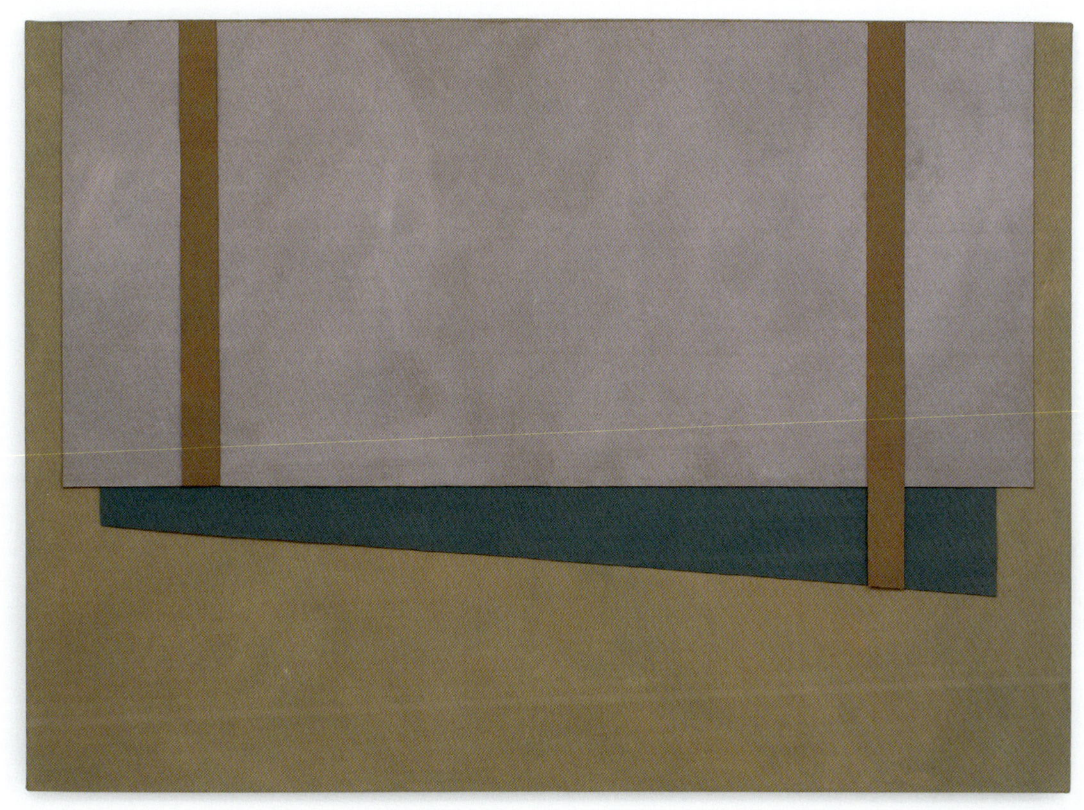

Caddo Day, 1974
Acrylic on canvas
60 × 84 in.
(152.4 × 213.4 cm)

Black March, 1974
Acrylic on canvas
66 × 108 in.
(167.6 × 274.3 cm)

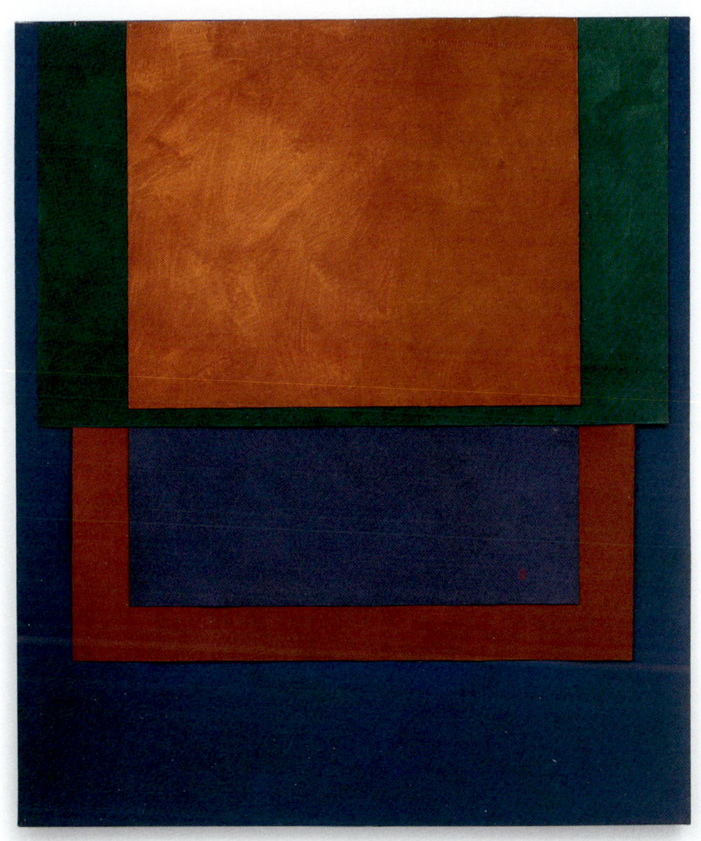

Balcony, 1975
Acrylic on canvas
84 × 72 in.
(213.4 × 182.9 cm)

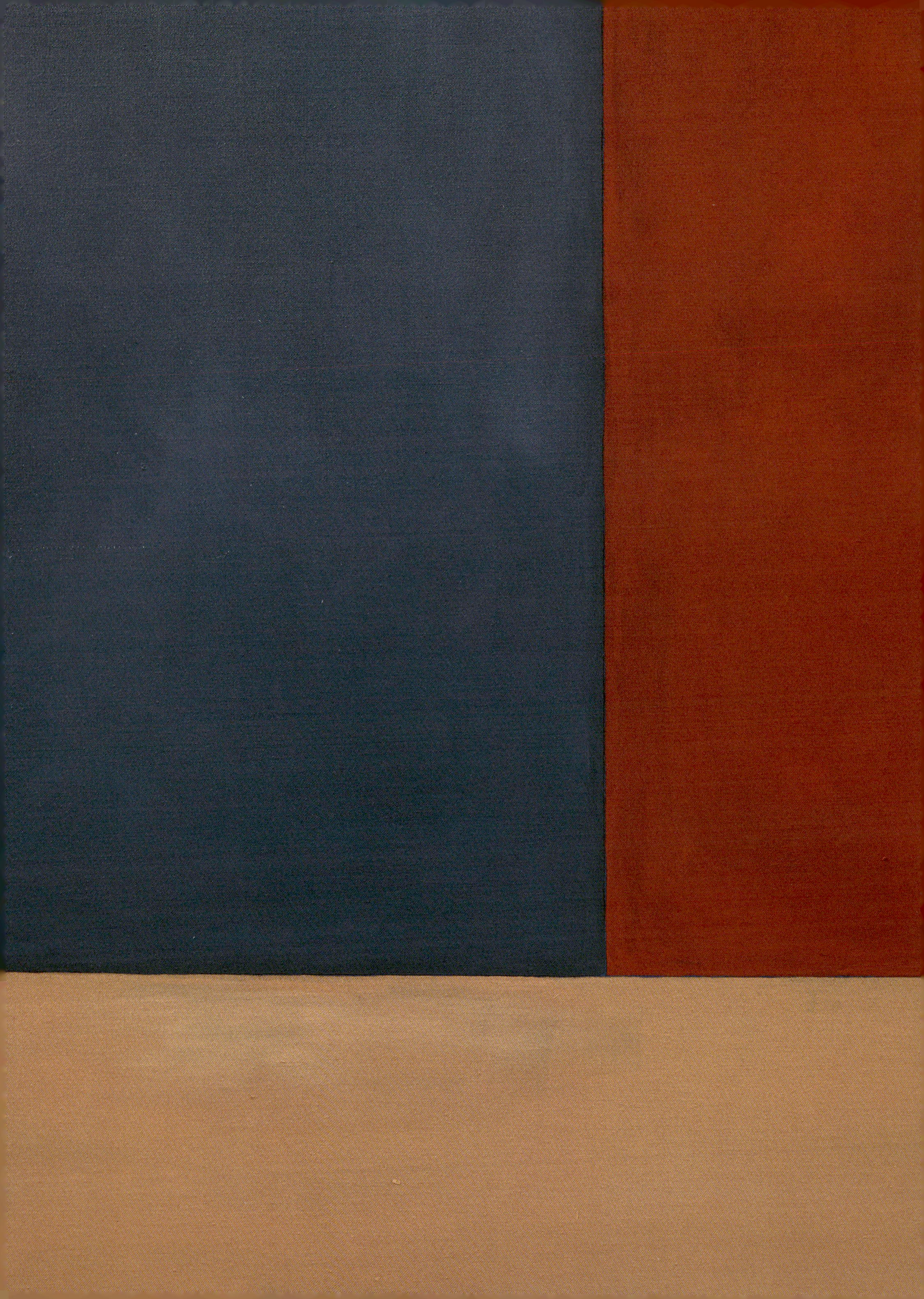

OIL ON CANVAS

For a brief period in the 1970s, Obering painted in the traditional medium of oil on canvas. These rectilinear compositions are exercises in the artist's mathematical understanding of proportions. Painted in velvety textures that highlight the artist's own hand, the paintings also suggest the artist's deft understanding of balance and composition. At the same time, the multipartite paintings reveal the artist's development as a colorist, often produced in a muted palette whose hues are built up to a nearly tactile depth.

Announcement, 1973
Oil on canvas
108.25 × 108.25 in.
(274.96 × 274.96 cm)

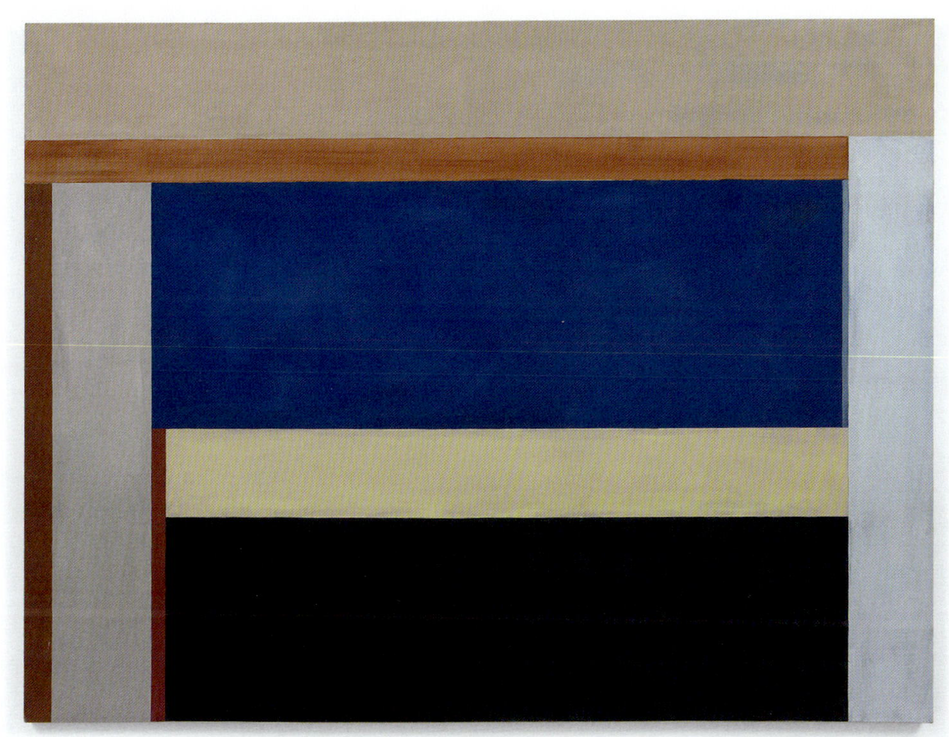

Big A, 1973
Oil on canvas
72×96 in.
(183×244 cm)

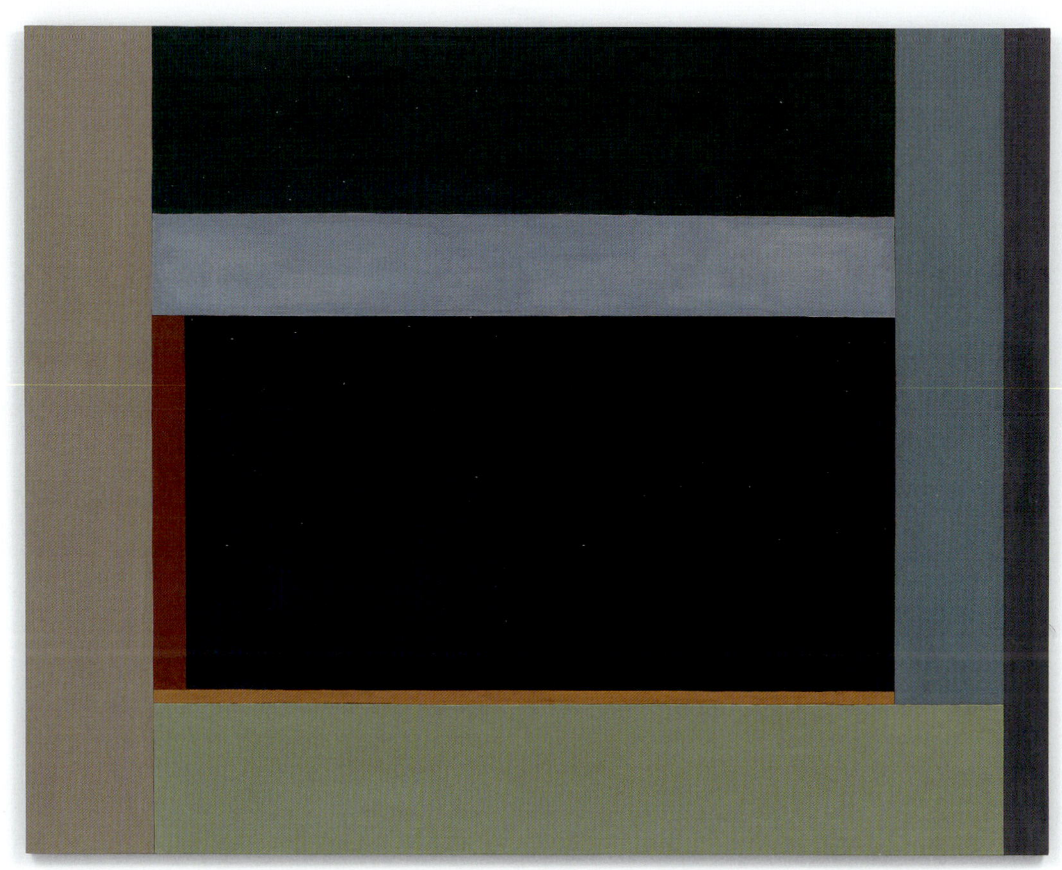

Wildwood, 1973
Oil on canvas
66×84 in.
(167.6×213.4 cm)

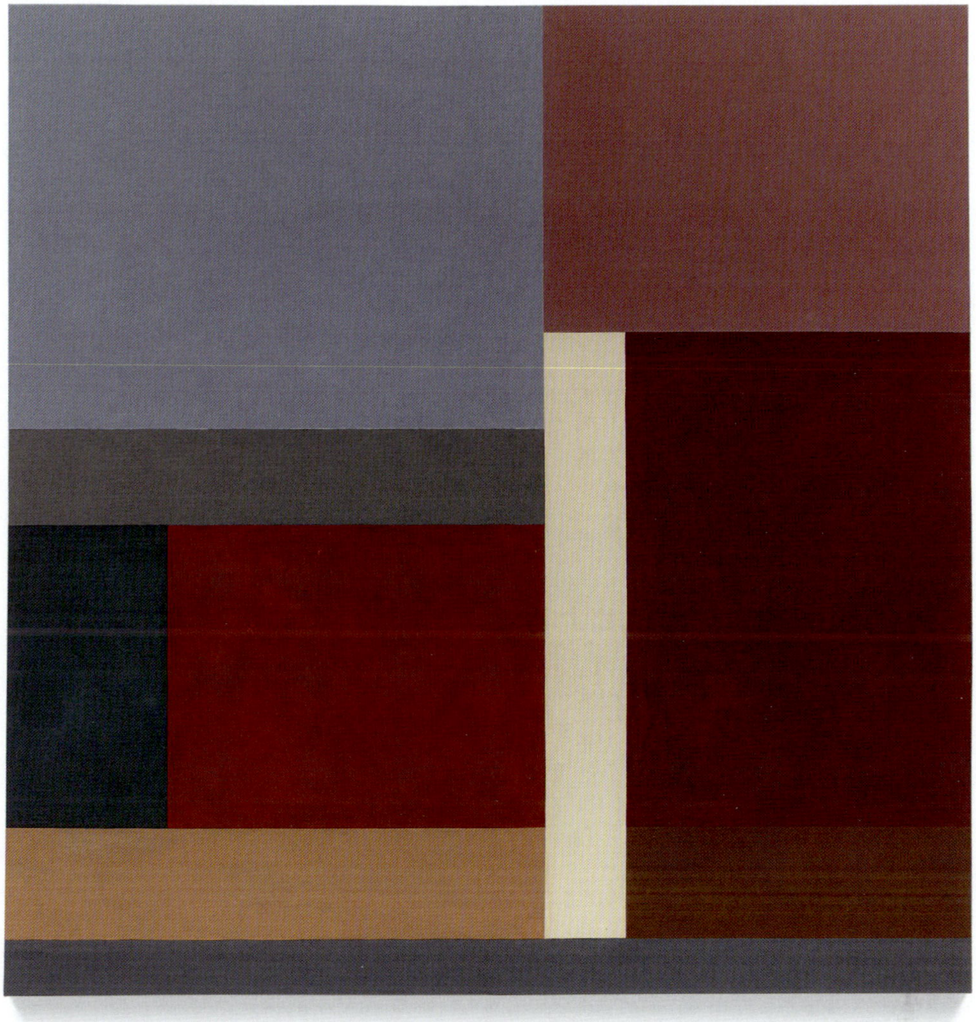

Announcement, 1973
Oil on canvas
108.25×108.25 in
(274.96×274.96 cm)

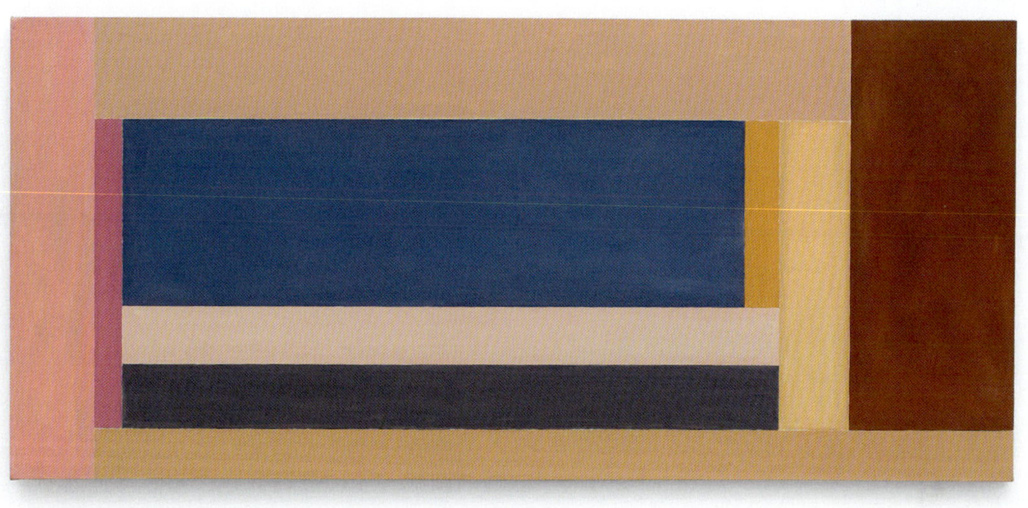

Through Blinds, 1973
Oil on canvas
32³⁄₁₆ × 72⅛ × 1⁵⁄₁₆ in.
(81.8 × 183.2 × 3.3 cm)

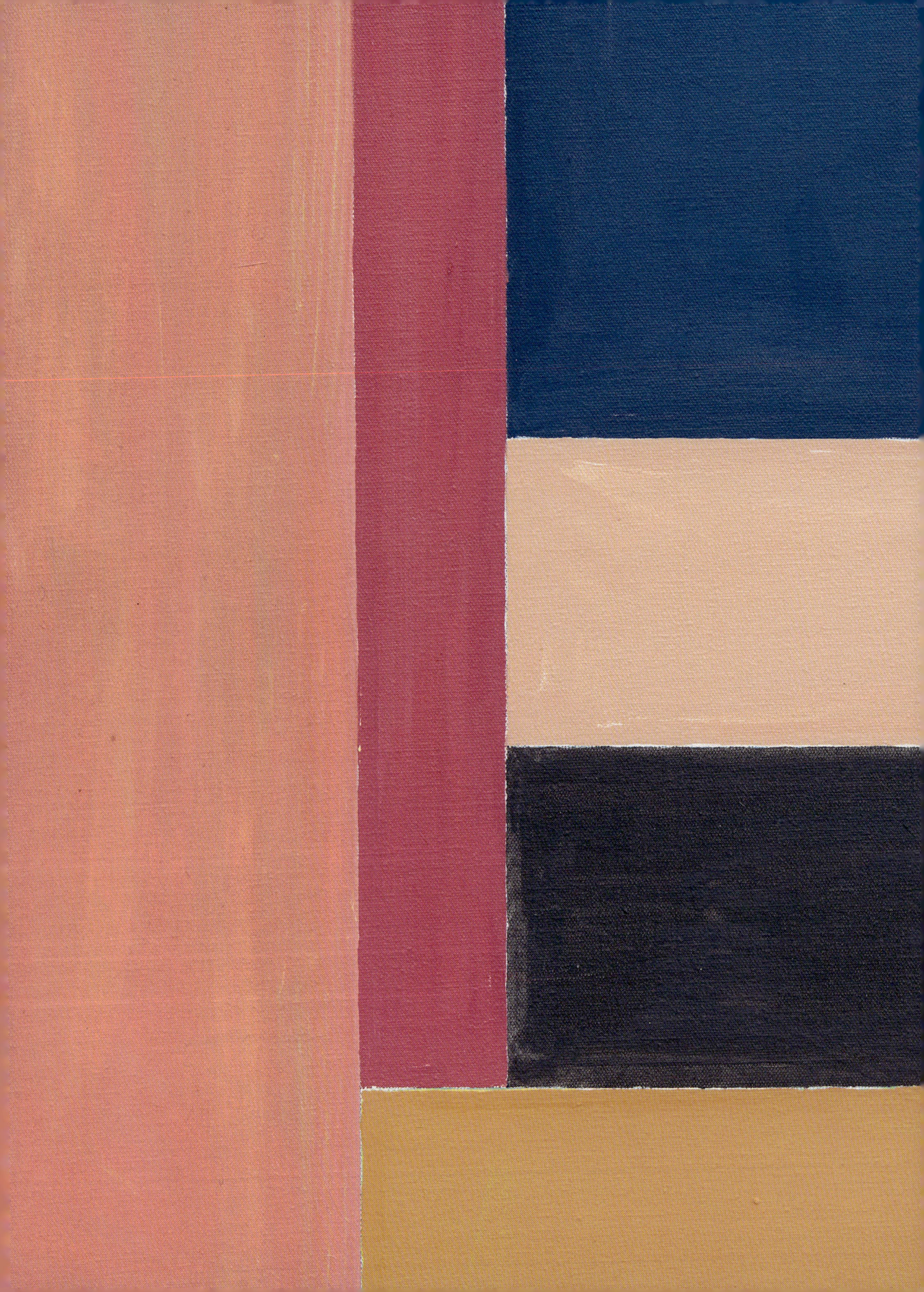

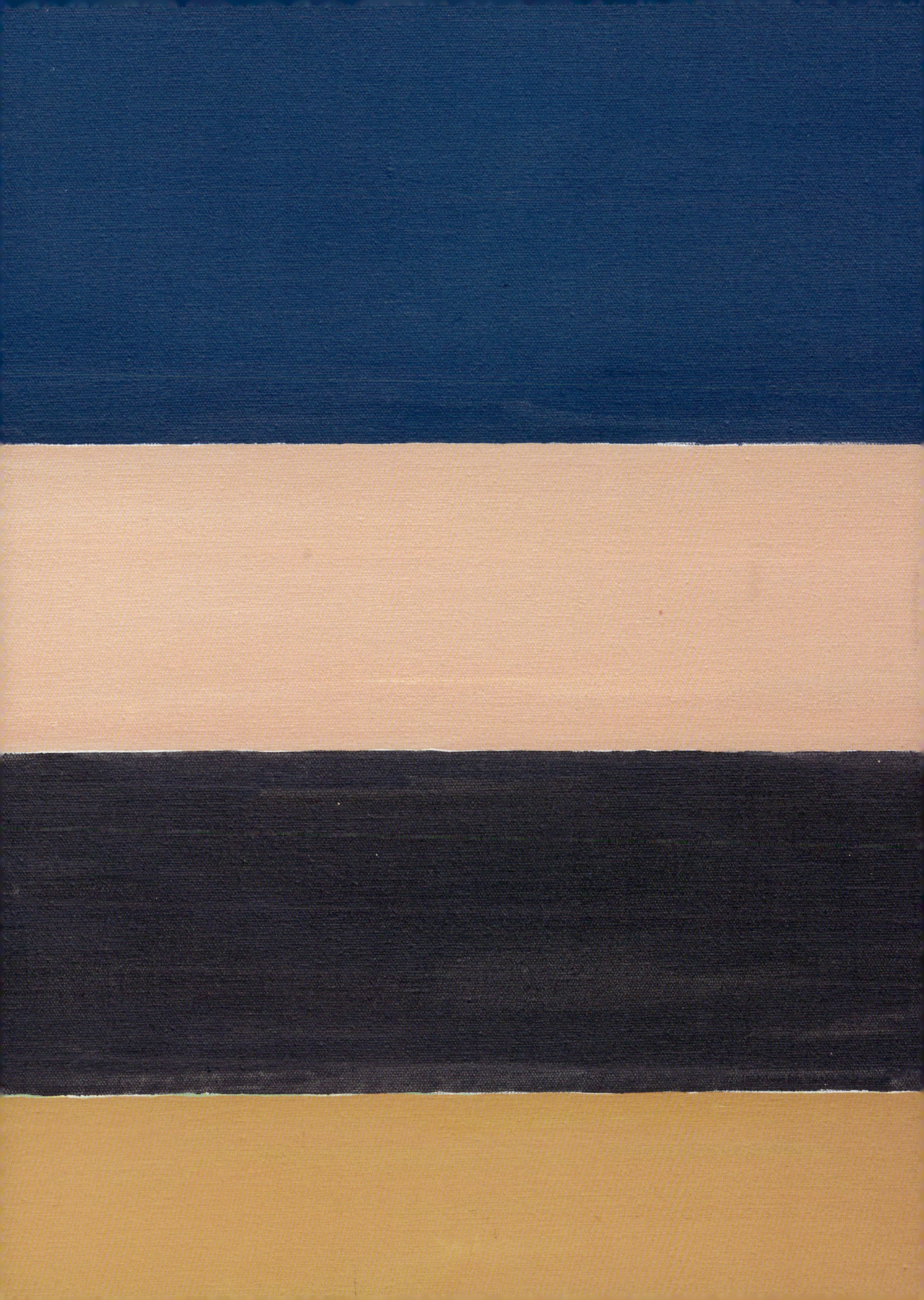

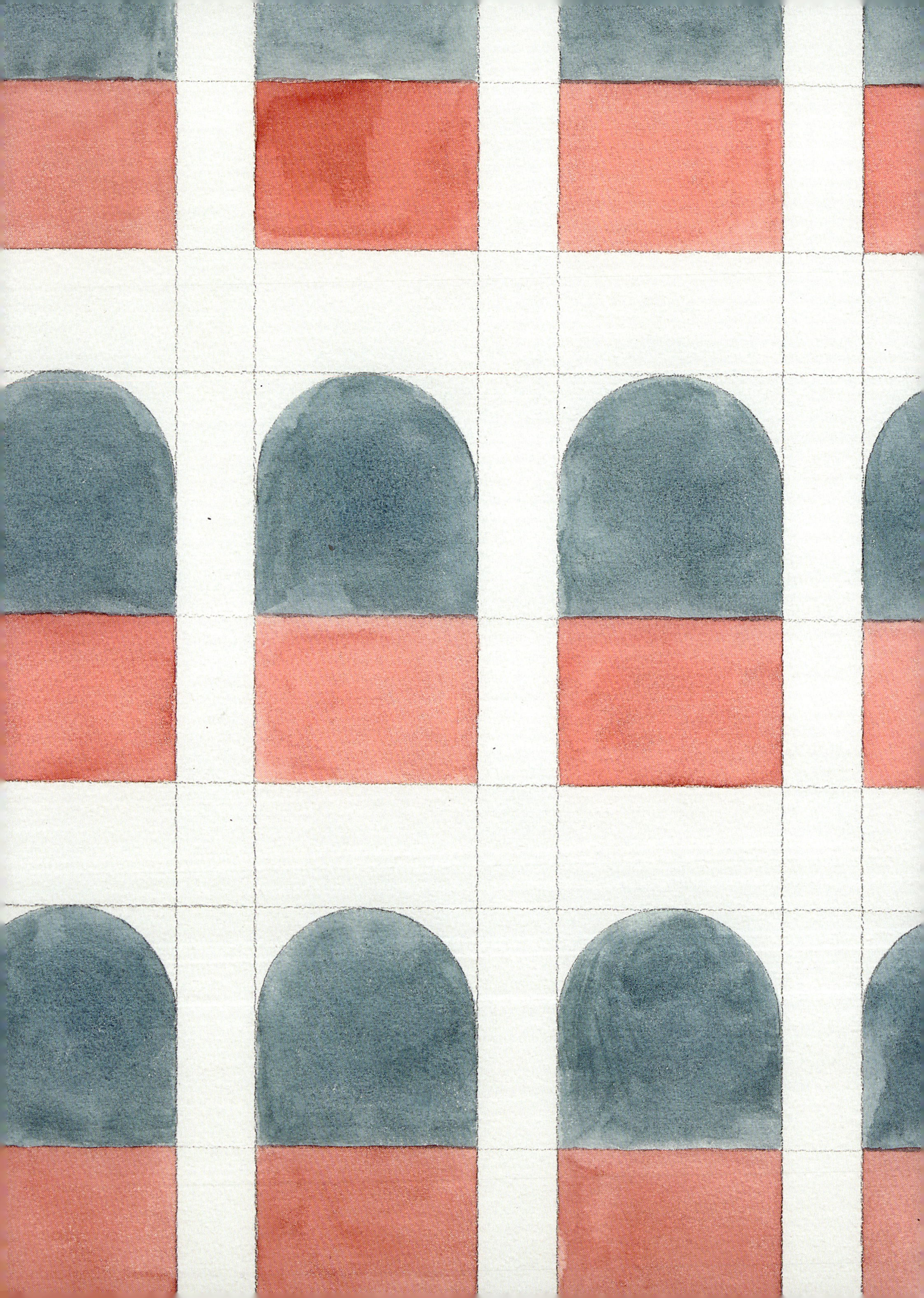

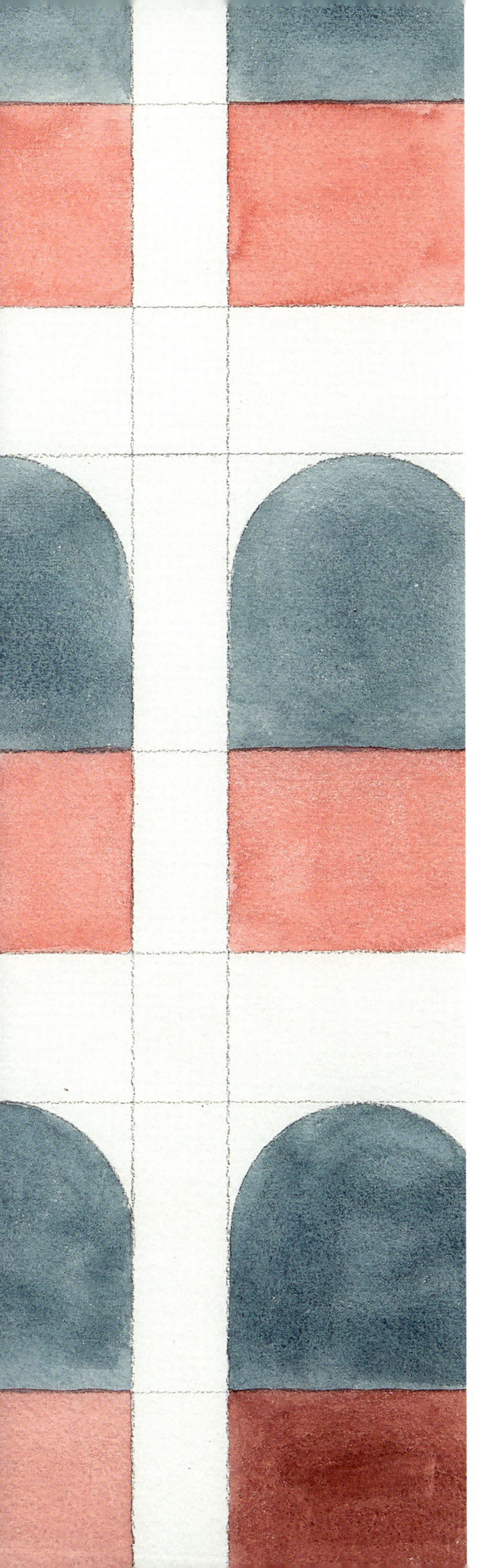

ARCH SERIES

Paintings from the Arch series, made up of simple curved panels—often pairs—and watercolors of varying scale, evoke windows through which a horizon line is visible. The arch shape, the foundation of so much architecture, poetically calls to mind myriad associations from bullets to tongues to tombstones. Each of the panels is spliced horizontally and painted in two colors applied in gestural and quick brushstrokes. At once inspired by the windows of the buildings of her Soho neighborhood as well the views she documented in Italy, the paintings toe the line between what the artist thought of as pure abstraction and the compositional elements of landscape. With the bifurcation occurring at different heights and within panels of various sizes, both squat and elongated, Obering invests in the possibility of roving viewpoints within the static art object. This series also marks the artist's ultimate use of oil paint before moving to tempera.

French Incarnation, 1976
Watercolor on paper
22.25 × 30 in.
(56.52 × 76.2 cm)

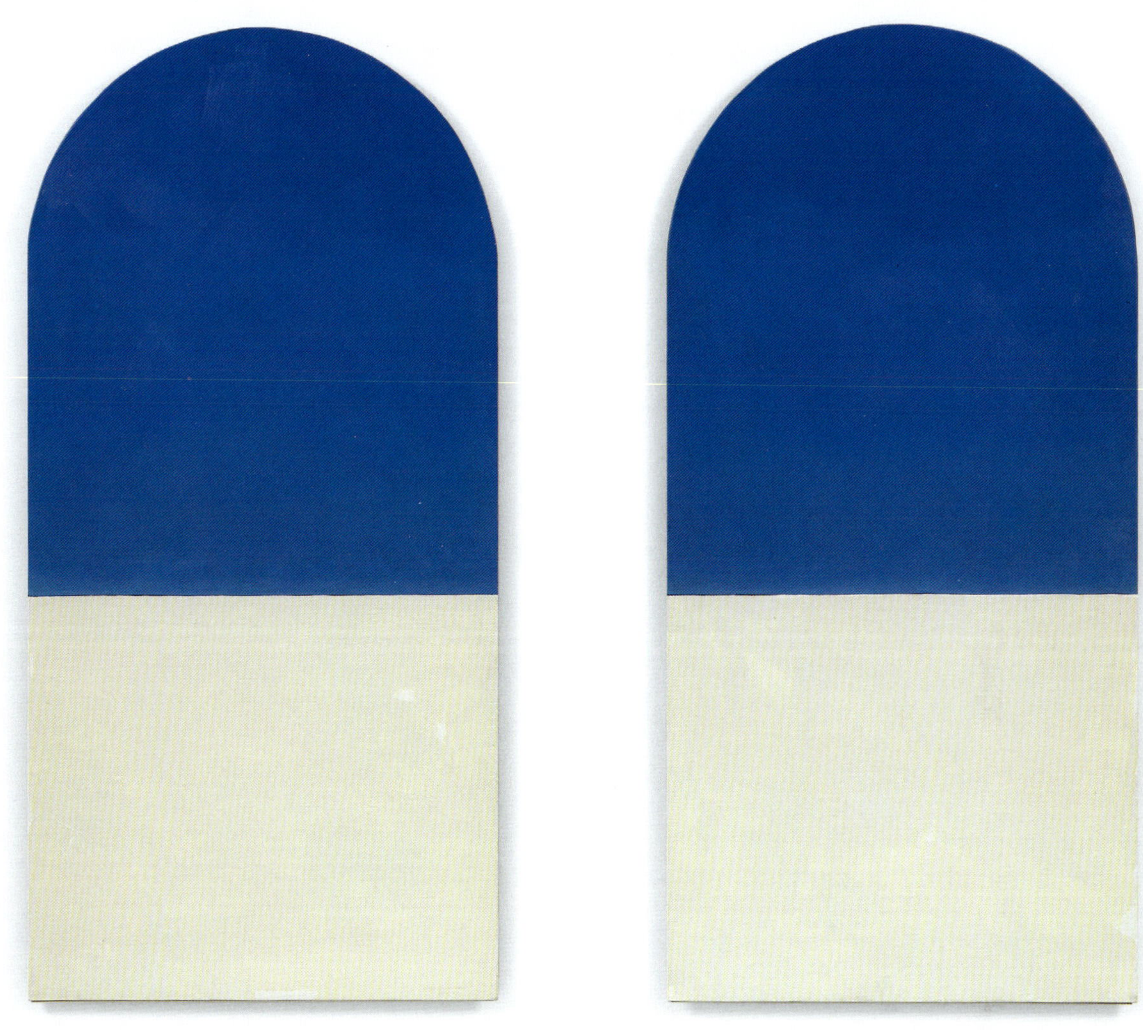

Dream Plane, 1975
Oil on Masonite
2 panels, 48×24 in. each
(121.92×60.96 cm)

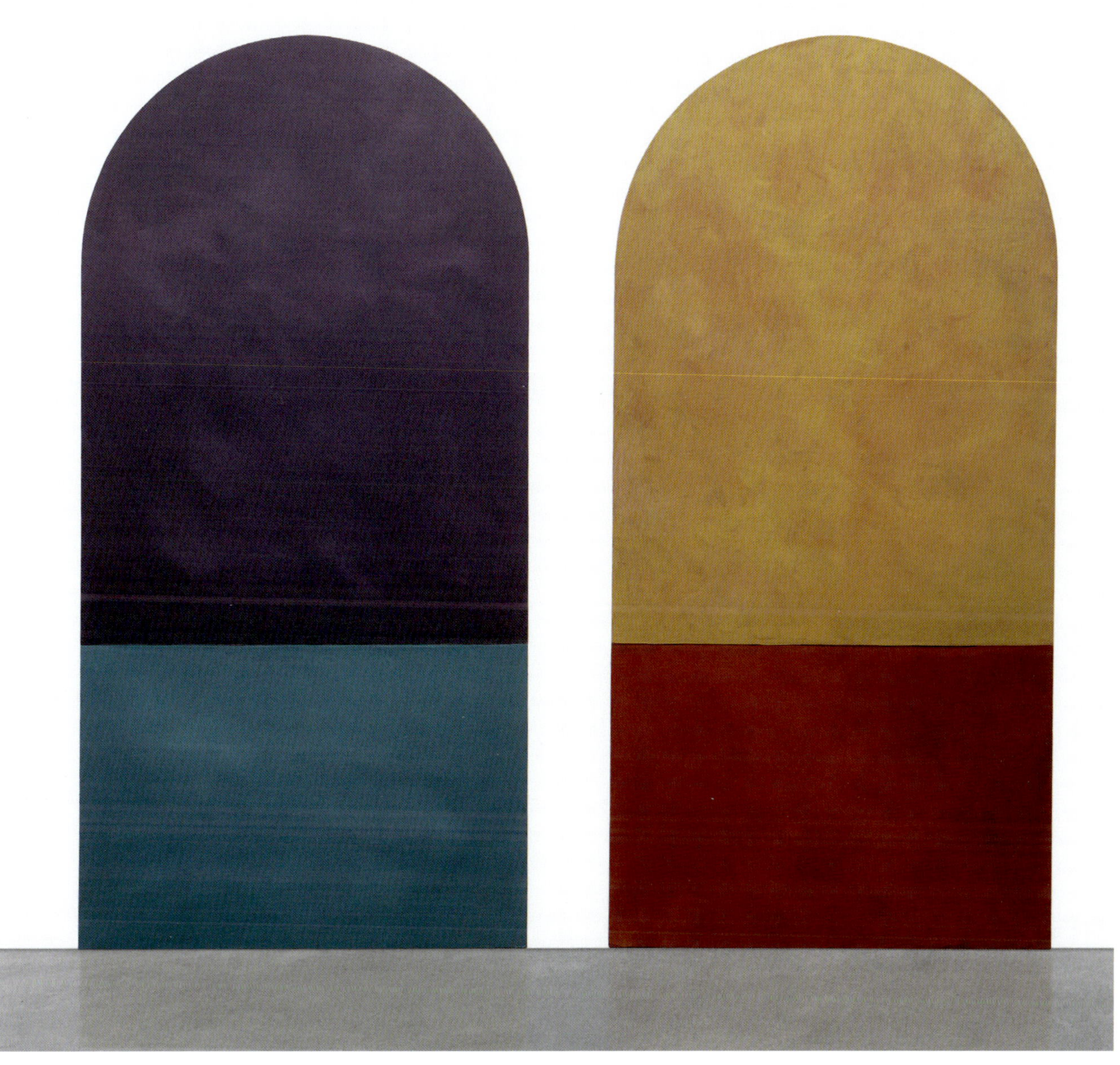

Outside and Inside, 1975
Oil on Masonite
2 panels, 72×36 in. each
(182.9×91.4 cm)

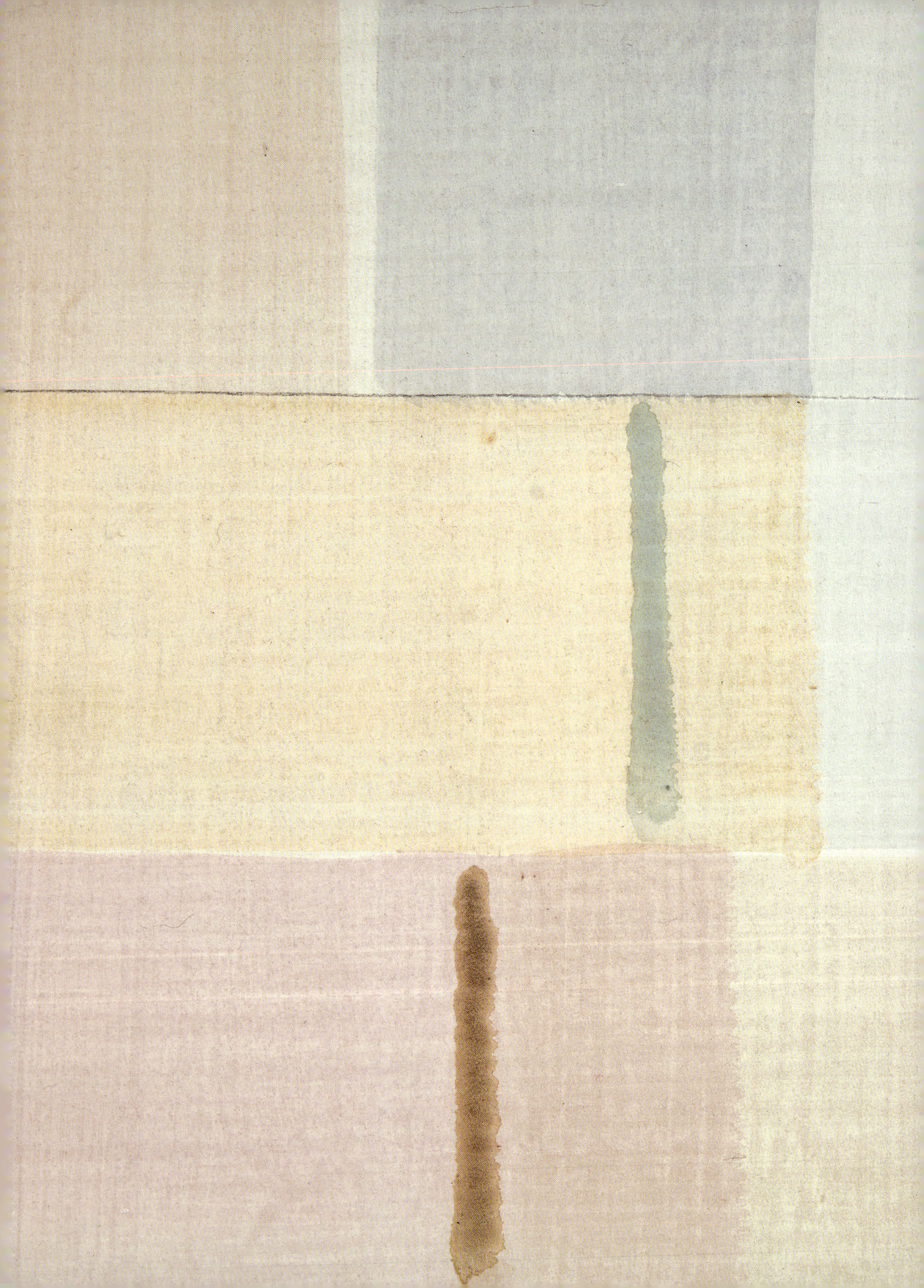

SETS SERIES

In the latter half of the 1970s, Obering painted a series of works that she hung in sets, each panel painted in egg tempera with short brushstrokes, the width of which was determined by the brush's size. Tempera allowed a translucency not seen in her acrylic and oil paintings, and highlighted Obering's process of painting in which the start and finish of each stroke are clearly delineated, creating a rhythm within the blocks of color. These paintings are clear indications of Obering's fascination with color relationships and the science of looking, to which the genre of landscape, and especially the function of the horizon line, has been central, all provided by the medium that would become her signature.

For Morandi, 1978
Egg tempera on Masonite
6 panels, 12×16 in. each
(30.48×40.64 cm)

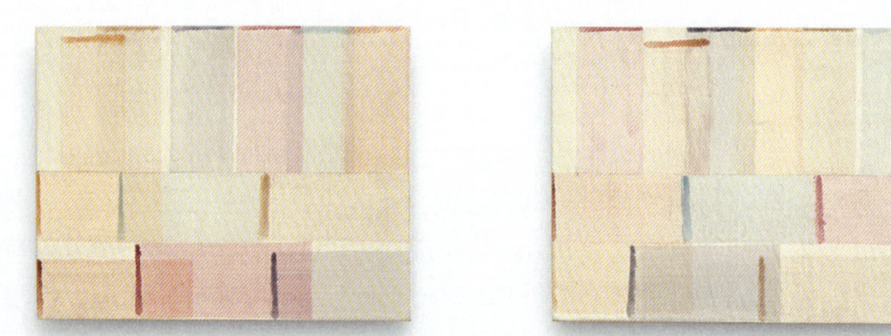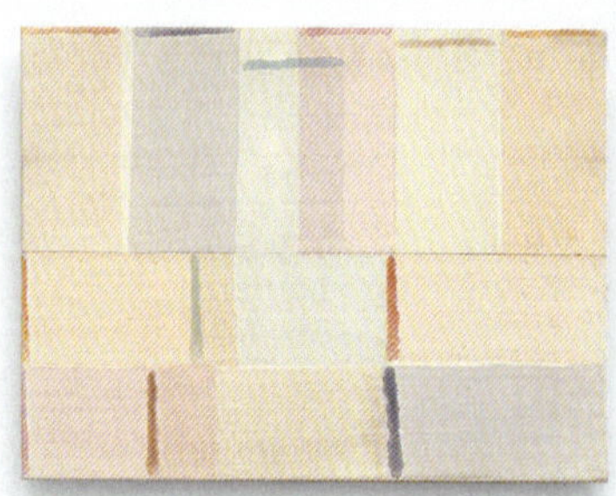

For Morandi, 1978
Egg tempera on Masonite
6 panels, 12×16 in. each
(30.48×40.64 cm)

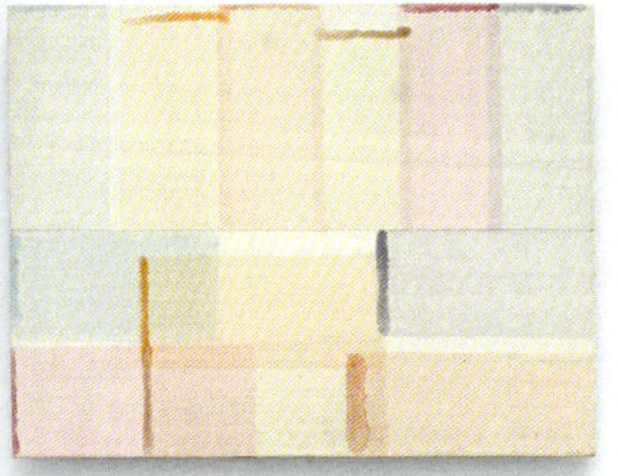
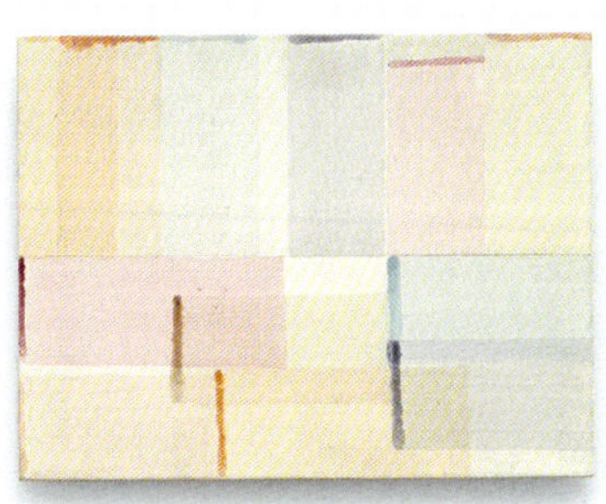
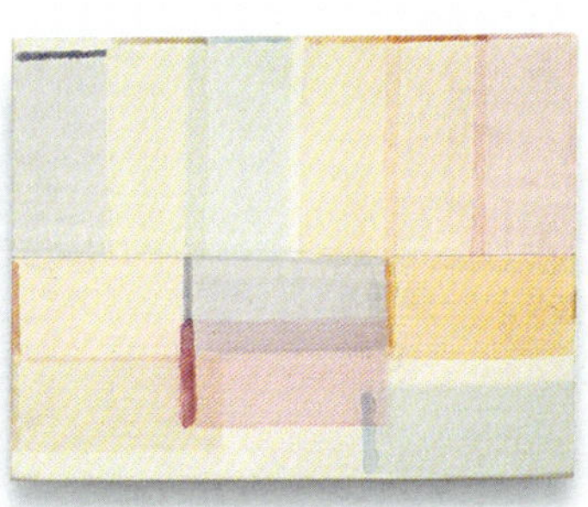

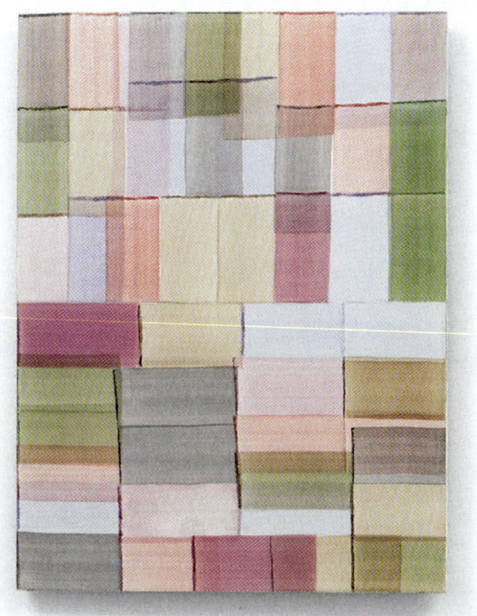
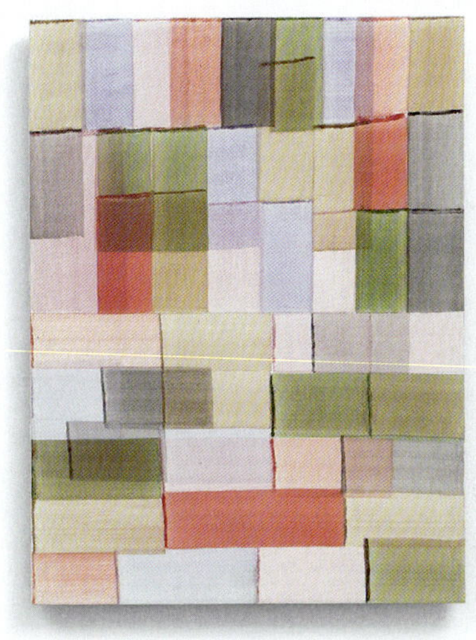

Paler I, 1978
Egg tempera on plywood
2 panels, 30×24 in. each
(76.2×60.96 cm)

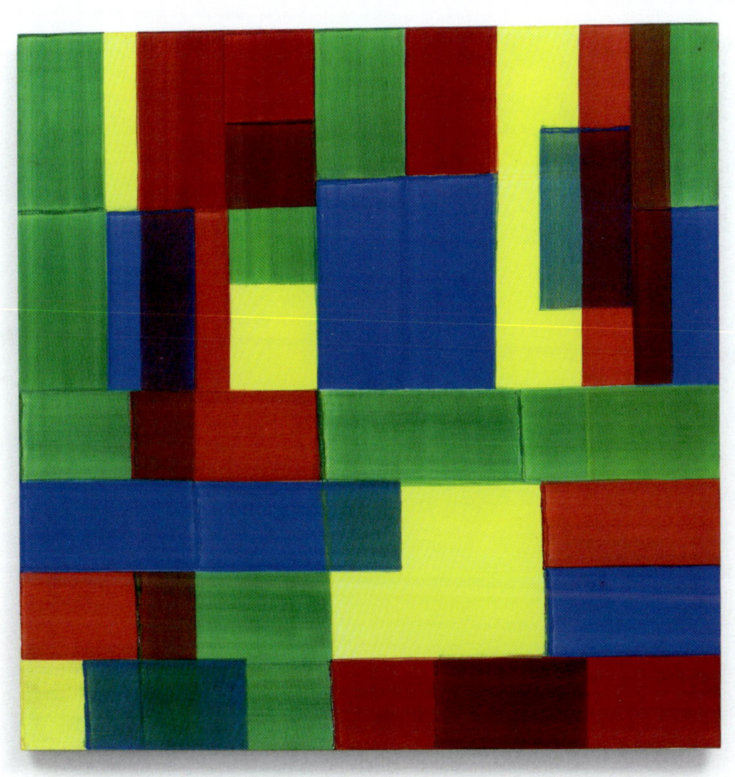

Big Bix, 1978
Egg tempera on
gessoed panel
48×48 in.
(121.9×121.9 cm)

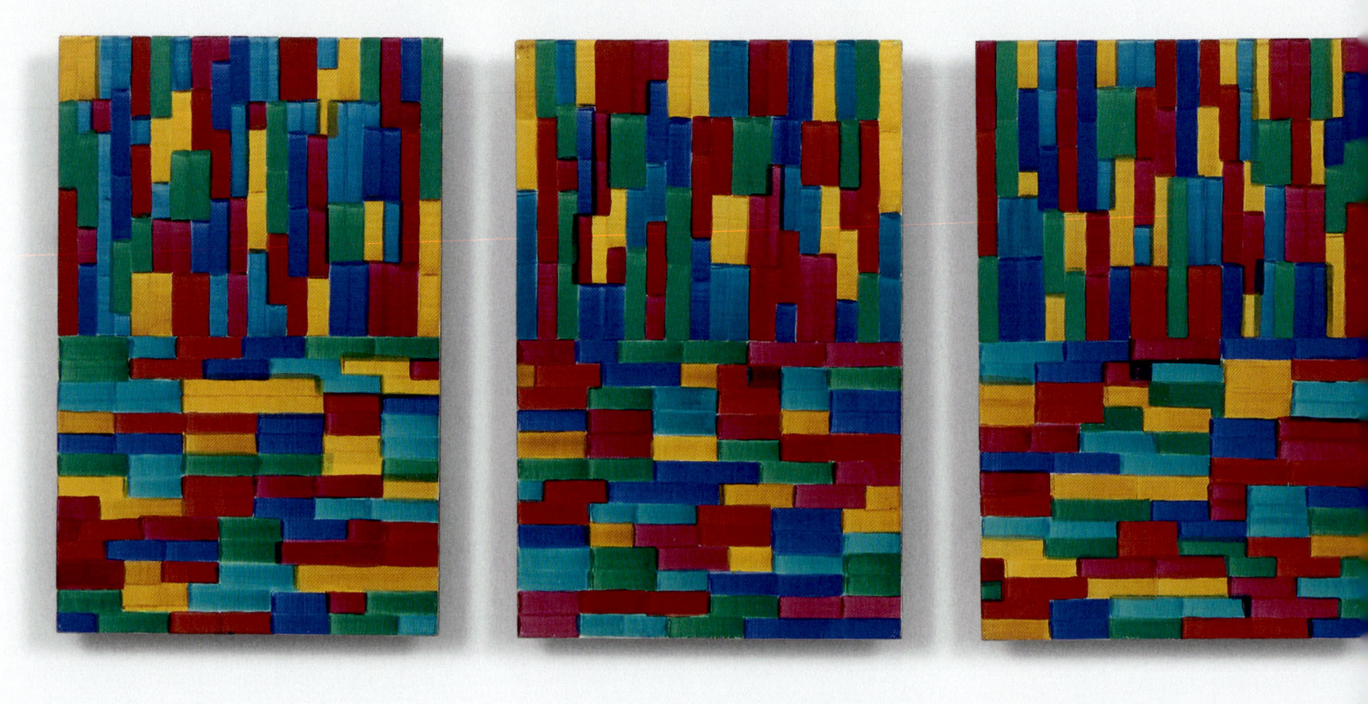

Jewels, 1977
Egg tempera on Masonite
6 panels, 8×12 in. each
(20.32×30.48 cm)

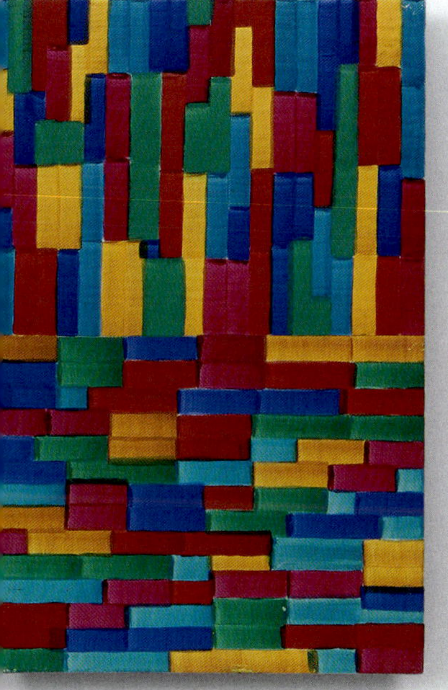
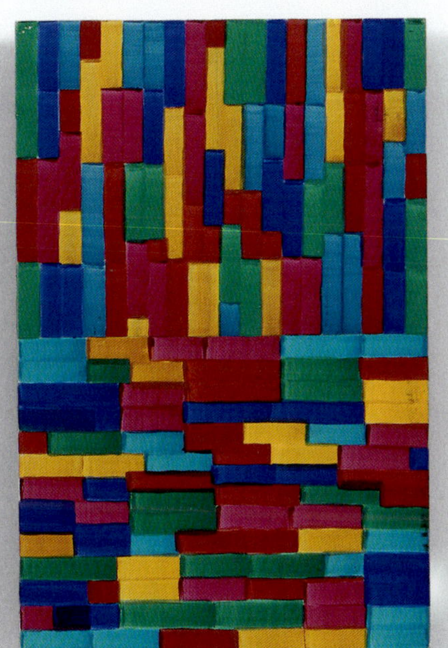
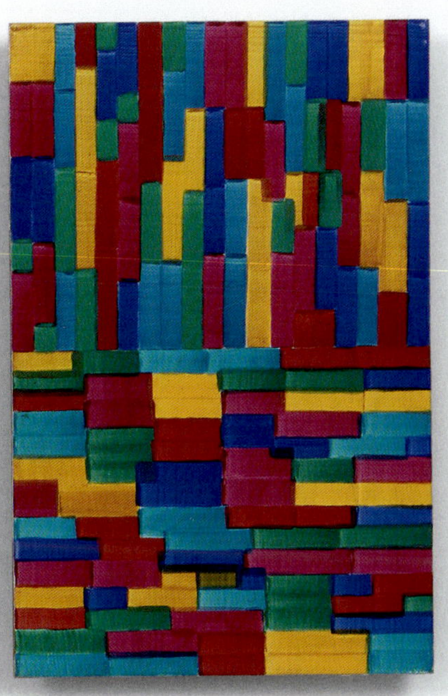

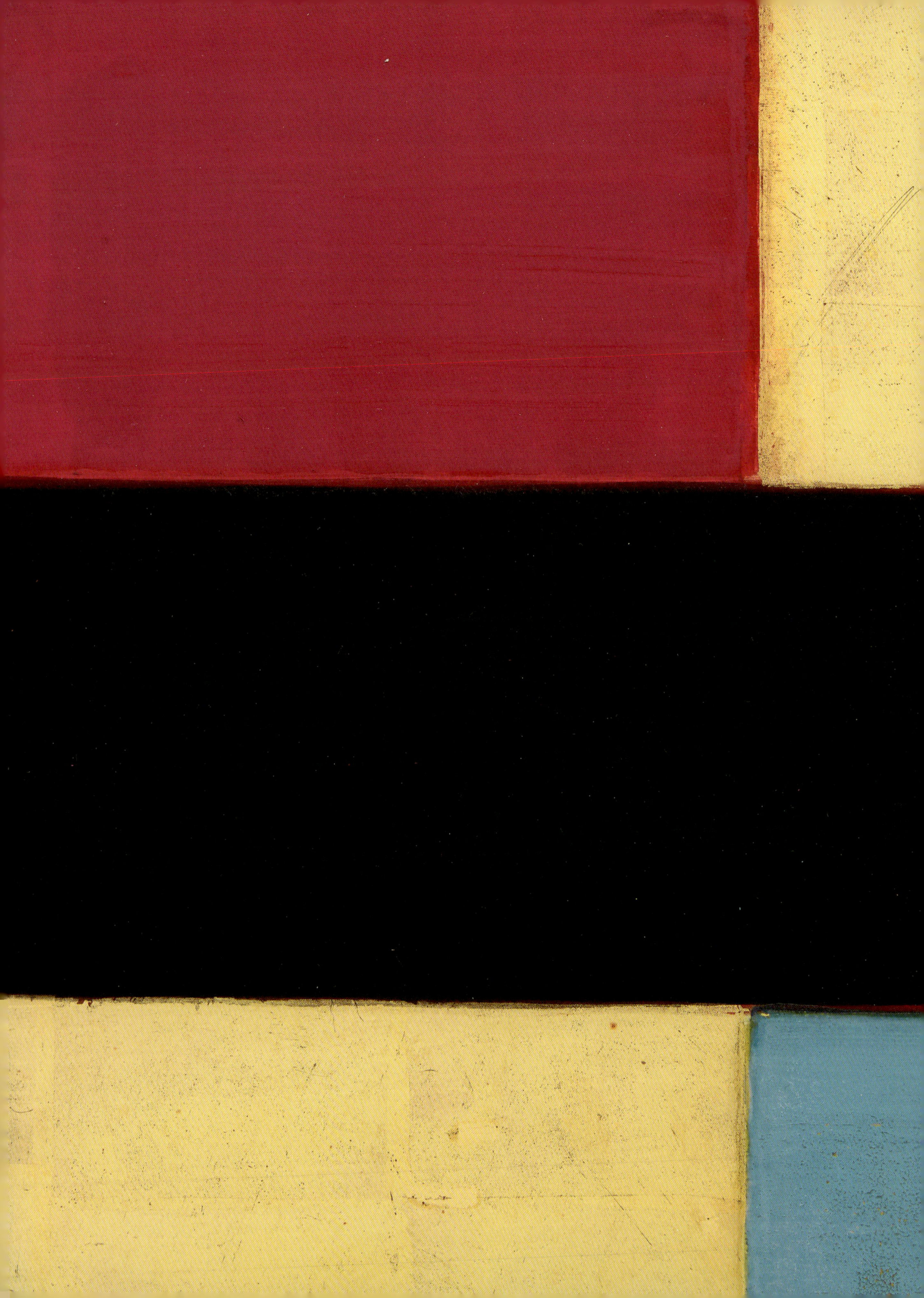

EARLY GOLDEN

Gold leaf makes its first marked appearance in the Early Golden series, alongside its counterpart, egg tempera. The paintings from this series are produced on Masonite, a new material at the time of the painting's production, cradled beneath their support in a gesture recalling tempera and gold leaf's Old Master origins. Undergoing training to gain knowledge of these mediums, this series sees the artist's earliest experimentation with the elements that reflect her ongoing interest in the Italian Renaissance and Byzantine art. The process of gold leafing is slow and tedious, with delicate strips of the metal leafed with a brush, moistened by lotion applied to the artist's own skin, acting like a palette, and finally adhered onto rabbit skin glue. Each Early Golden painting is intimately sized, an indication of the artist's humble yet sophisticated first processes with these ancient materials.

Bridge, 1979
Egg tempera and gold
leaf on gessoed panel
27 × 21 in.
(68.58 × 53.34 cm)

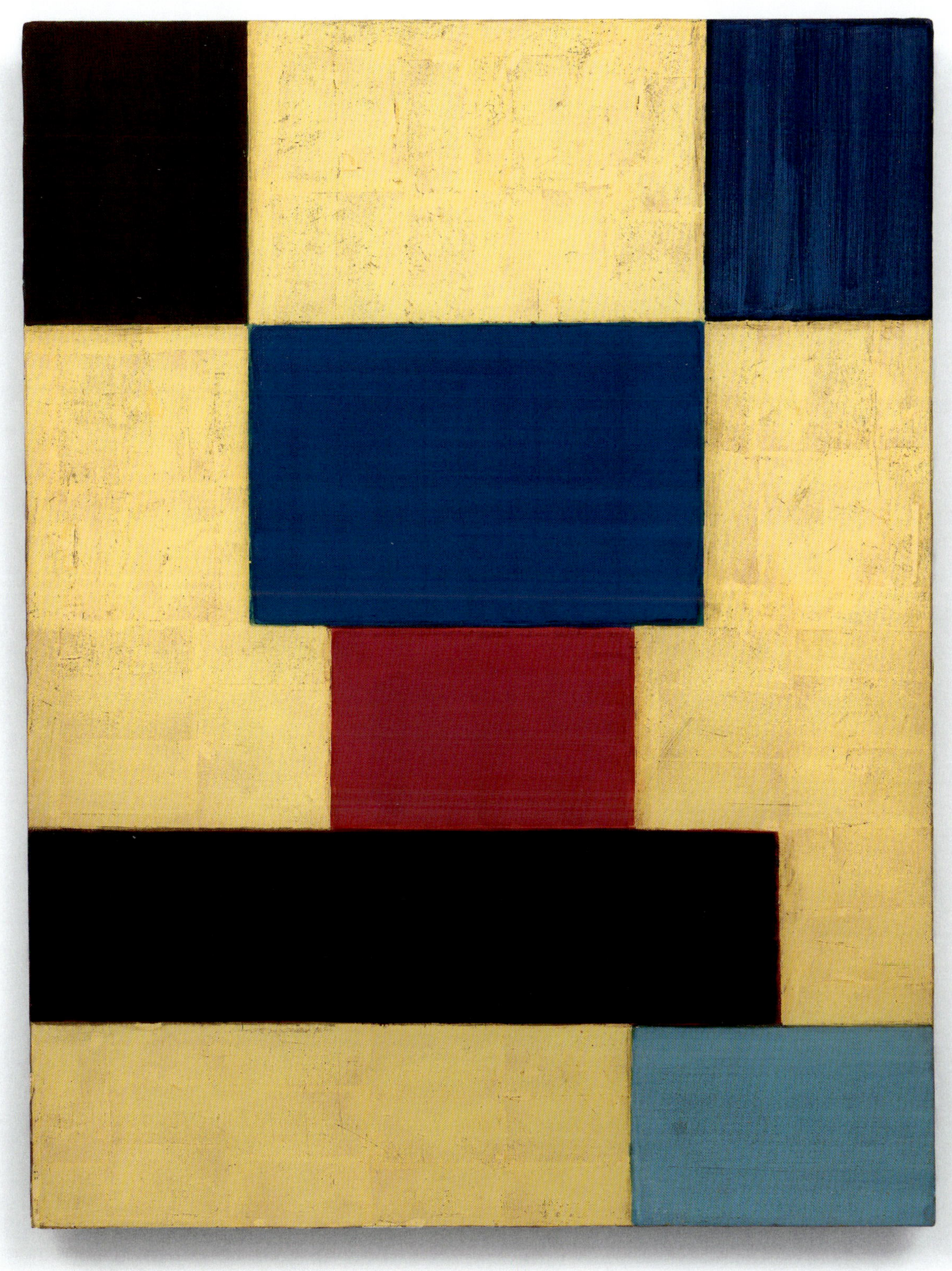

Bridge, 1979
Egg tempera and gold
leaf on gessoed panel
27×21 in.
(68.58×53.34 cm)

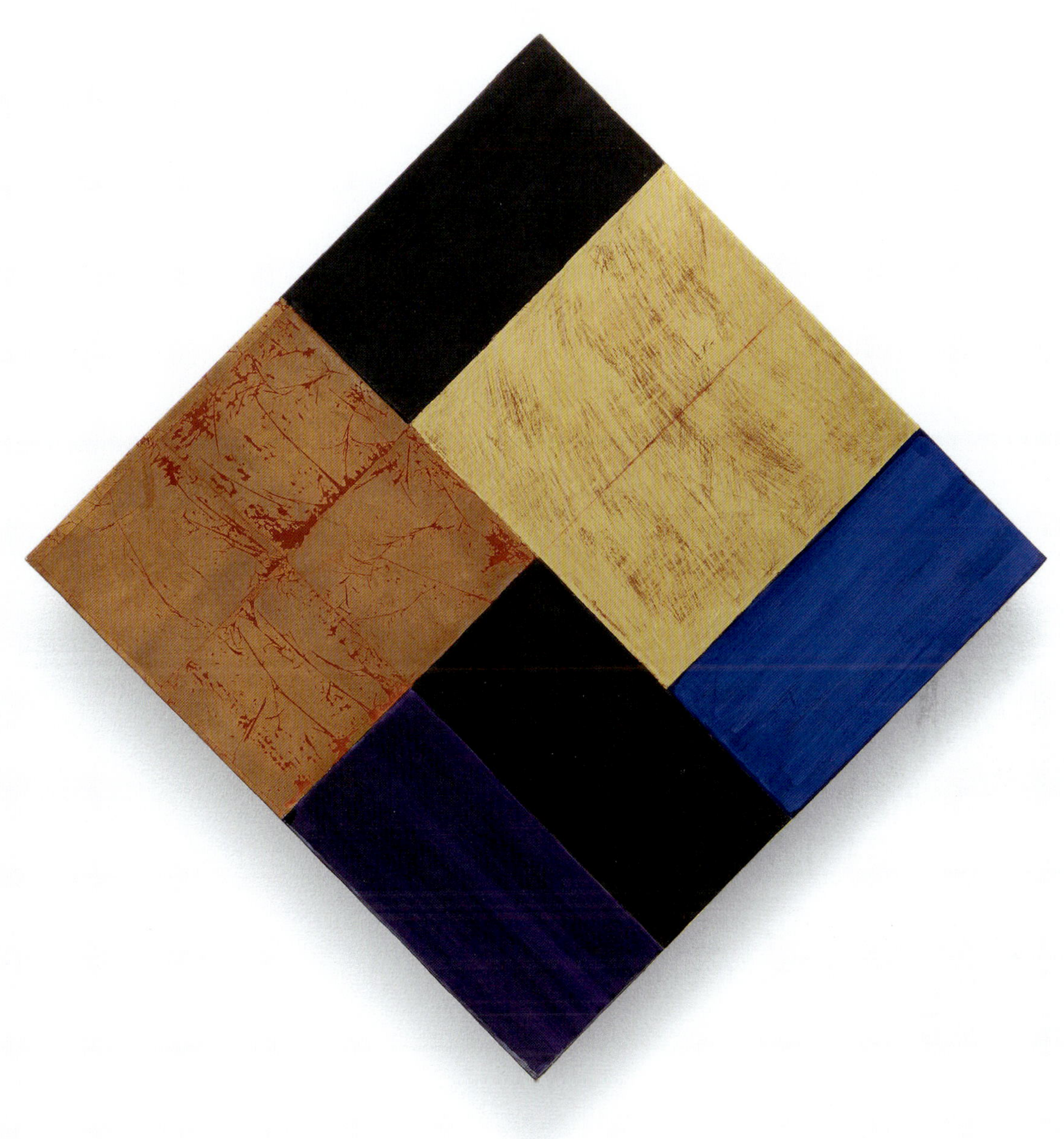

Byrd Fair Park, 1980
Egg tempera and gold leaf
on gessoed panel
21¾×21¾ in.
(55.2×55.2 cm)

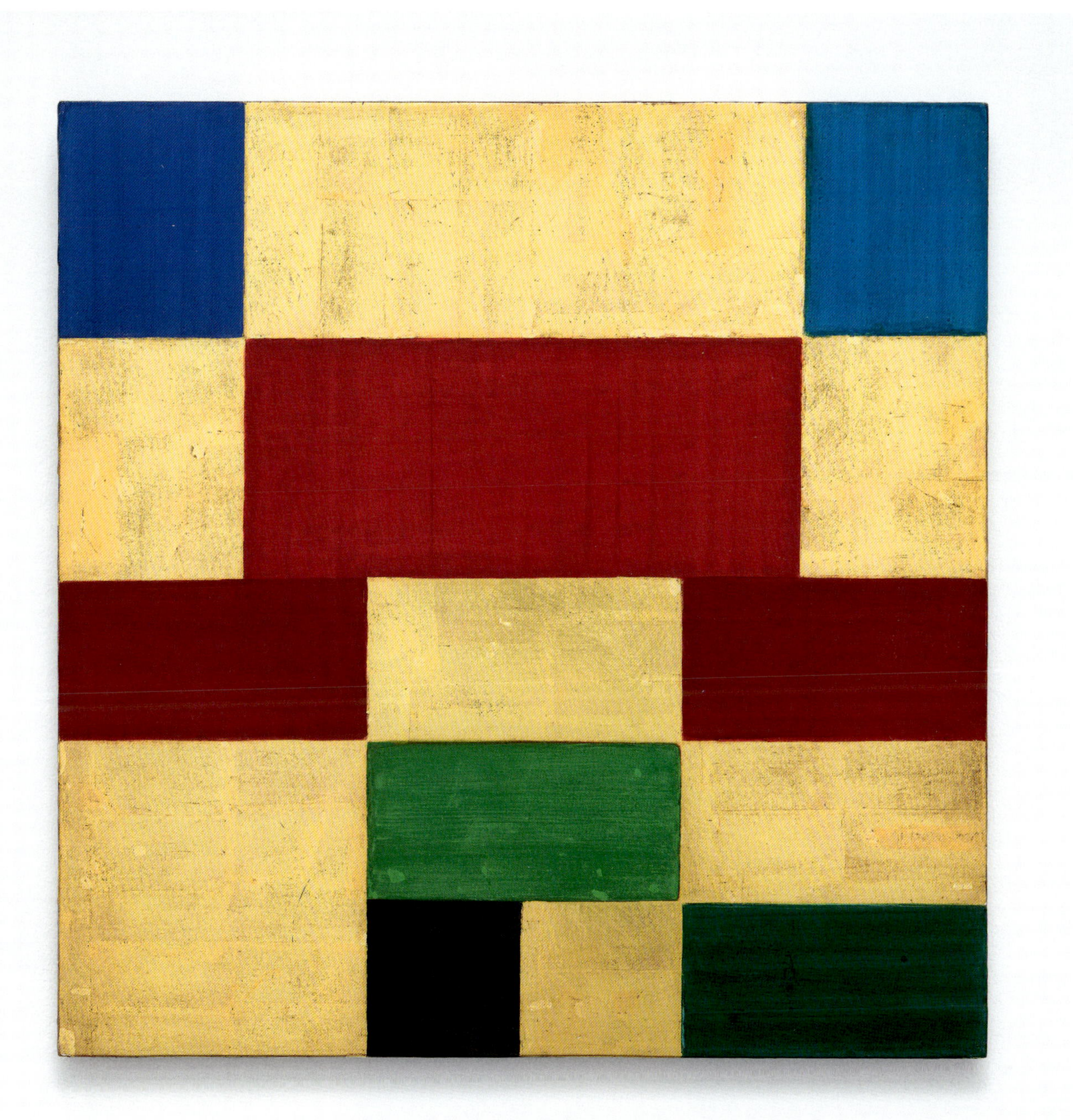

Cricket, 1979
Egg tempera and gold
leaf on gessoed Masonite
21×21 in.
(53.3×53.3 cm)

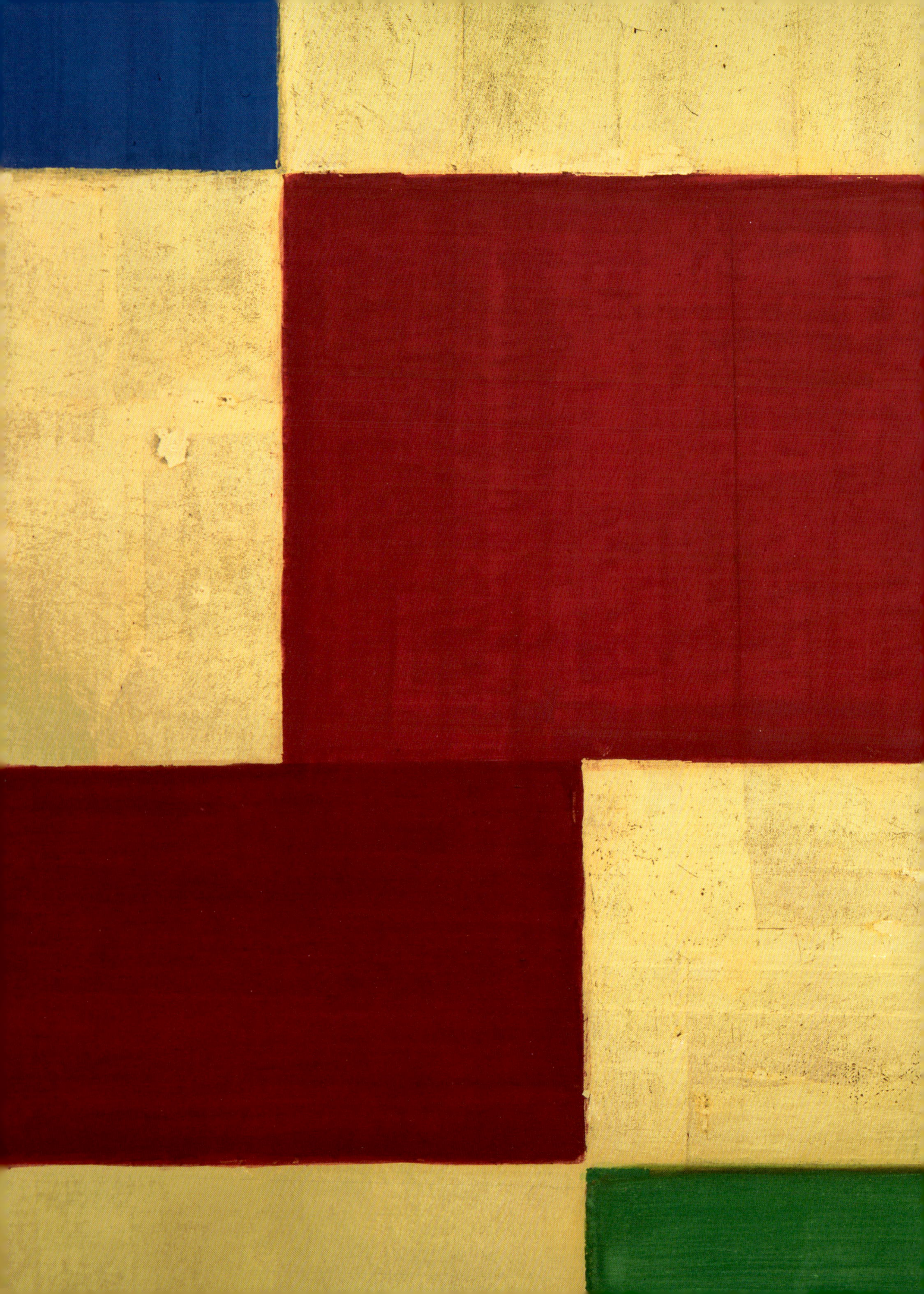

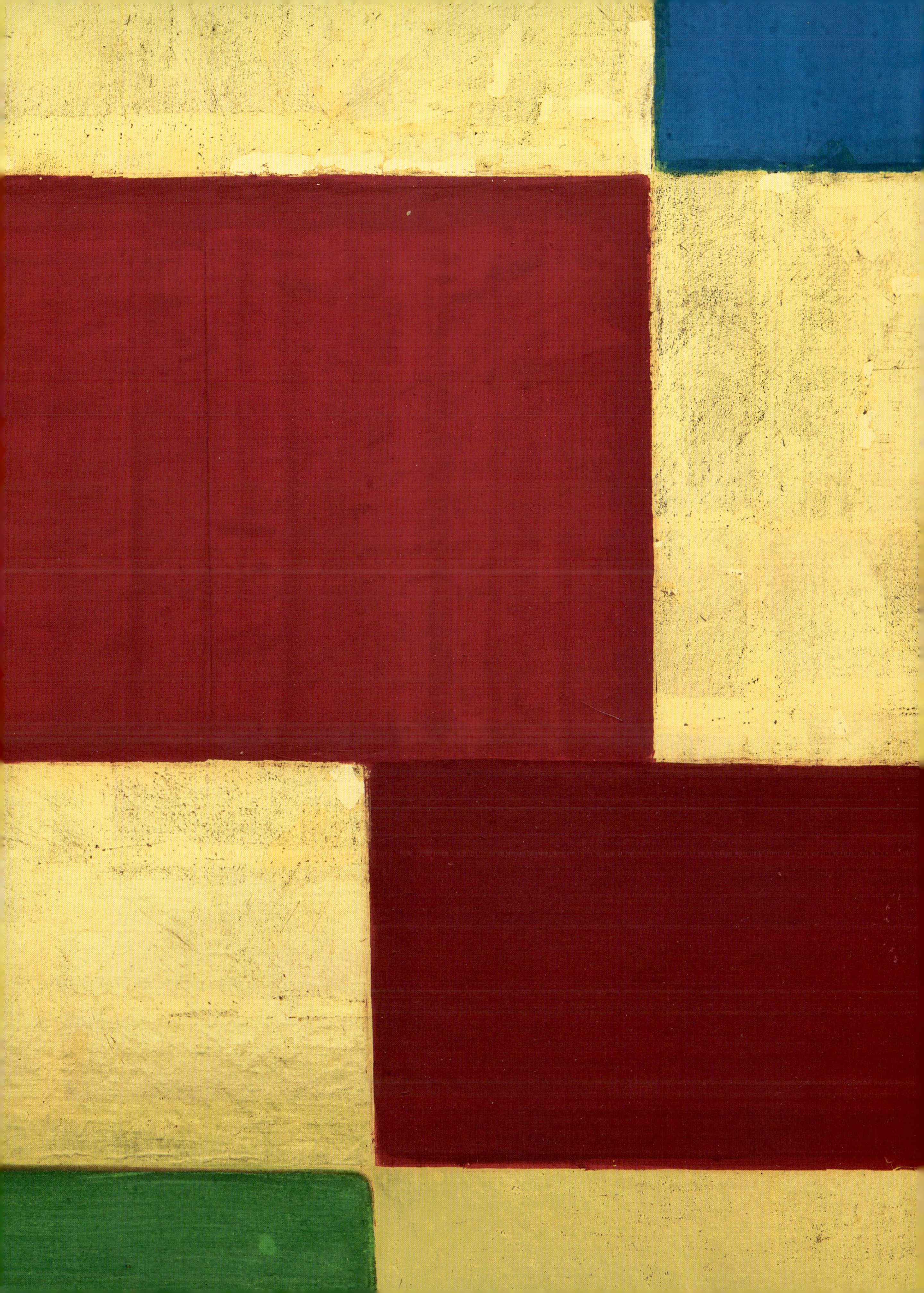

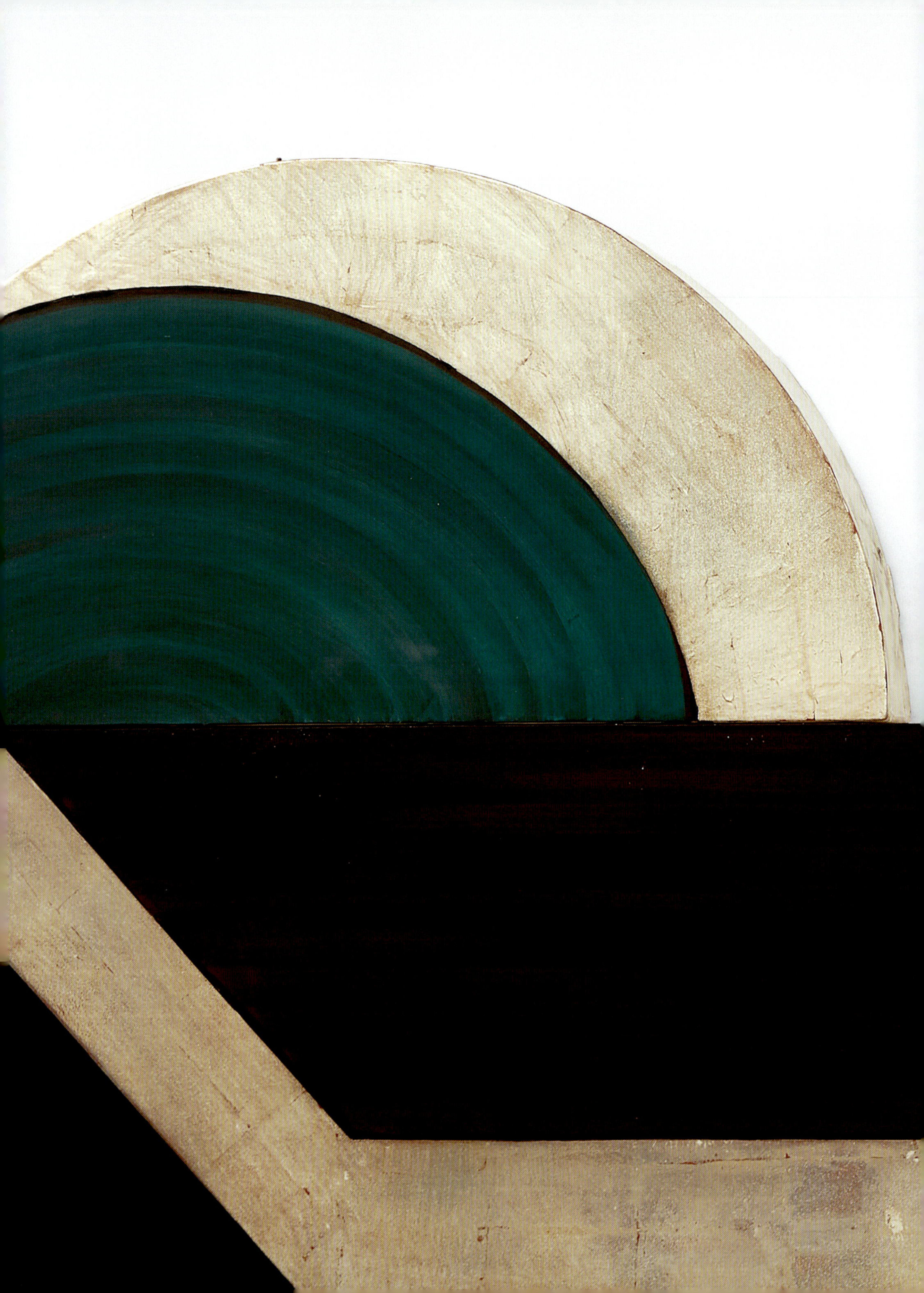

1980s WORK

COSMIC SERIES
QUANTUM CHROMODYNAMICS SERIES

In the 1980s, Obering extended her visual vocabulary to panels of different shapes. Circular panels painted in stripes of tempera and gold leaf suggest waxing moons; a jagged beam, like a lightning bolt, is a nod to a positively charged atomic particle. During this decade, the notion of abstraction extends to include ideas both too massive and too minute to be perceived optically, from particle physics to planetary movements. Science, Obering is suggesting, is a construct wed to abstraction. The natural landscape, an ongoing concern of the artist's, is much too complex to be limited to its illustration.

Streamline, 1981
Egg tempera, gold leaf,
and white gold leaf on
gessoed panel
24×84 in
(61×213.4 cm)

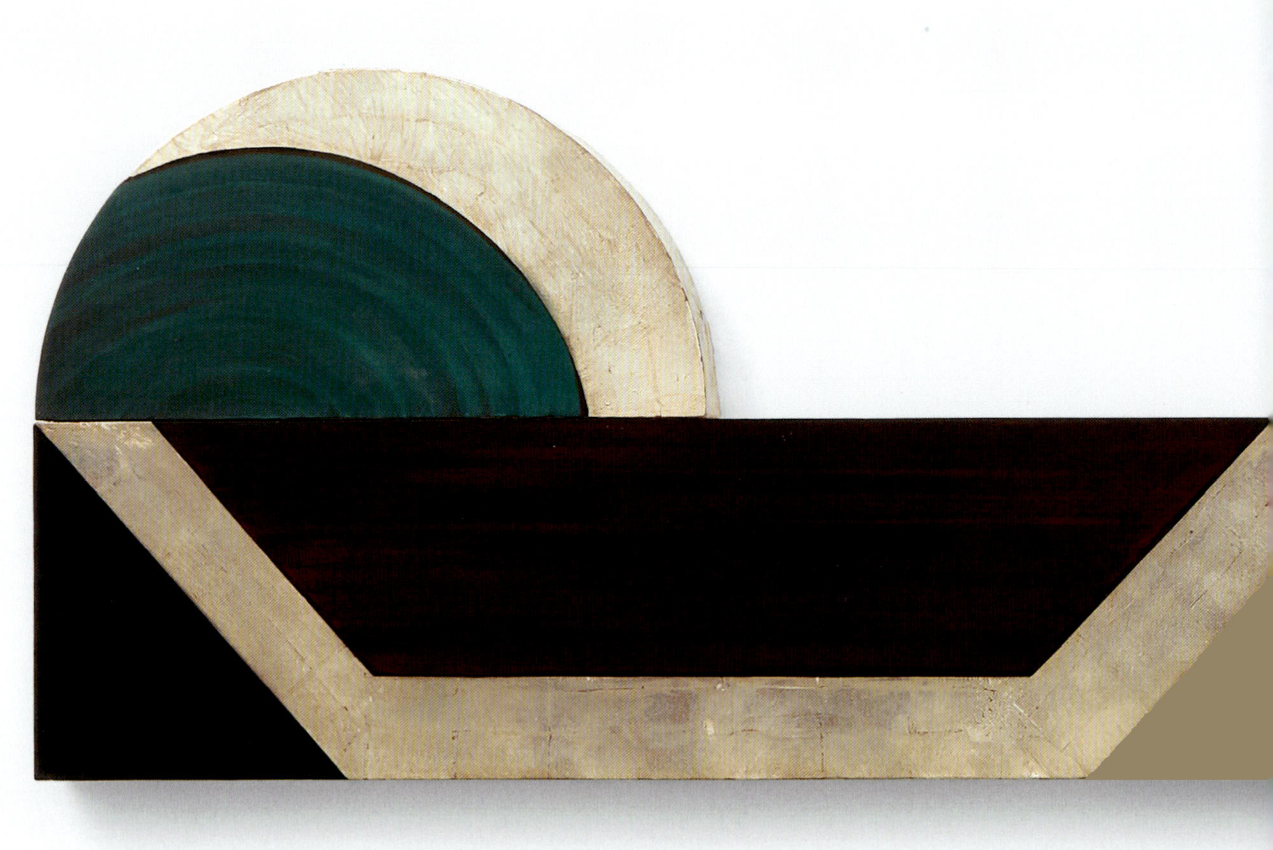

Streamline, 1981
Egg tempera, gold leaf,
and white gold leaf on
gessoed panel
24×84 in
(61×213.4 cm)

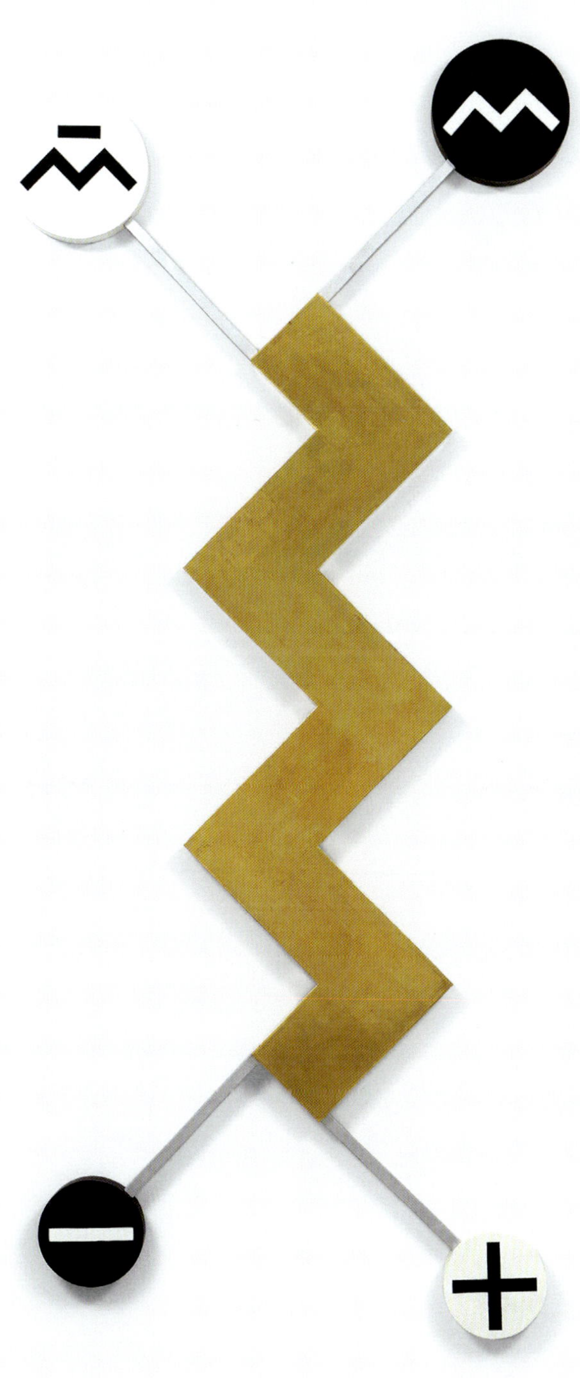

Muon Maker, 1987
Egg tempera and gold leaf
on gessoed panel
107×47 in.
(271.8×119.4 cm)

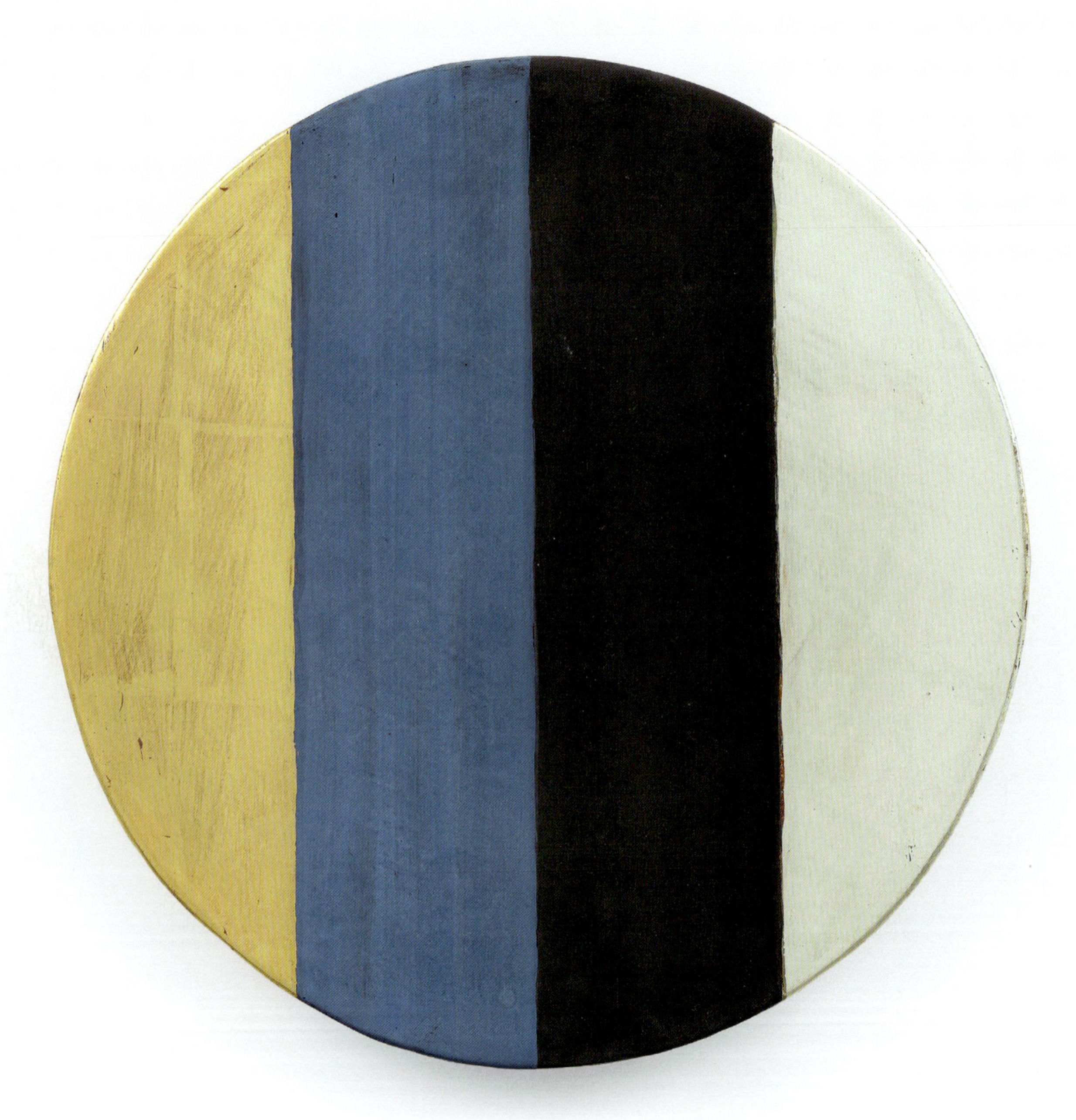

Four Houses of the Sun I, 1983
Egg tempera, gold leaf and
white gold leaf on gessoed panel
12 in. diameter each
(30.48 cm diameter each)

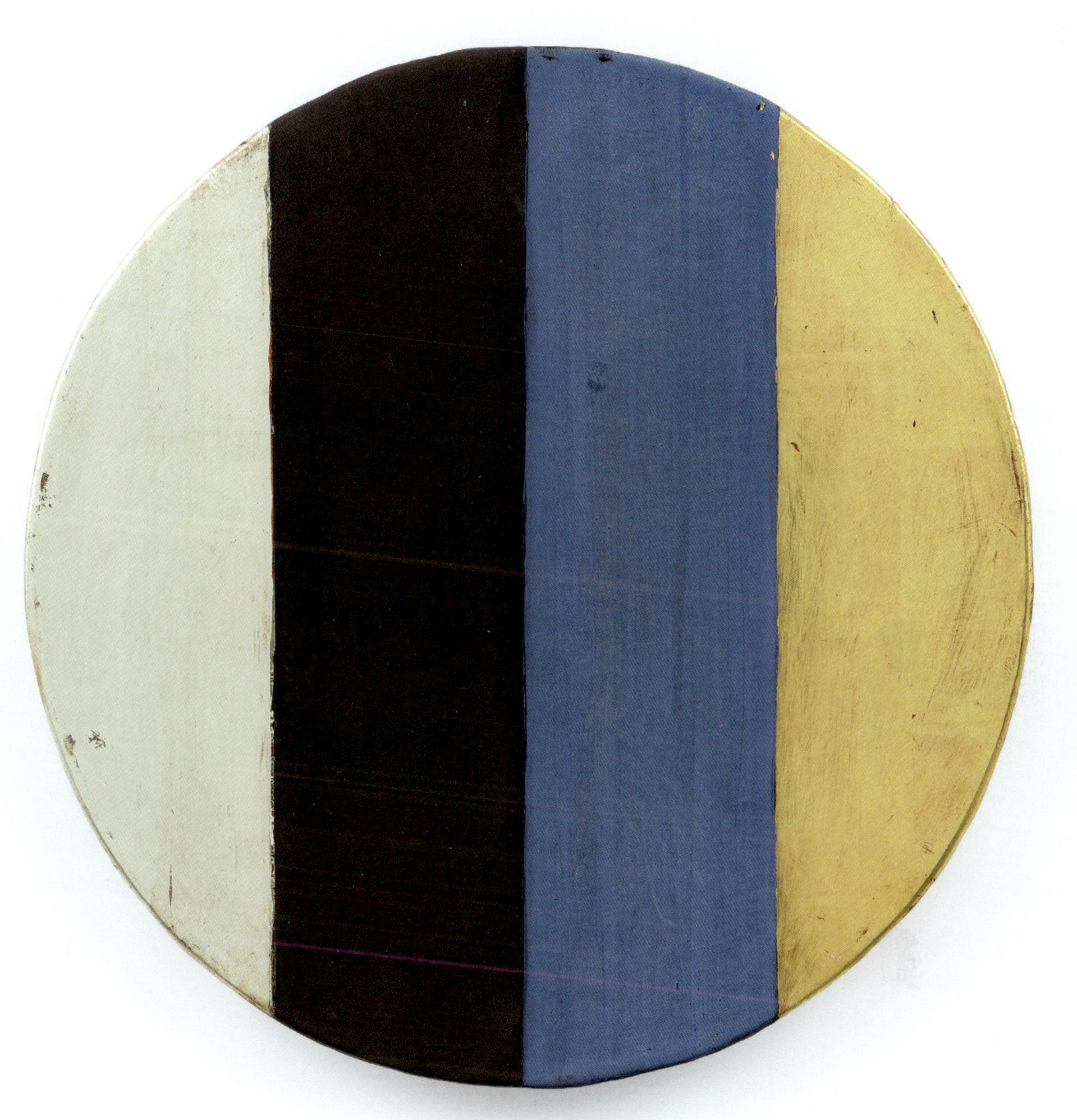

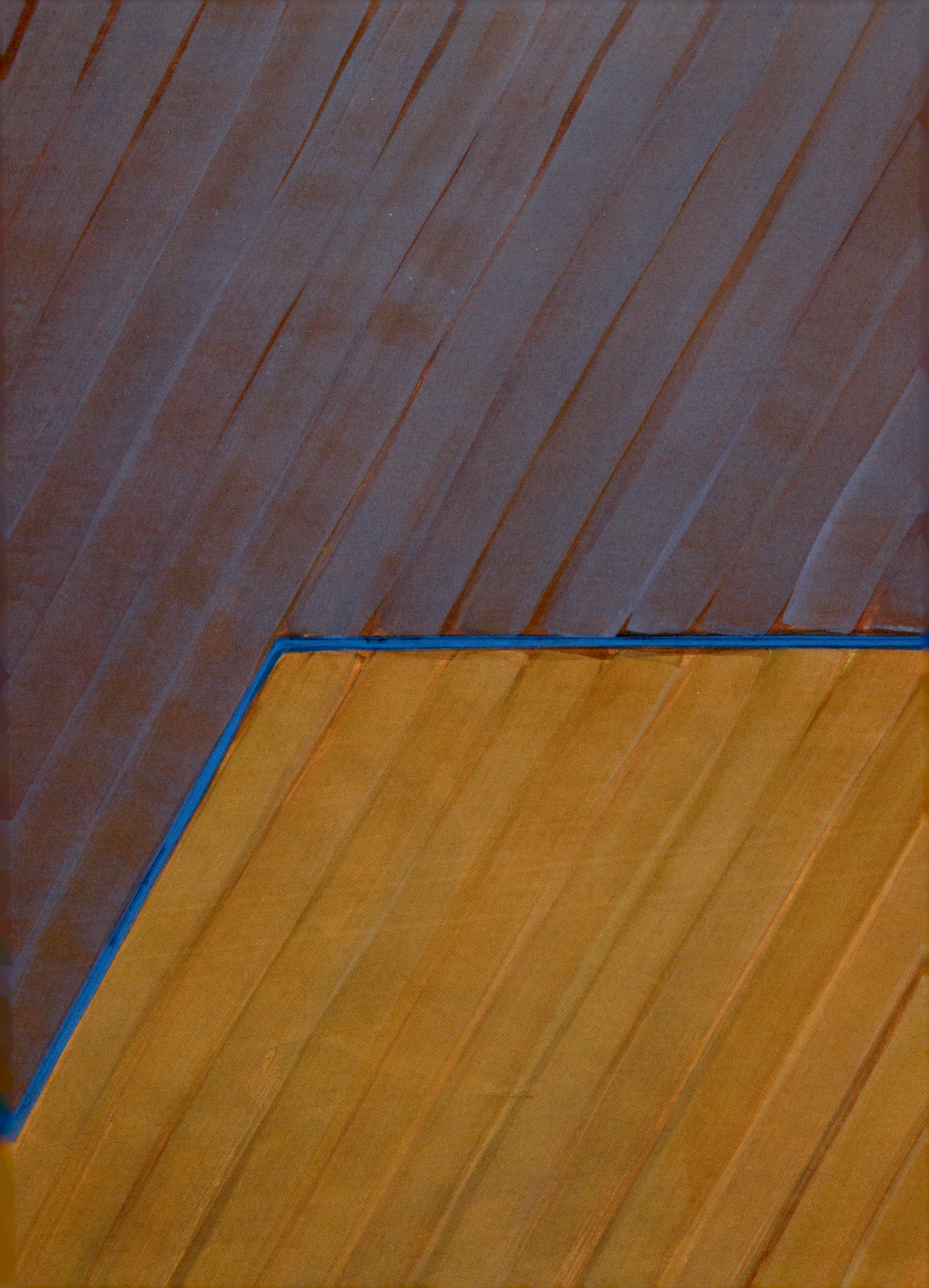

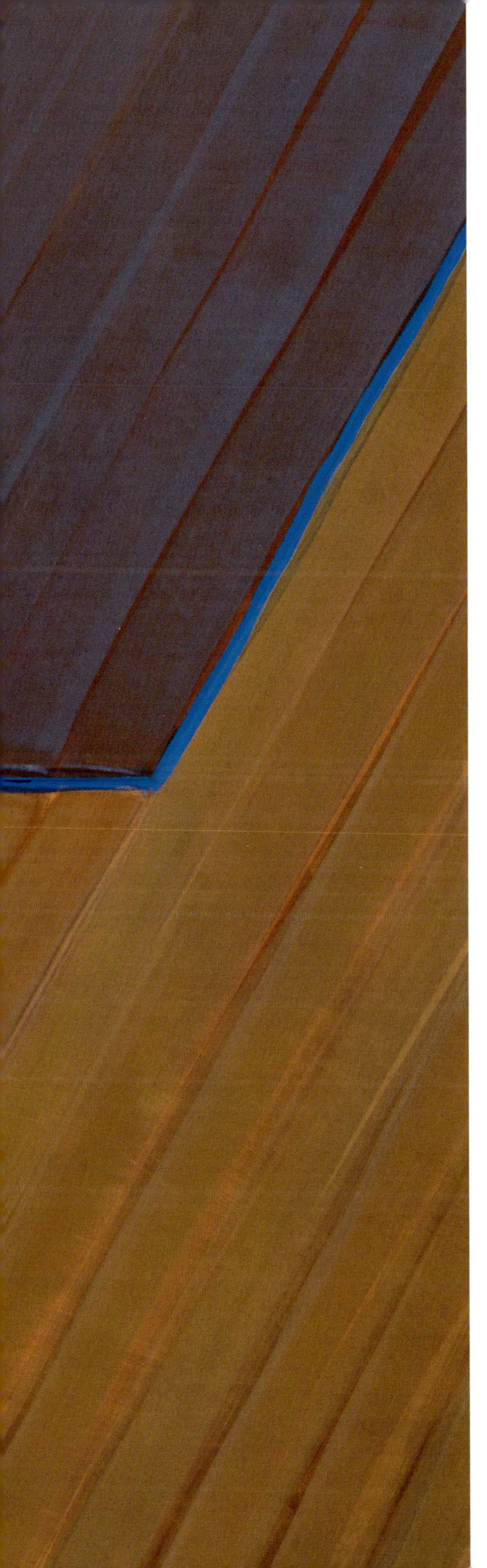

REPTILE SERIES

Obering's wide range of interests, from science and math to art history and psychology, is highlighted in the many notebooks she kept, detailing her thoughts as she worked through materials and composition in her painting. One such series, Reptile, directly correlates to a term in geometry, "rep-tile," in which a particular shape is composed of smaller copies of itself. Equations written in pencil in the margins of a geometry book from her library illustrate Obering's continued focus on scale, but also color relationships as the tempera fields delineate and highlight the composite shapes. Notably, the tile work—tessellation—Obering admired in ancient Italian architecture is derived from this theory. Each painting's title is a play on words in which Obering references reptiles: *Snake Prince, Tortoise, Blue Runner*. Gilded along their edges, the Reptile series paintings reflect a halo onto the wall, an indication of Obering's interest in activating the space beyond the pictorial plane.

Reptile, 1985
Egg tempera on gessoed
panel with copper leaf edge
42.5 × 47.5 in.
(107.95 × 120.65 cm)

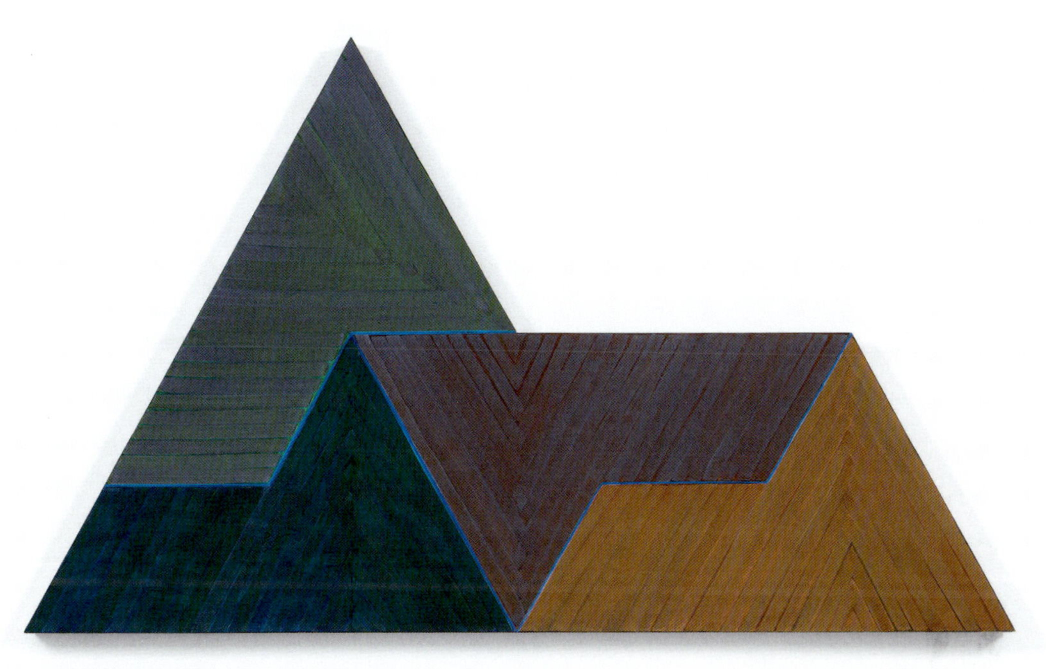

Reptile, 1985
Egg tempera on gessoed
panel with copper leaf edge
42.5×47.5 in.
(107.95×120.65 cm)

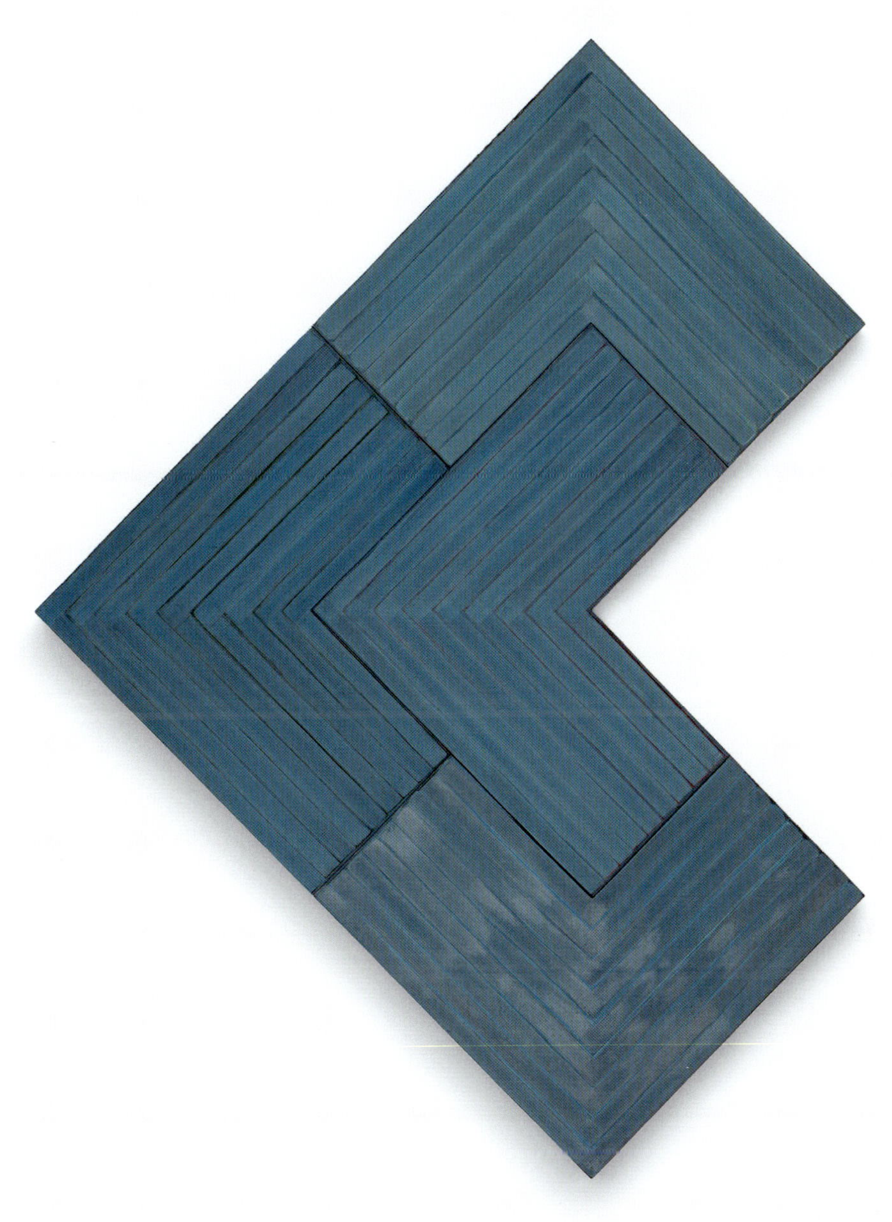

Blue Runner, 1985
Egg tempera on gessoed
panel with aluminum leaf edge
66×60 in.
(167.6×152.4 cm)

Plell, 1986
Egg tempera on gessoed
panel with aluminum leaf edge
24 × 41½ in.
(61 × 105.4 cm)

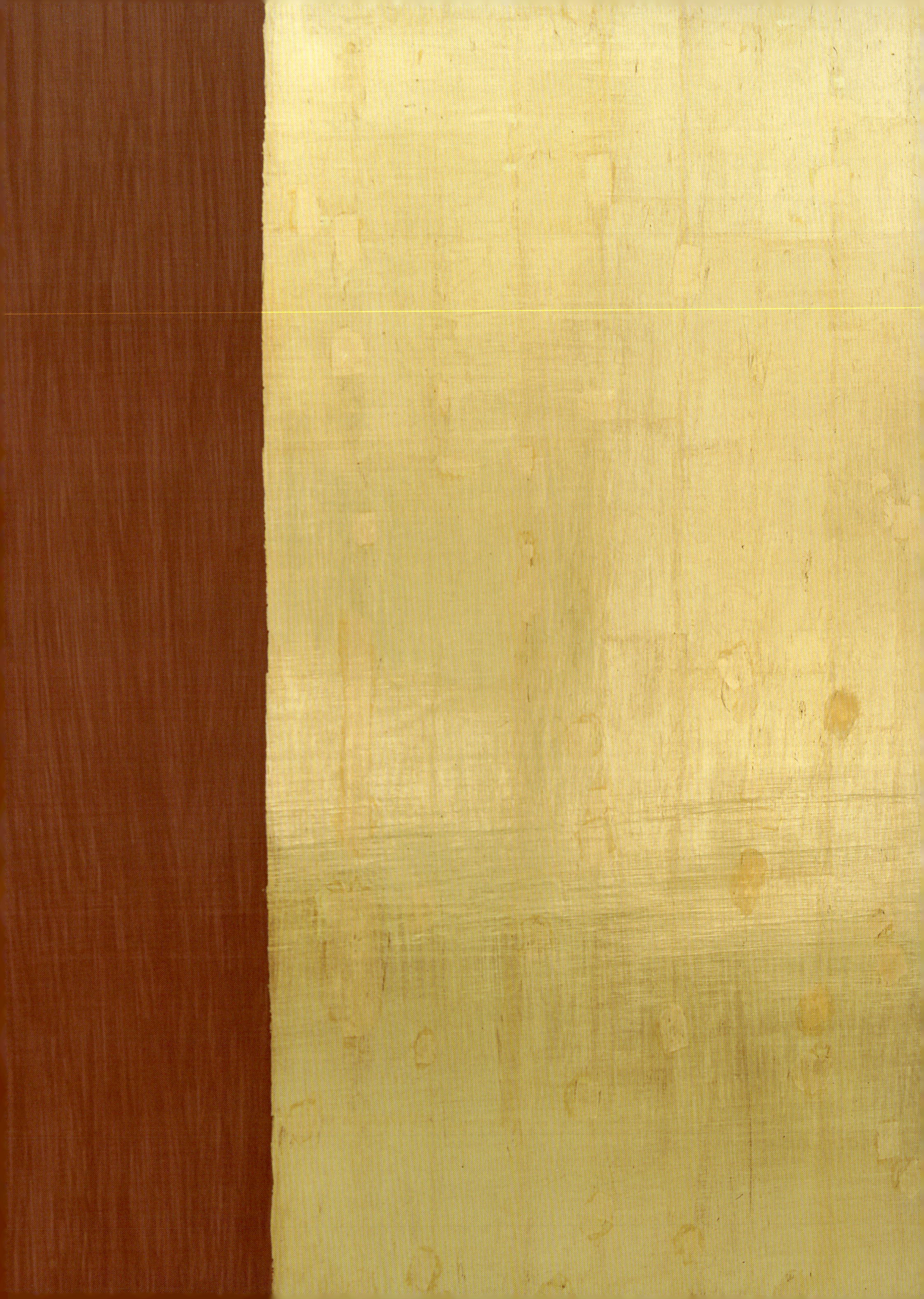

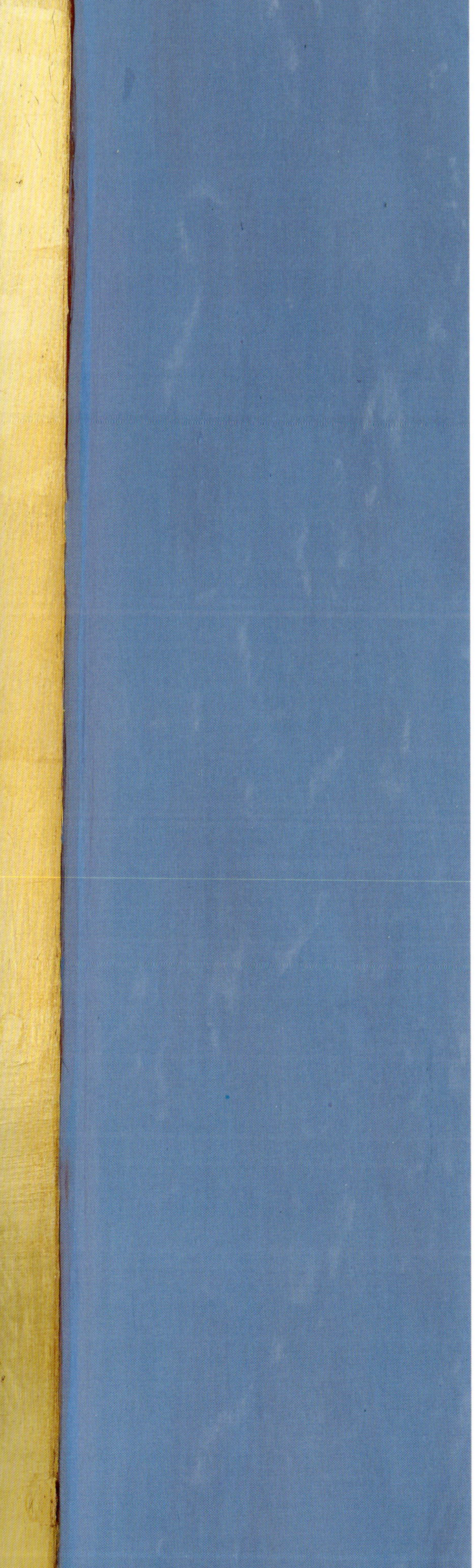

MATERIAL PAINTINGS

Beginning in the late 1980s, Obering produced the Material paintings, horizontal and square arrangements on Masonite that reveal the artist's process borrowed from Renaissance techniques. Each quadrant illustrates an element key to the production of Italian altarpieces: gesso, gilding clay, egg tempera, gold leaf, and the support itself. These elegant rectilinear paintings bring to the fore materials that would otherwise be concealed in the finished work of art, giving precedence to the deft construction and tactility with which the artist herself became engrossed. Laid clearly in a grid, each stratum of a painting, generally concealed through their layering, is exposed, unburdened from the needs of representation. In the Slip series, a square is suspended atop underlayers of color, metal leaf, and gilding clay in a nod to both Josef Albers' investigations of shape and color and the typically obscured material employed.

Untitled III, 1986
Egg tempera, gold leaf and
red gilding clay on gessoed panel
47⅞ × 59⅞ in.
(121.9 × 152.4 cm)

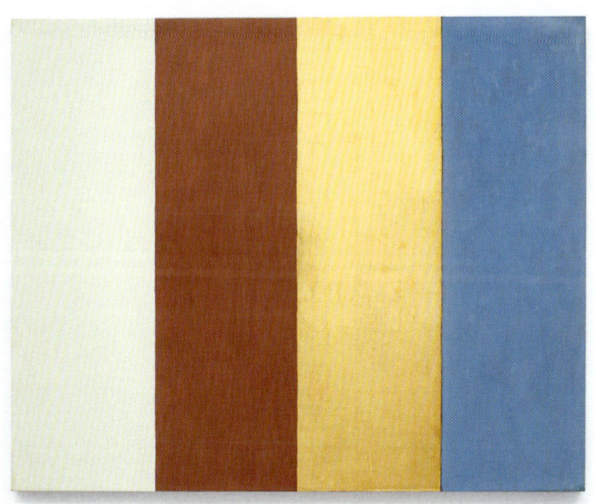

Untitled III, 1986
Egg tempera, gold leaf and
red gilding clay on gessoed panel
47⅞×59⅞ in.
(121.9×152.4 cm)

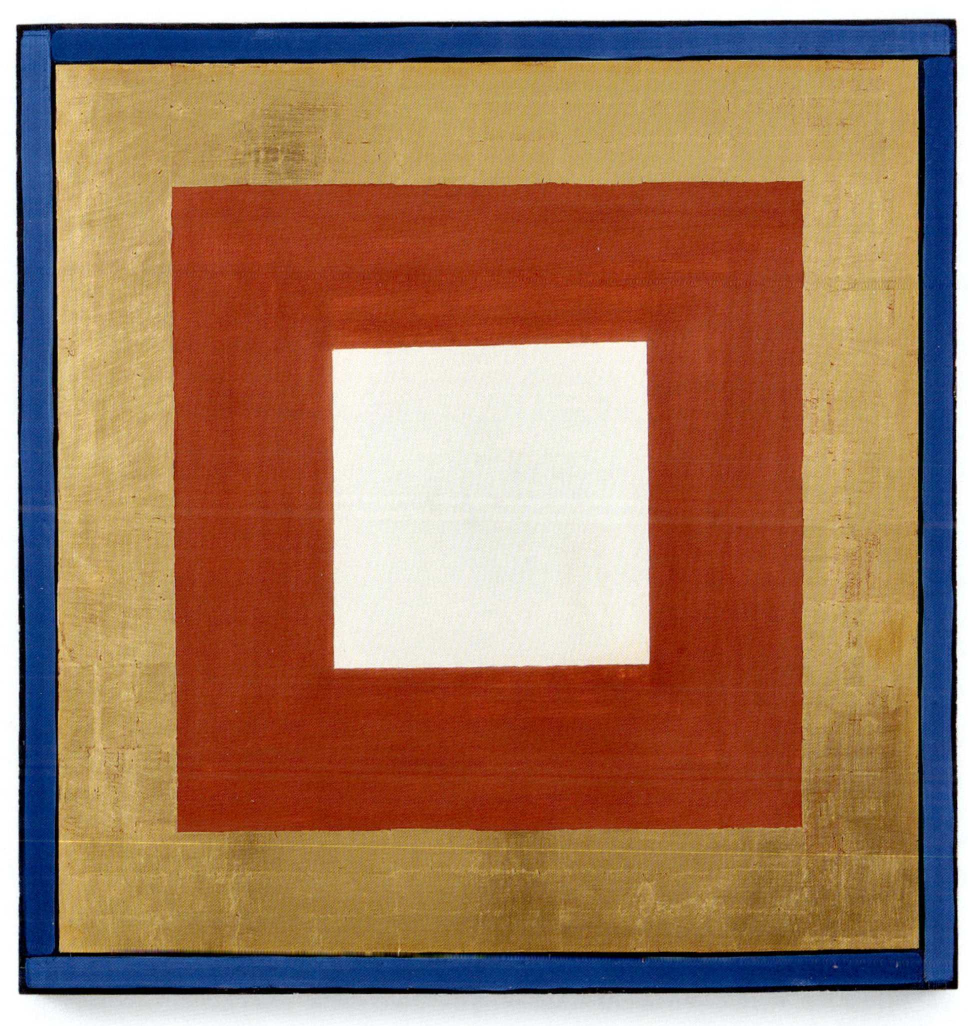

Blue Border, 1986
Egg tempera, gold leaf and
red gilding clay on gessoed panel
36×36 in.
(91.4×91.4 cm)

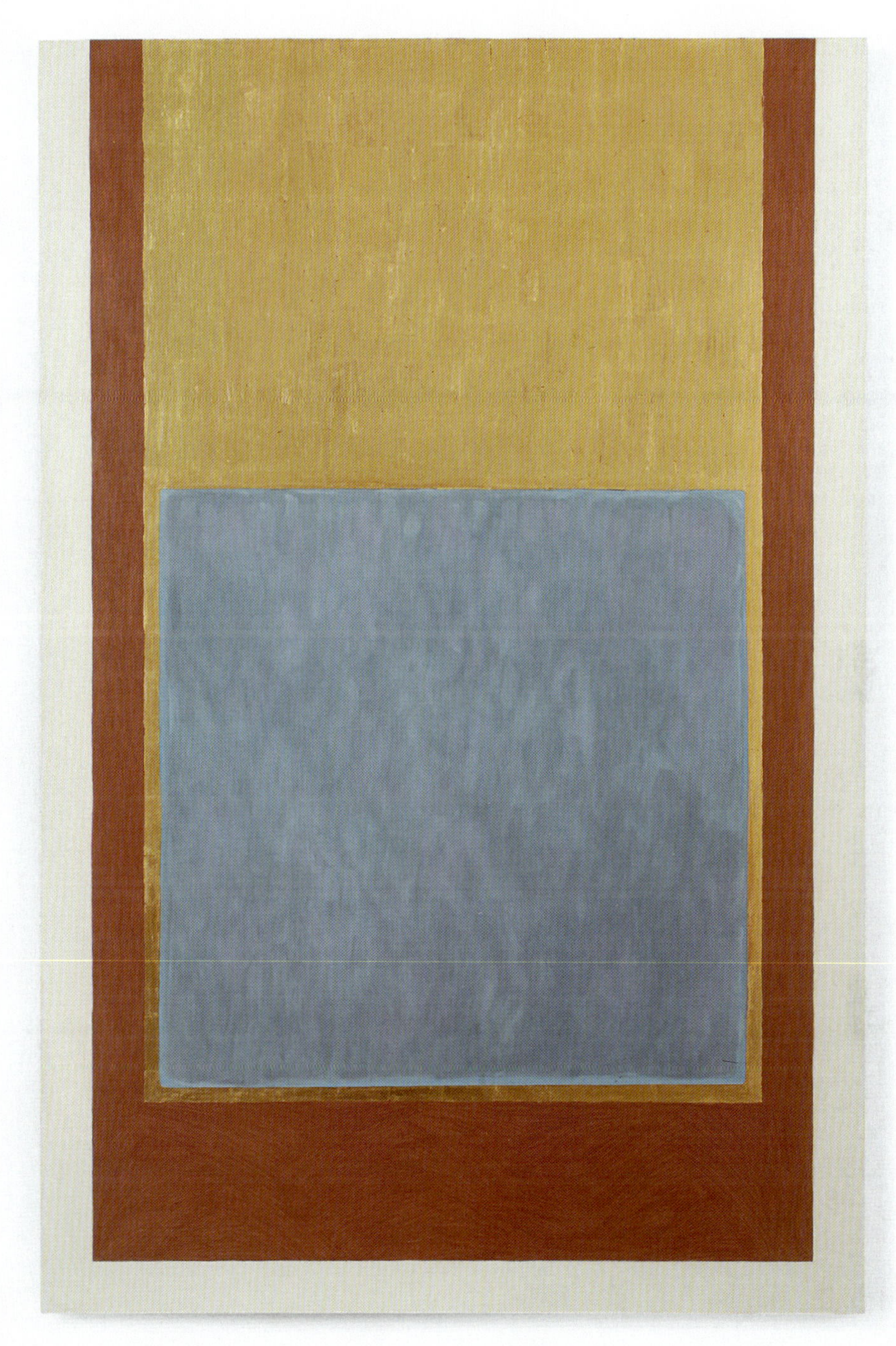

Slip, 1989
Egg tempera, gold leaf and
red gilding clay on gessoed panel
72×48 in.
(152.4×121.9 cm)

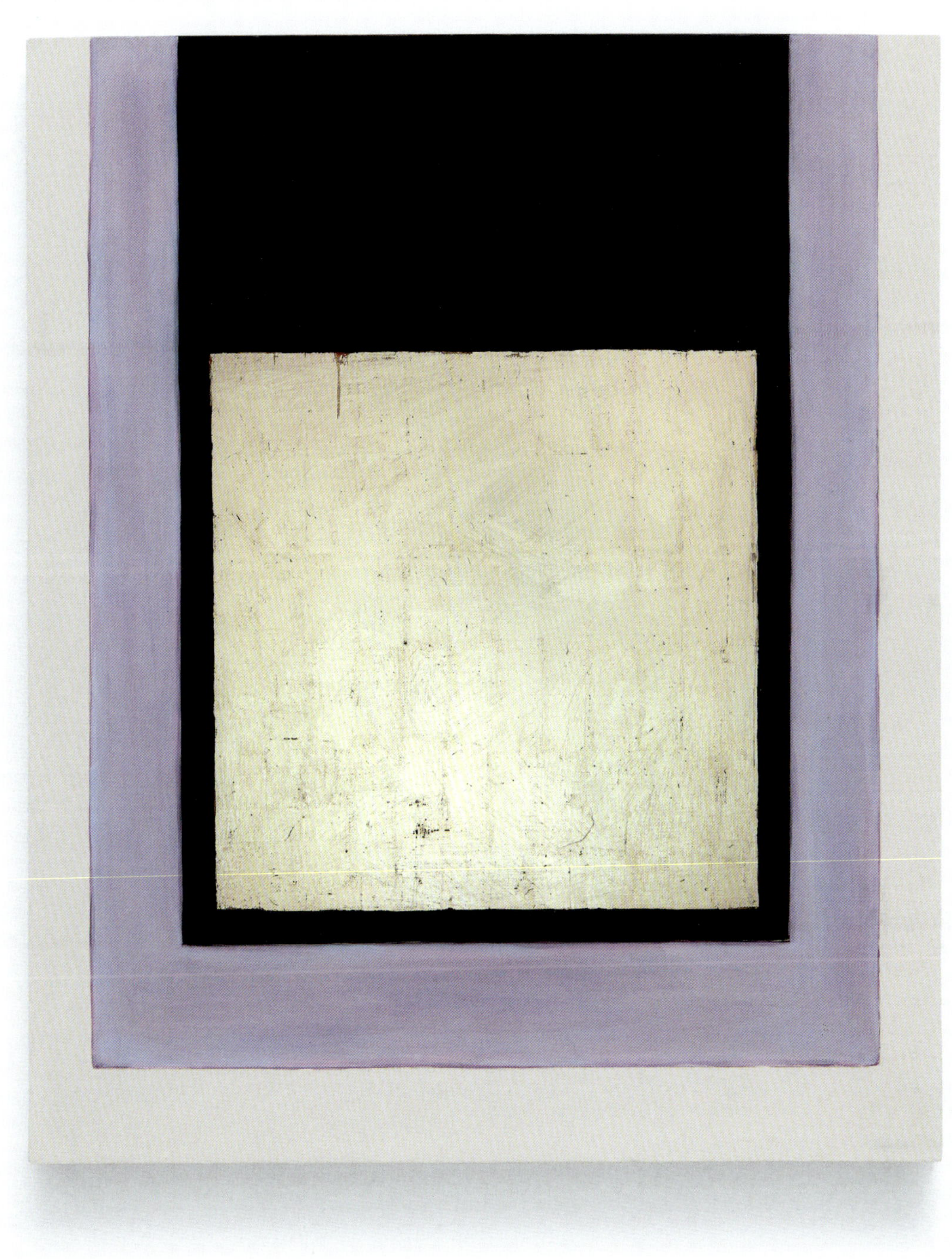

Slip II, 1990
Egg tempera and gold leaf
on gessoed panel
36×30 in.
(91.4×76.2 cm)

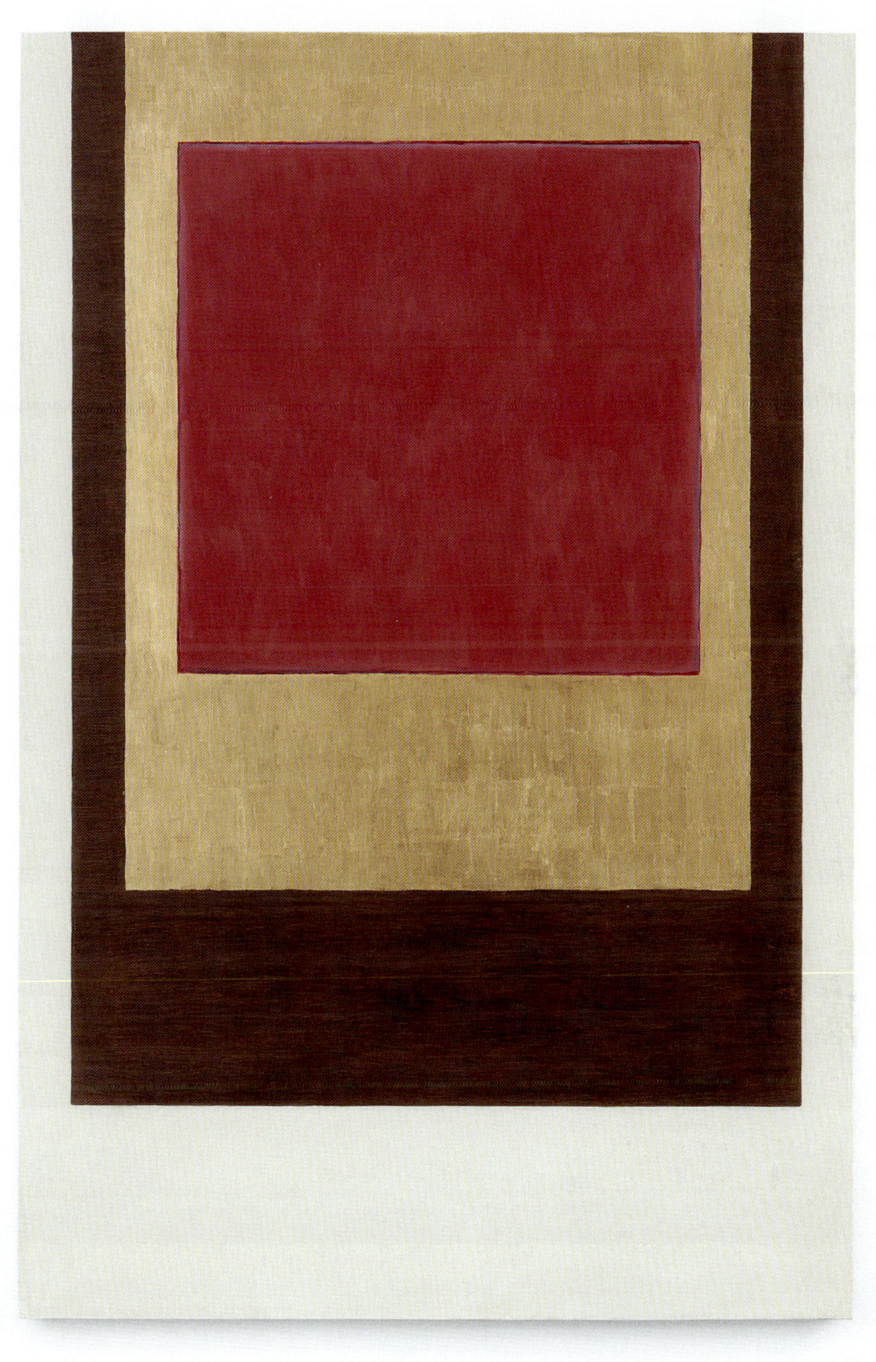

Hanging Pieces, 1989
Egg tempera, gold leaf and red
gilding clay on gessoed panel
72×48 in.
(182.9×121.9 cm)

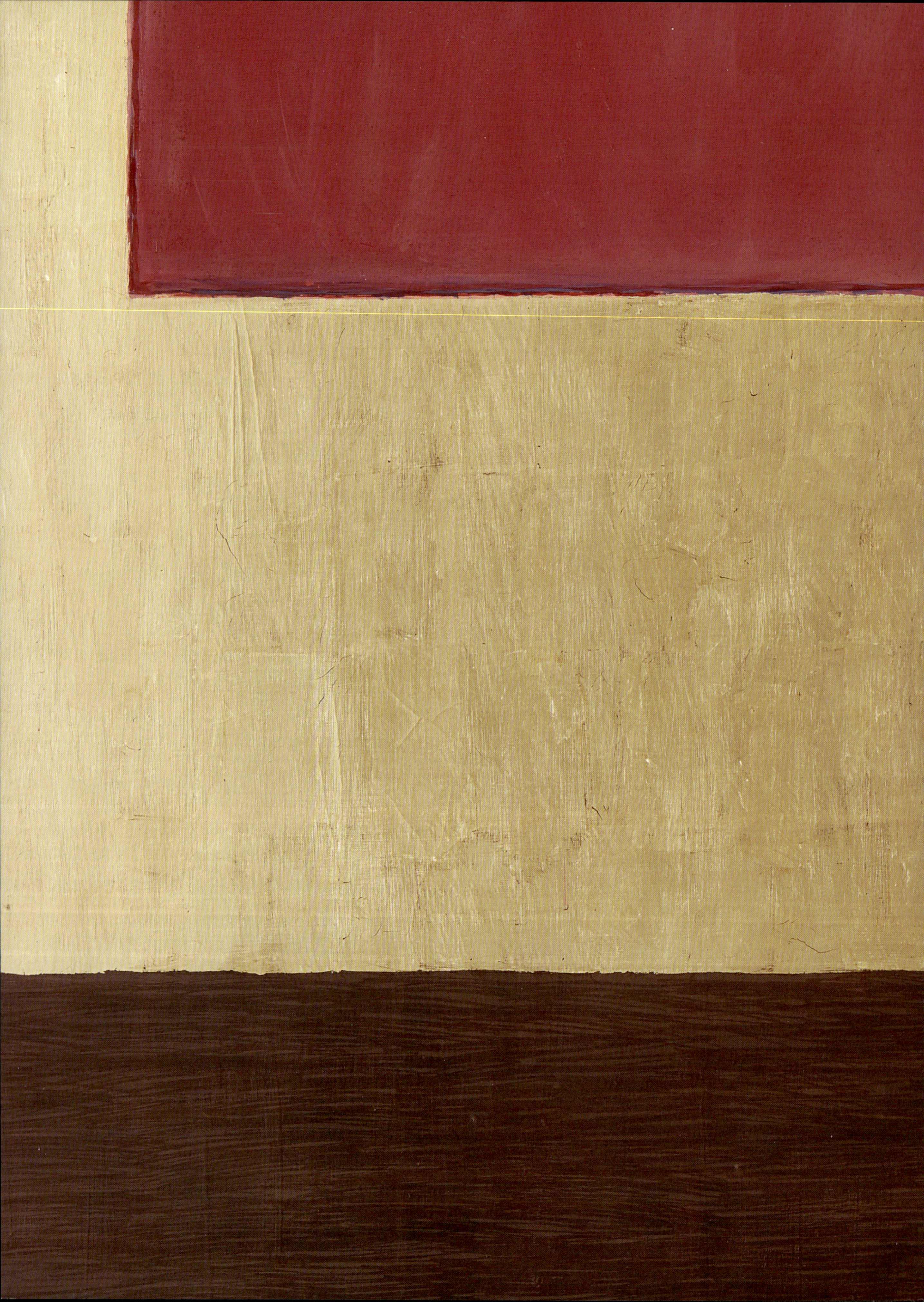

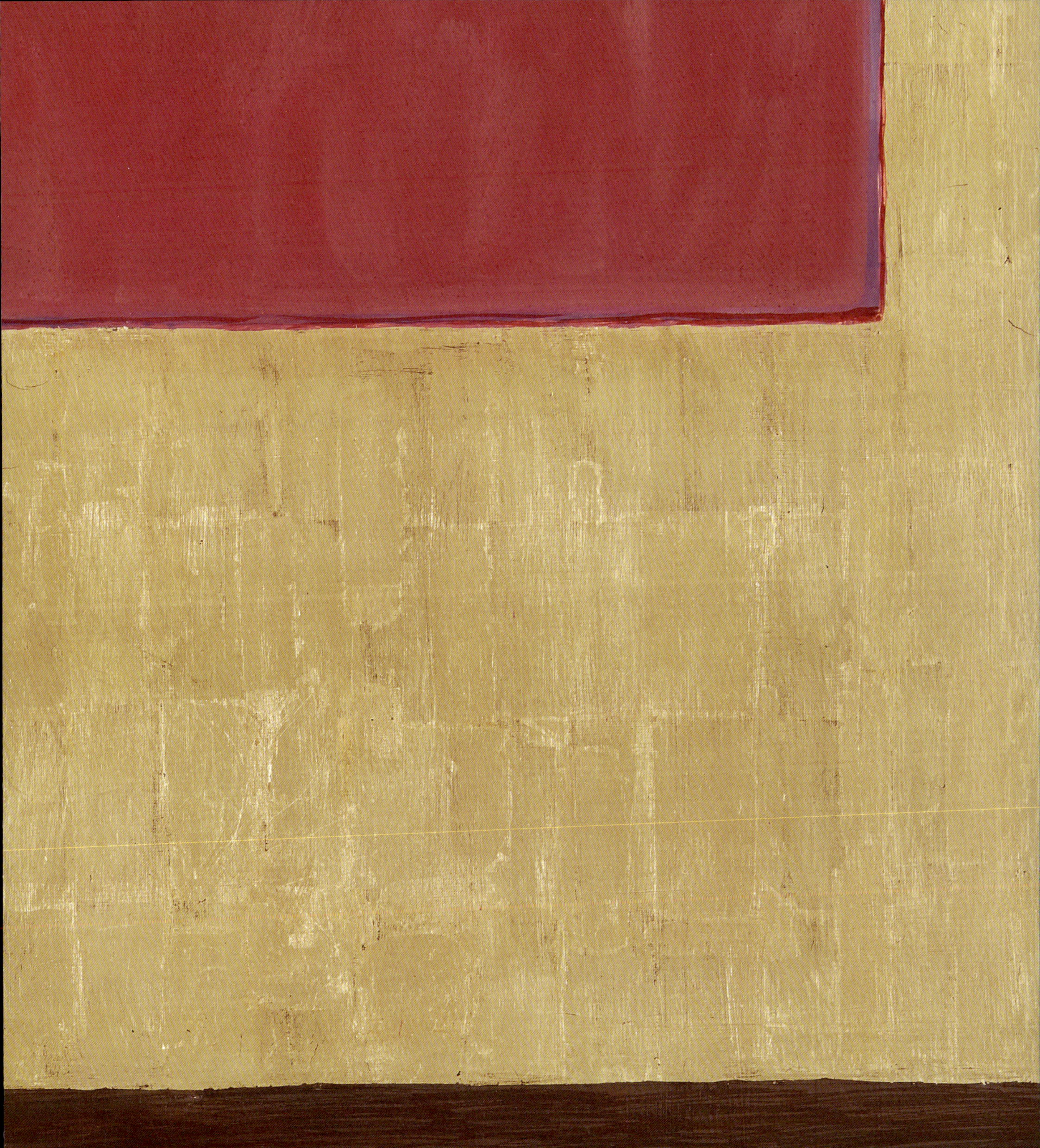

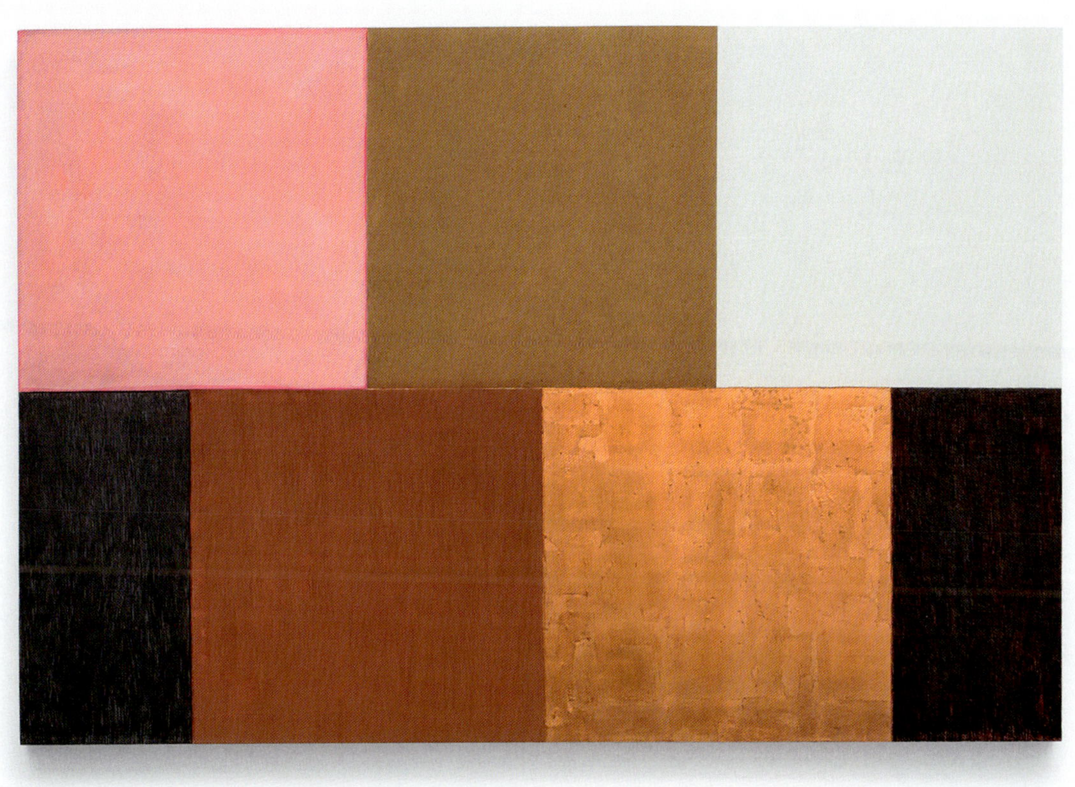

Blocked, 1990
Egg tempera, copper leaf,
gilding clay and graphite on
gessoed panel
48×72×2.5 in.
(121.9×182.9×6.4 cm)

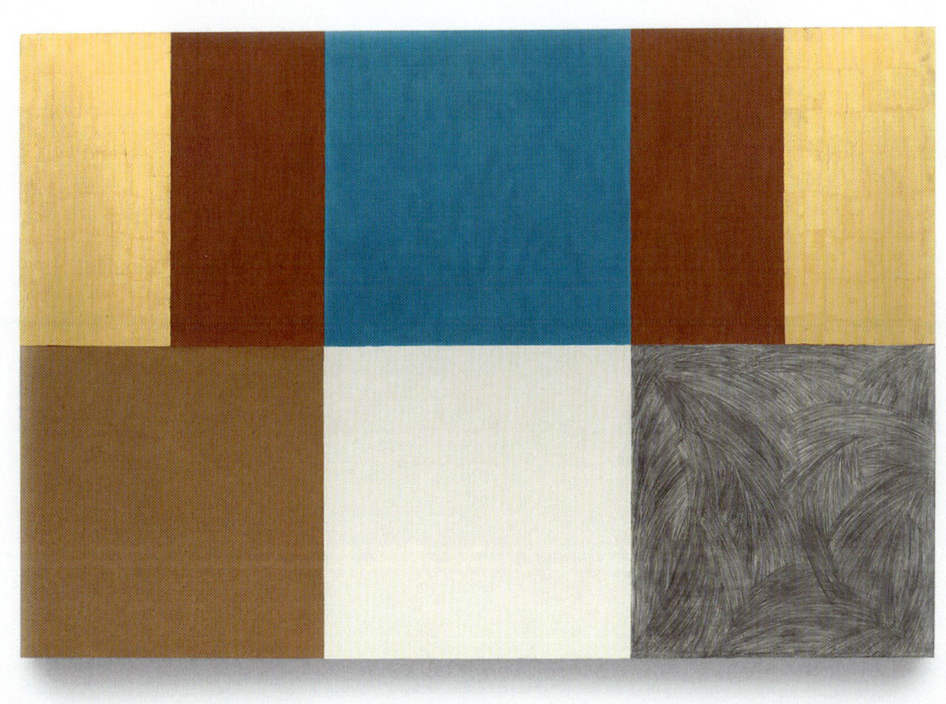

Archangel, 1990
Egg tempera, gold leaf,
graphite, and gilding clay
on gessoed panel
48×72 in.
(121.9×182.8 cm)

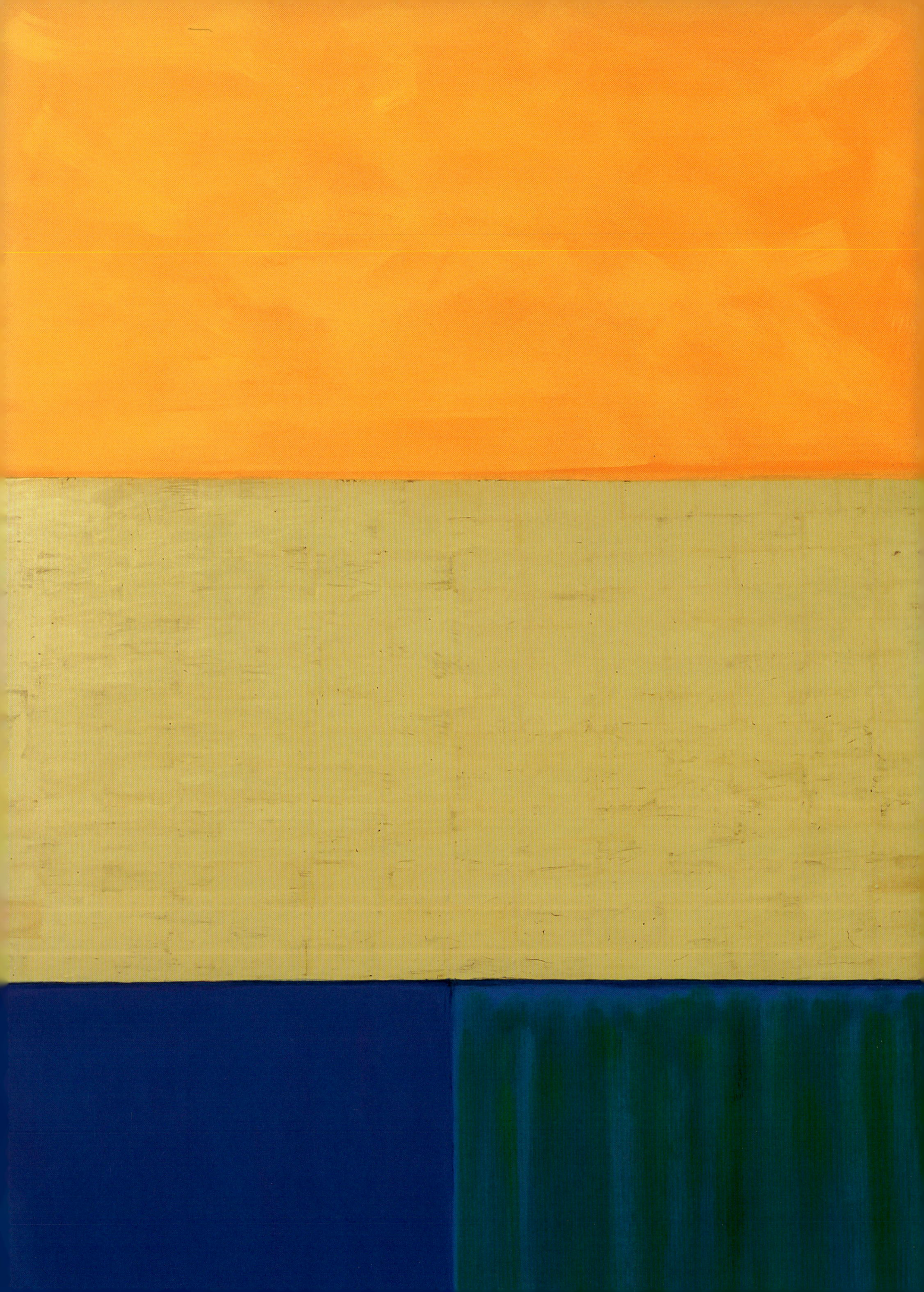

HORIZONTAL & VERTICAL

H&V, short for Horizontal & Vertical, are paintings most often composed of two panels, hung to touch, and bifurcated laterally in their composition. The results are two types of recessions operating on an axis: the vertical one made up of a physical slicing and the horizontal one produced optically by color and composition. The series continues Obering's long standing concern with landscape, offering a horizon line that delineates the direction of the grid, an exercise first employed in the Sets series and Arch series. Simple choices, composed of Obering's signature materials of tempera and gold leaf, produce lush effects and the suggestion of depth in an otherwise flat arena.

A 2 + Y 2, 1992
Egg tempera and gold leaf
on gessoed panel
2 panels, 84 × 84 inches overall
(213.4 × 213.4 cm)

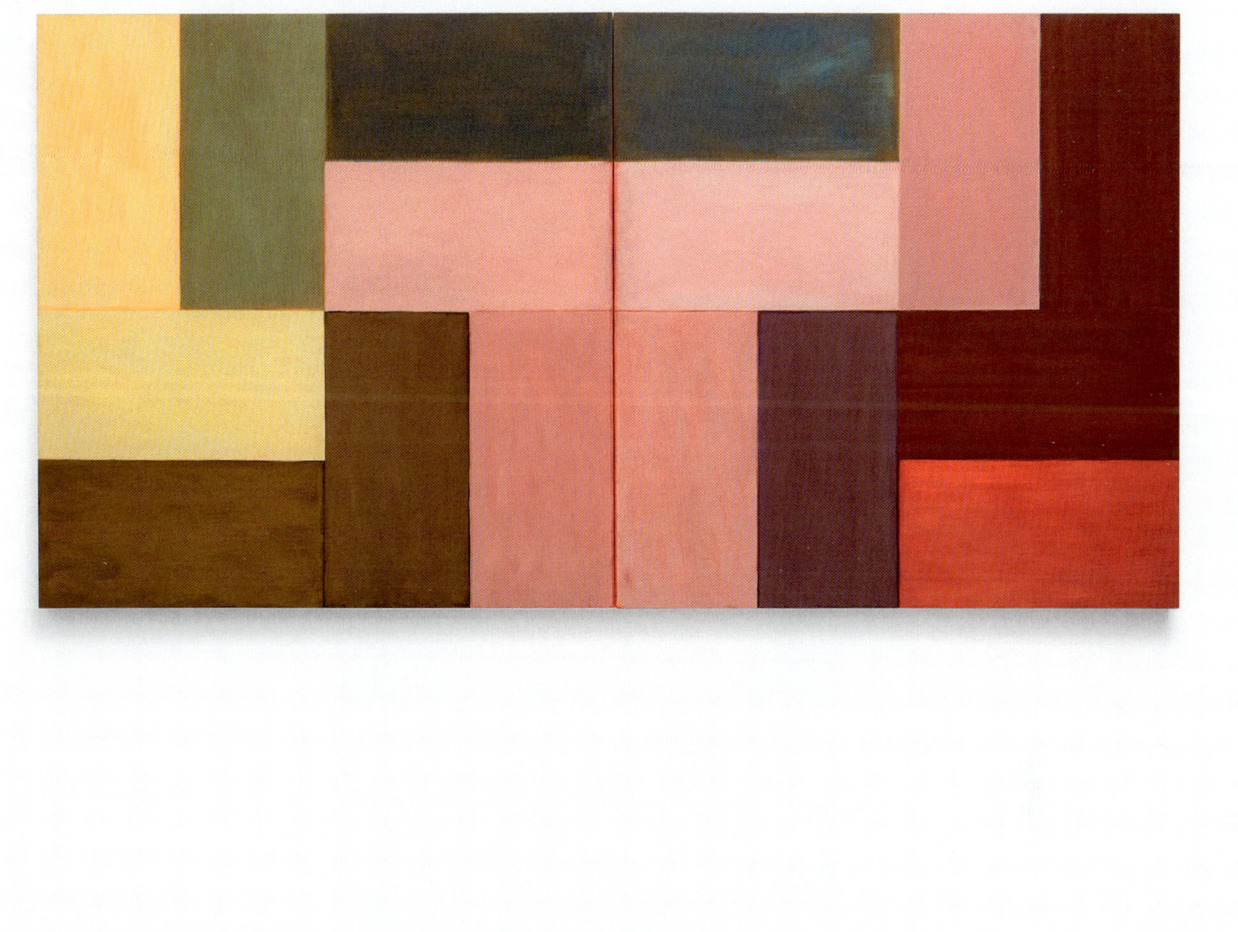

Club II, 1992
Egg tempera on gessoed panel
Diptych, each panel
48×48×2.75 in.
(121.9×121.9×7 cm)

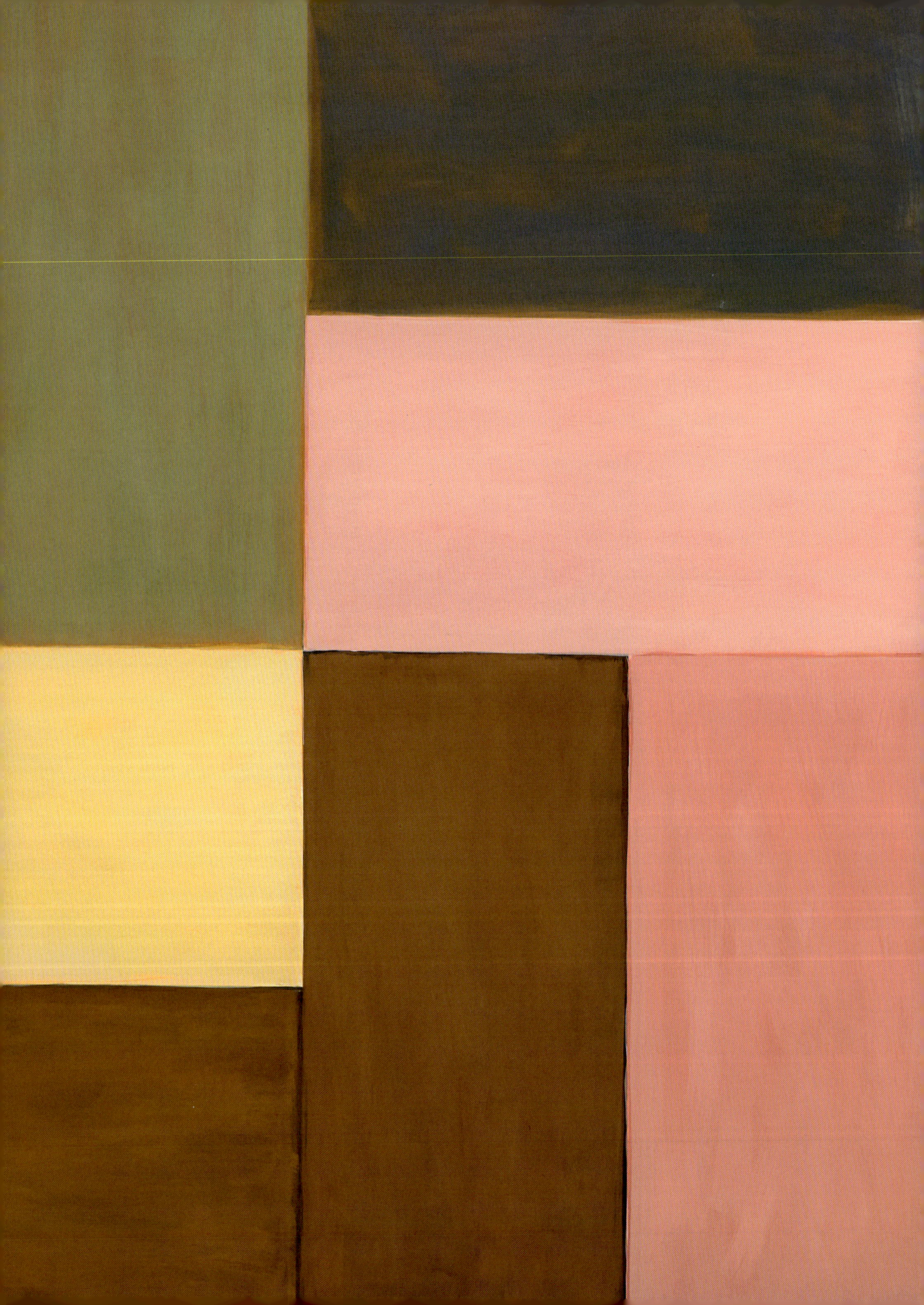

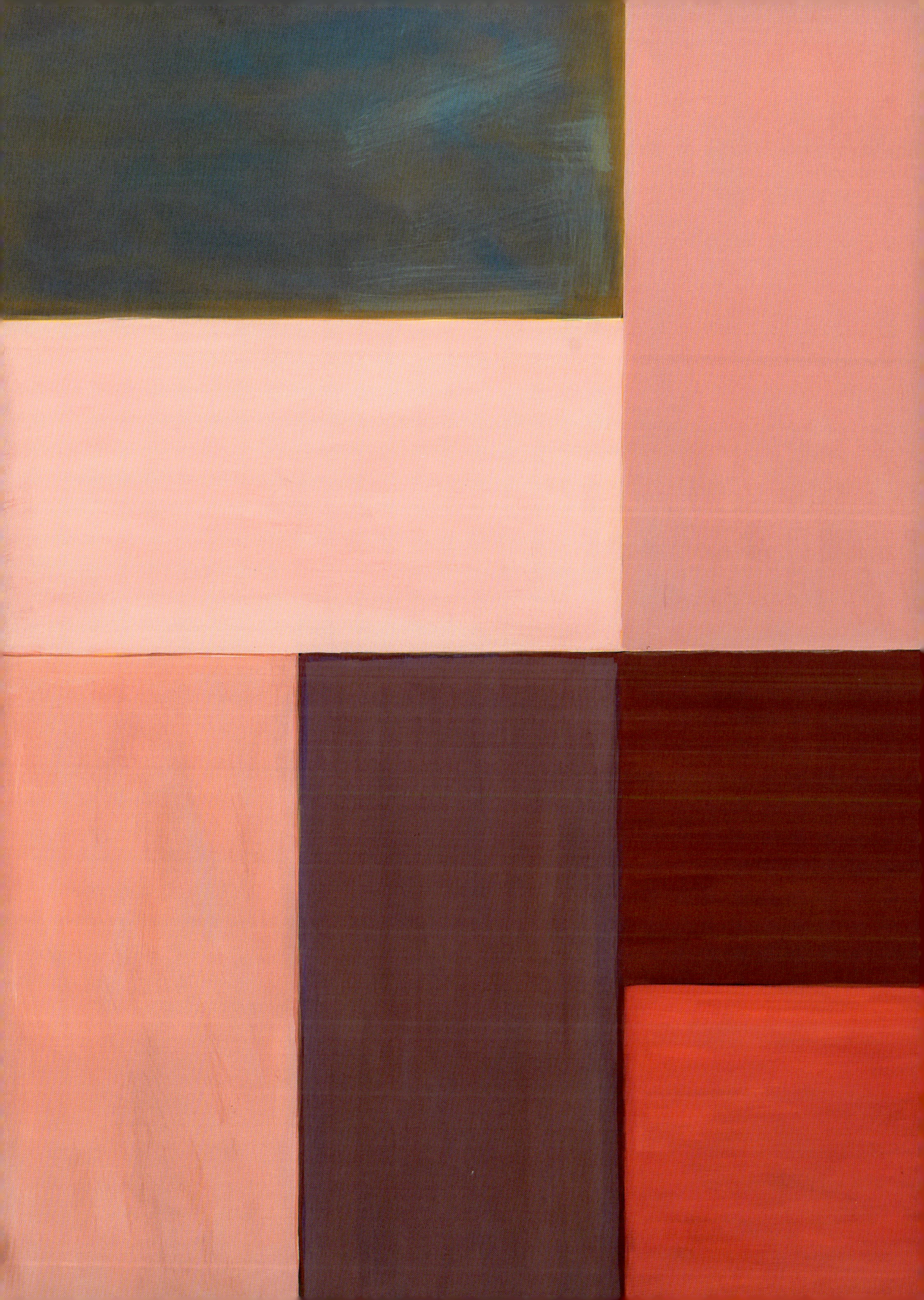

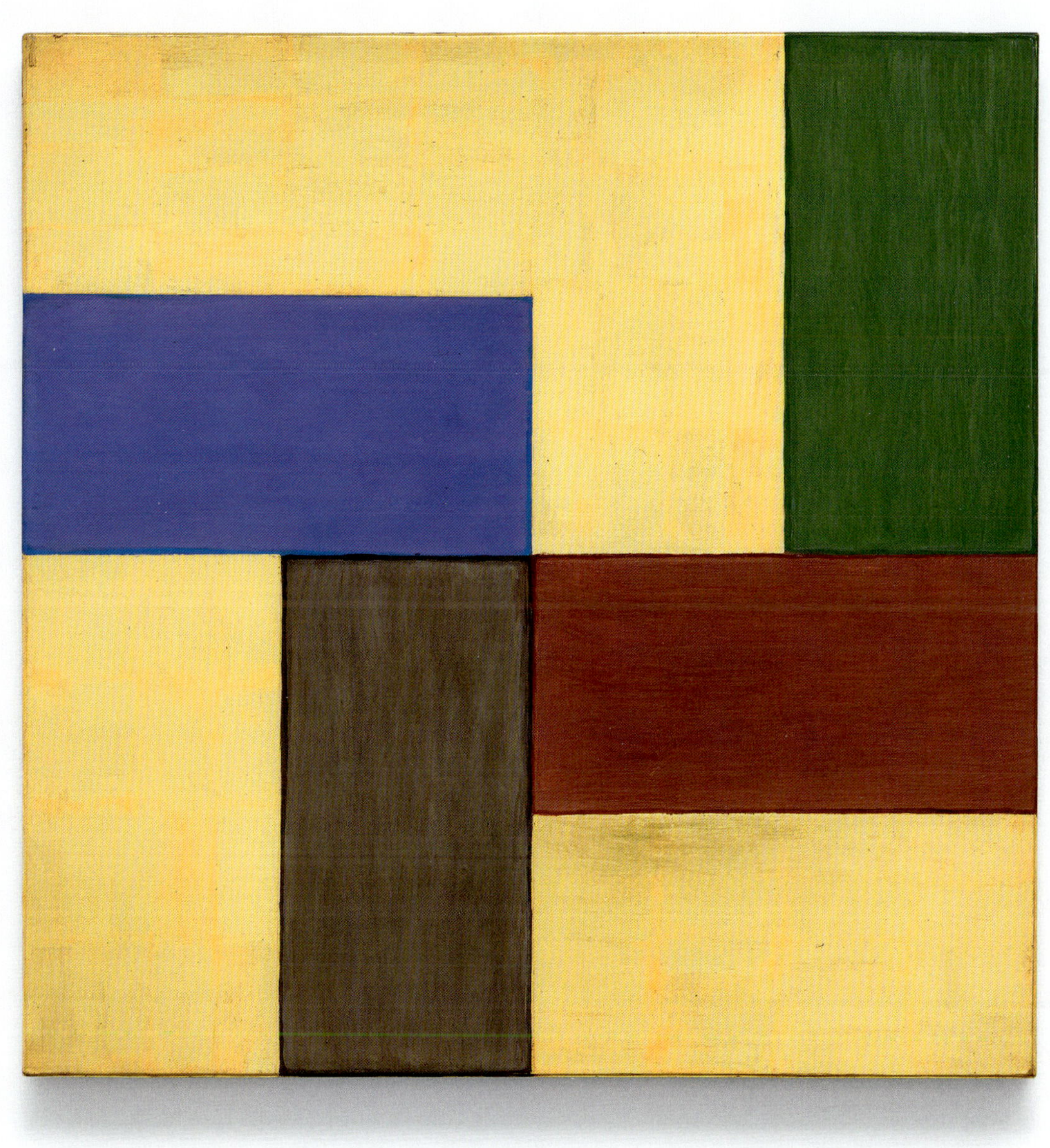

Luna d'autunno, 1992
Egg tempera and gold leaf
on gessoed panel
24 × 24 in.
(61 × 61 cm)

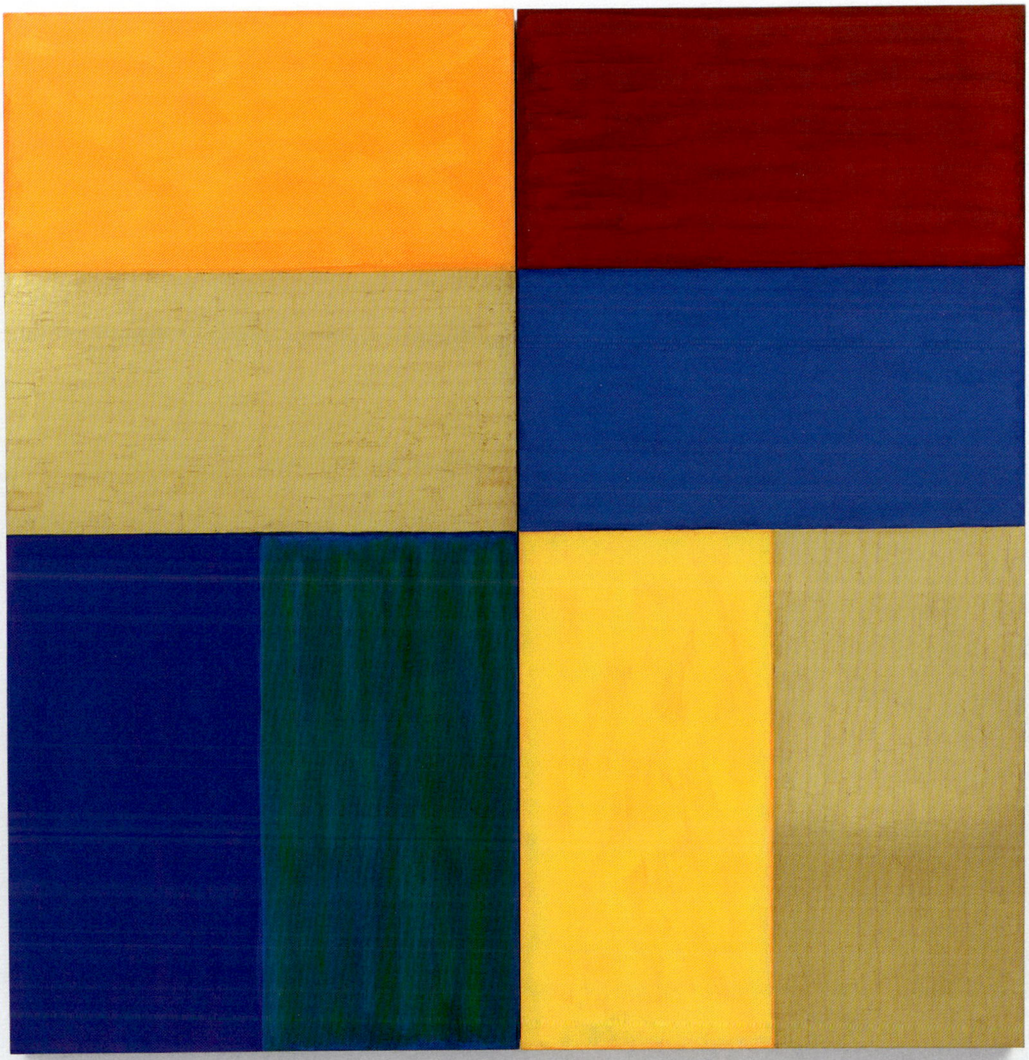

A 2 + Y 2, 1992
Egg tempera and gold leaf
on gessoed panel
2 panels, 84×84 inches overall
(213.4×213.4 cm)

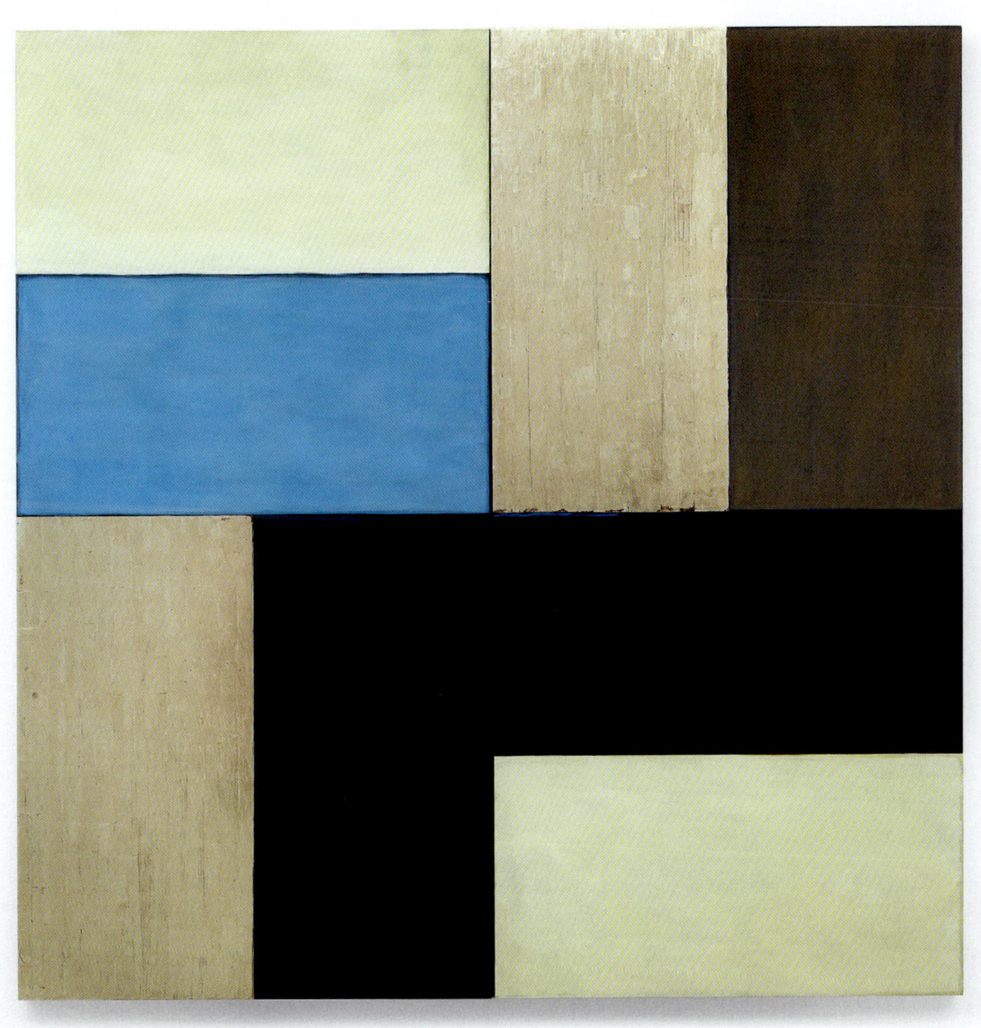

Winter, 1992
Egg tempera and white gold leaf
on gessoed panel
84×84 in
(213.4×213.4 cm)

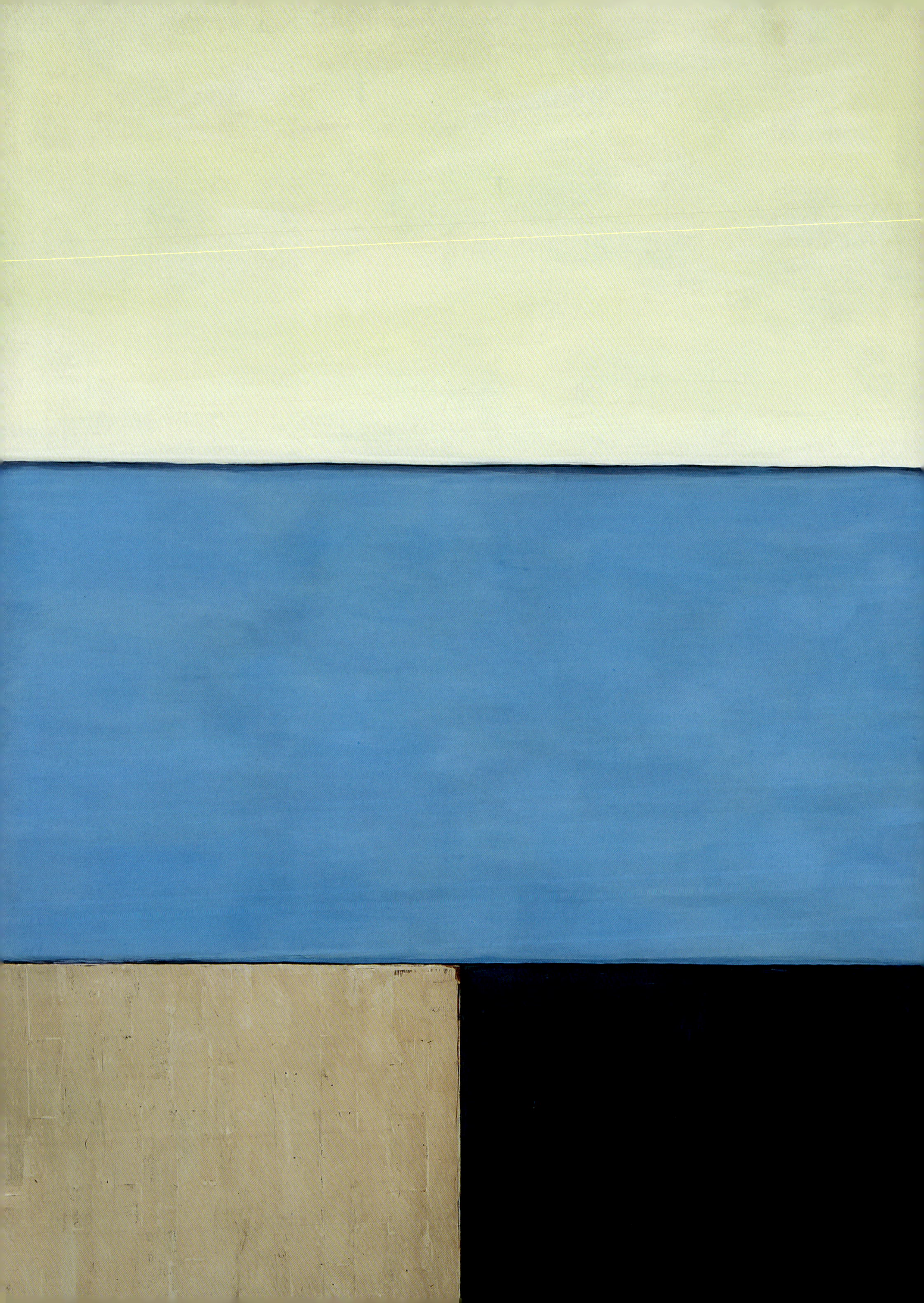

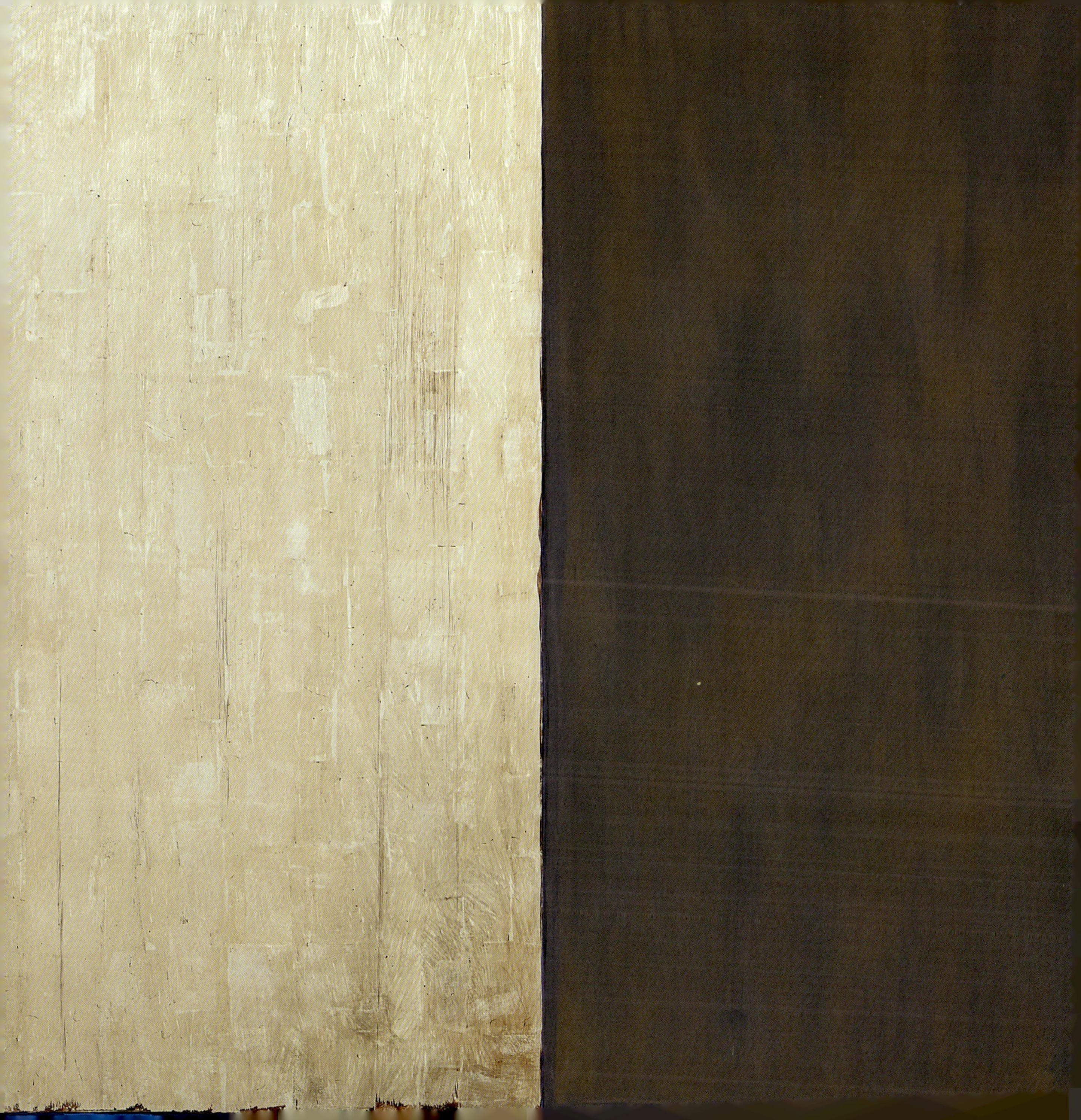

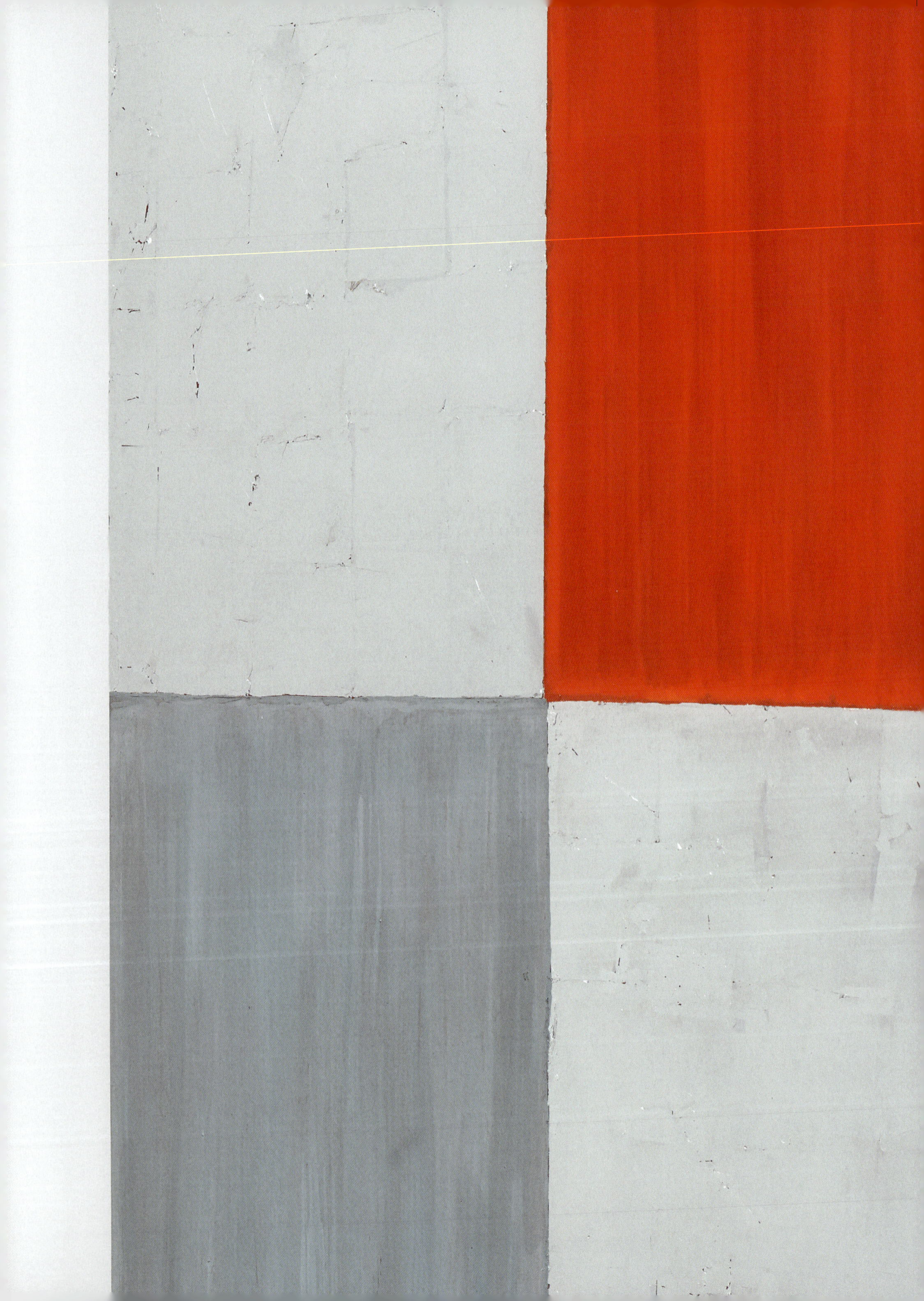

PER SERIES

The boxlike paintings in the Per series are generally six inches deep, with gilding and tempera wrapping around the front and sides of the panels in balanced compositions. Abutting chromatic rectangles of tempera and gold leaf contrast with one another in simple equilibriums within the palette of fourteenth- and fifteenth-century Italian Medieval and Renaissance painters. The title of each painting in the series is a dedication in the form of an acronym, the P an abbreviation of per (Italian for "for"). The Per series is both an exercise in chromatic relationships and a tacit indication of the artist's many intimate connections and inspirations.

PD, 1994
Egg tempera, white gold leaf, and aluminum leaf on gessoed panel
48×24 in.
(121.9×61 cm)

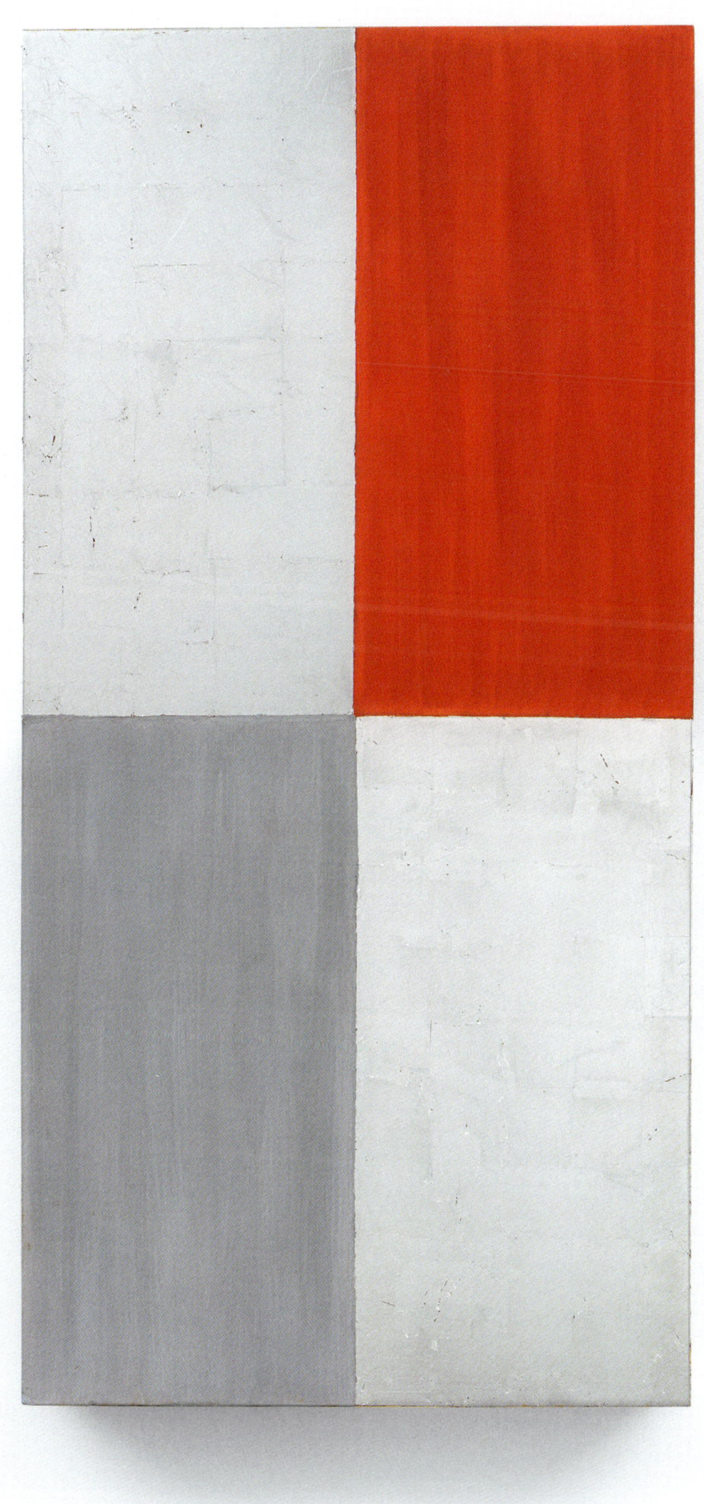

PD, 1994
Egg tempera, white gold
leaf, and aluminum leaf on
gessoed panel
48×24 in.
(121.9×61 cm)

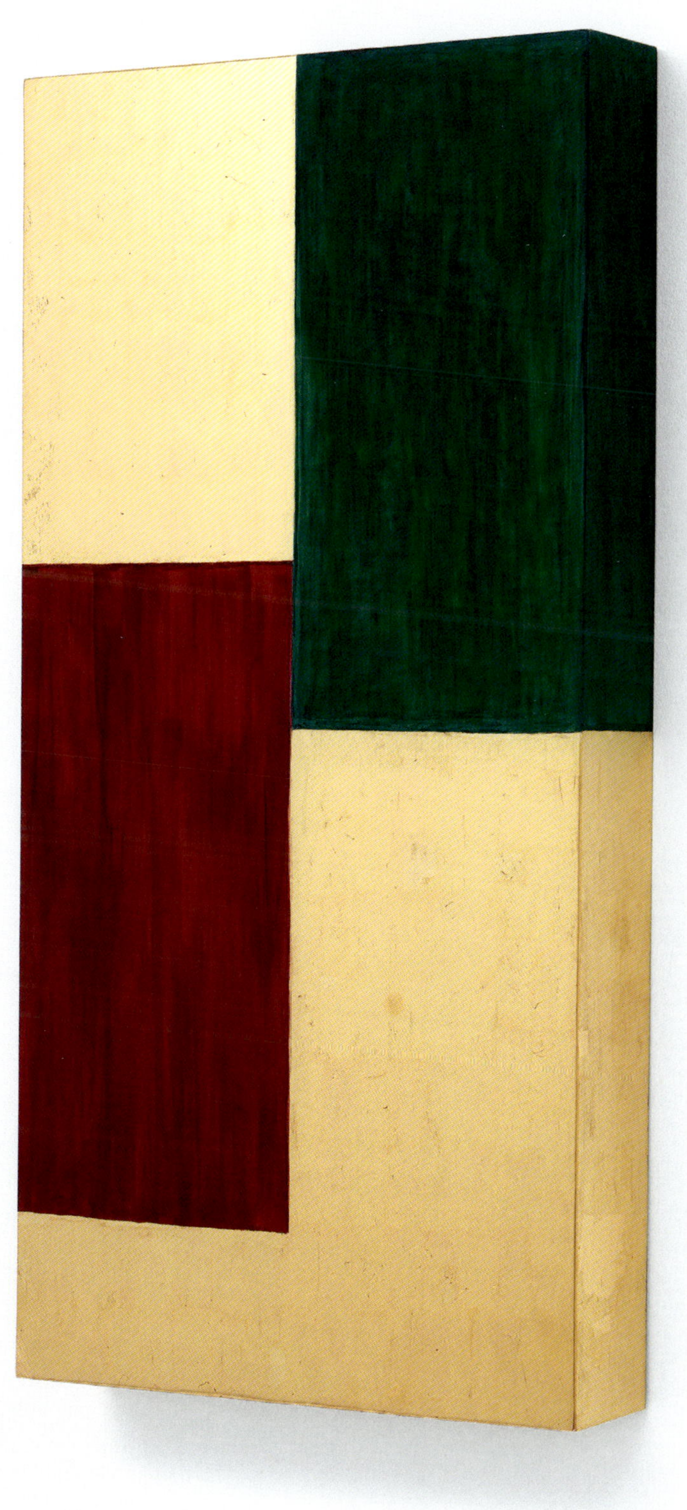

PM, 1994
Egg tempera and gold leaf
on gessoed panel
48×24 in.
(121.9×61 cm)

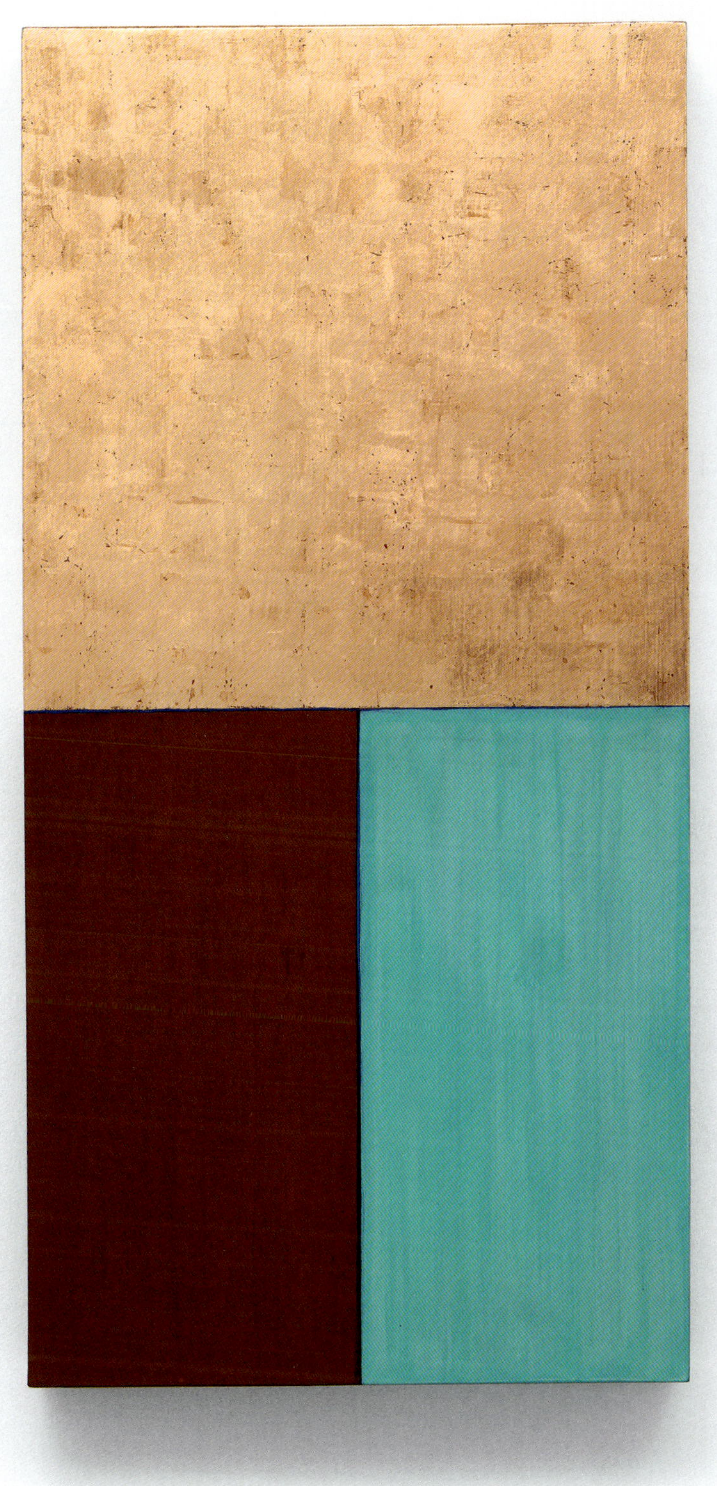

PMB, 1994
Egg tempera, copper leaf
and white gold leaf on
gessoed panel
48×24 in.
(121.9×61 cm)

STEPPED SERIES

The Stepped paintings unfurl cascading compositions over multiple panels or within a single shaped, rhythmic panel. A systematic tempo is produced through the repetition of block-like shapes that dip and stagger not unlike piano keys. Typically composed of Masonite, gold leaf, and egg tempera, the paintings' objecthood is forefronted, beckoning the viewer to treat the paintings as reliefs or altars, and to adjust themselves physically to view them. Integral to each composition is a particular system devised from proportions taken from both the painted panels and the spaces produced on the wall between them.

Sail On (For Hyde), 1998
Egg tempera and gold leaf
on gessoed panel
5 panels, 24×24 in. to 36×24 in. each
(61×61 cm to 91.4×61 cm each)

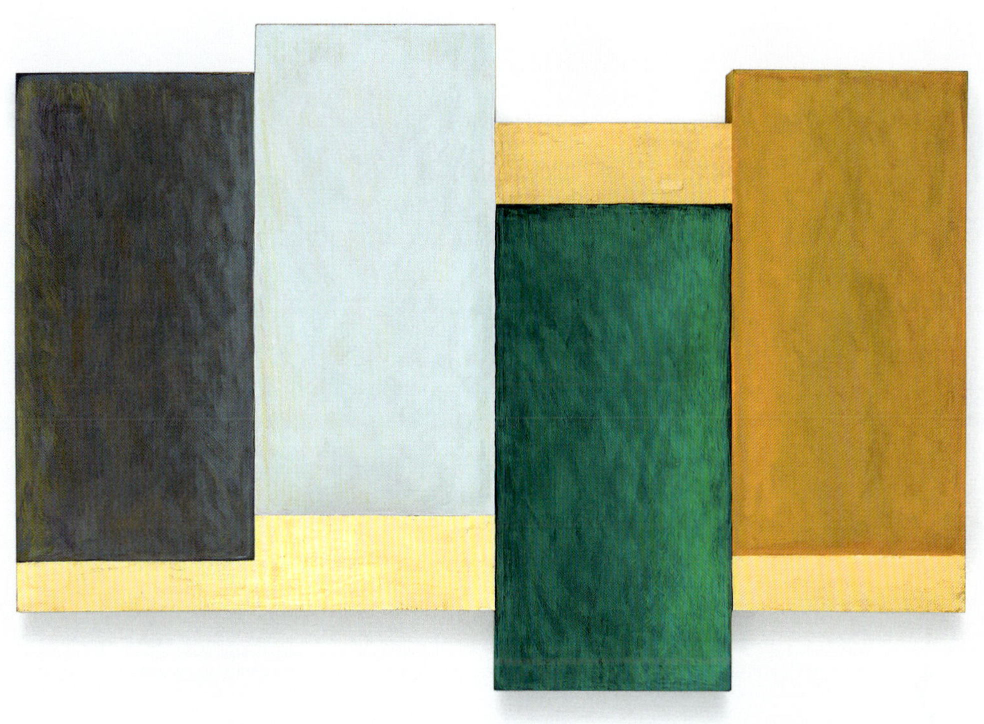

PF, 1997
Egg tempera and gold leaf
on gessoed panel
40⅞×60×5⅞ in.
(103.8×152.4×14.9 cm)

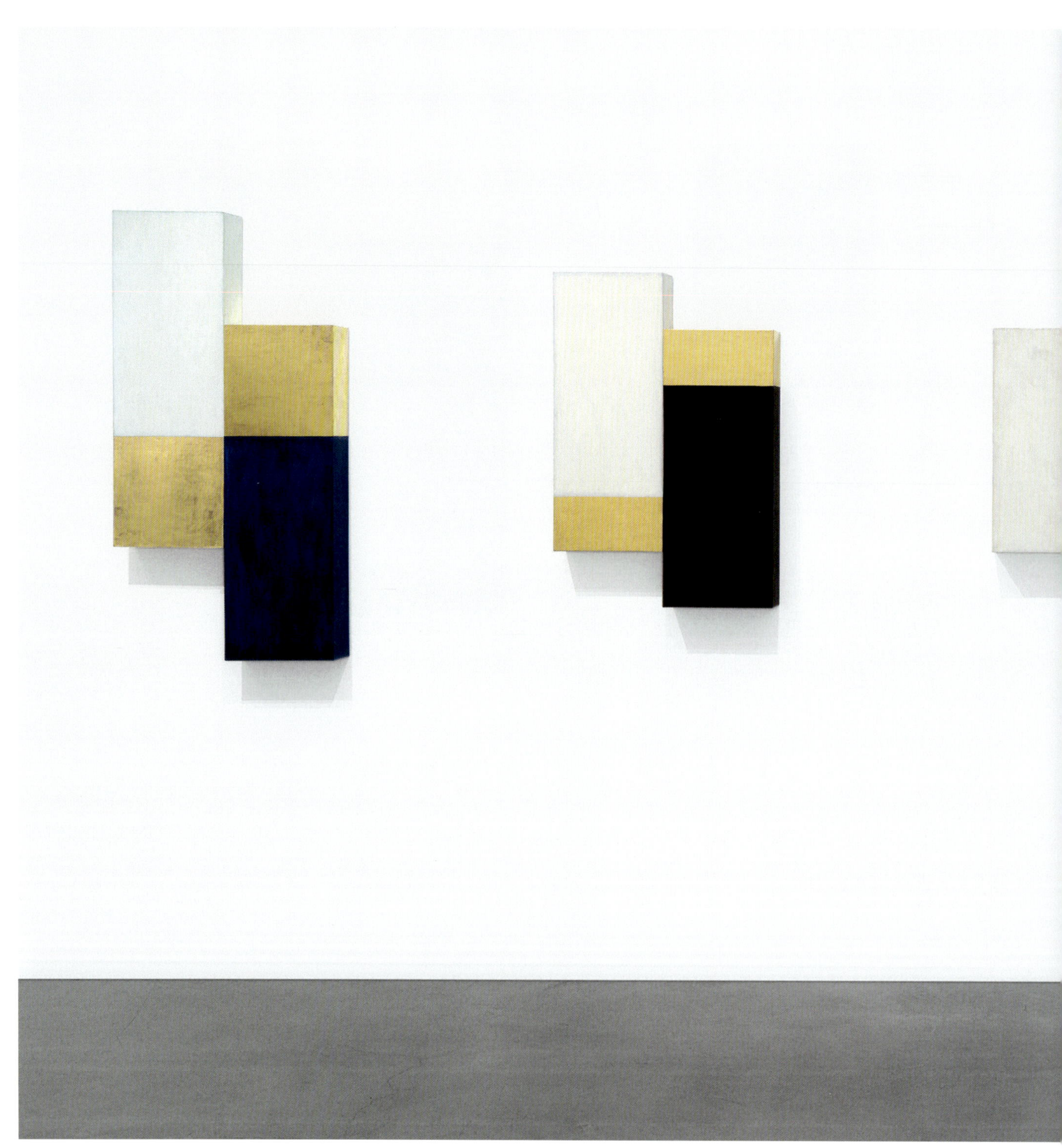

Sail On (For Hyde), 1998
Egg tempera, gold leaf
on gessoed panels
Dimensions variable (5 panels,
24×24 in to 36×24 in each)
(61×61 cm to 91.4×61 cm each)

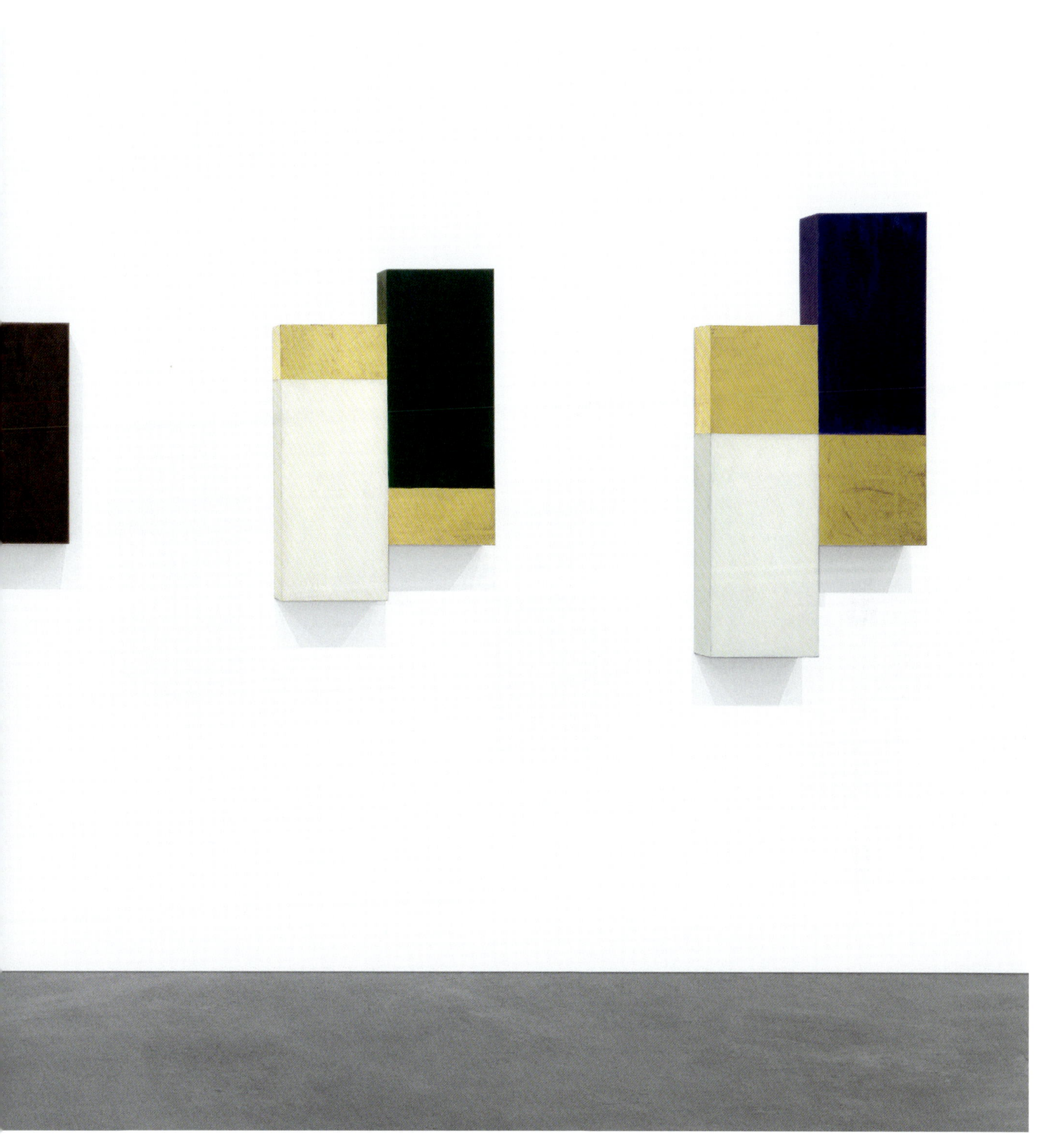

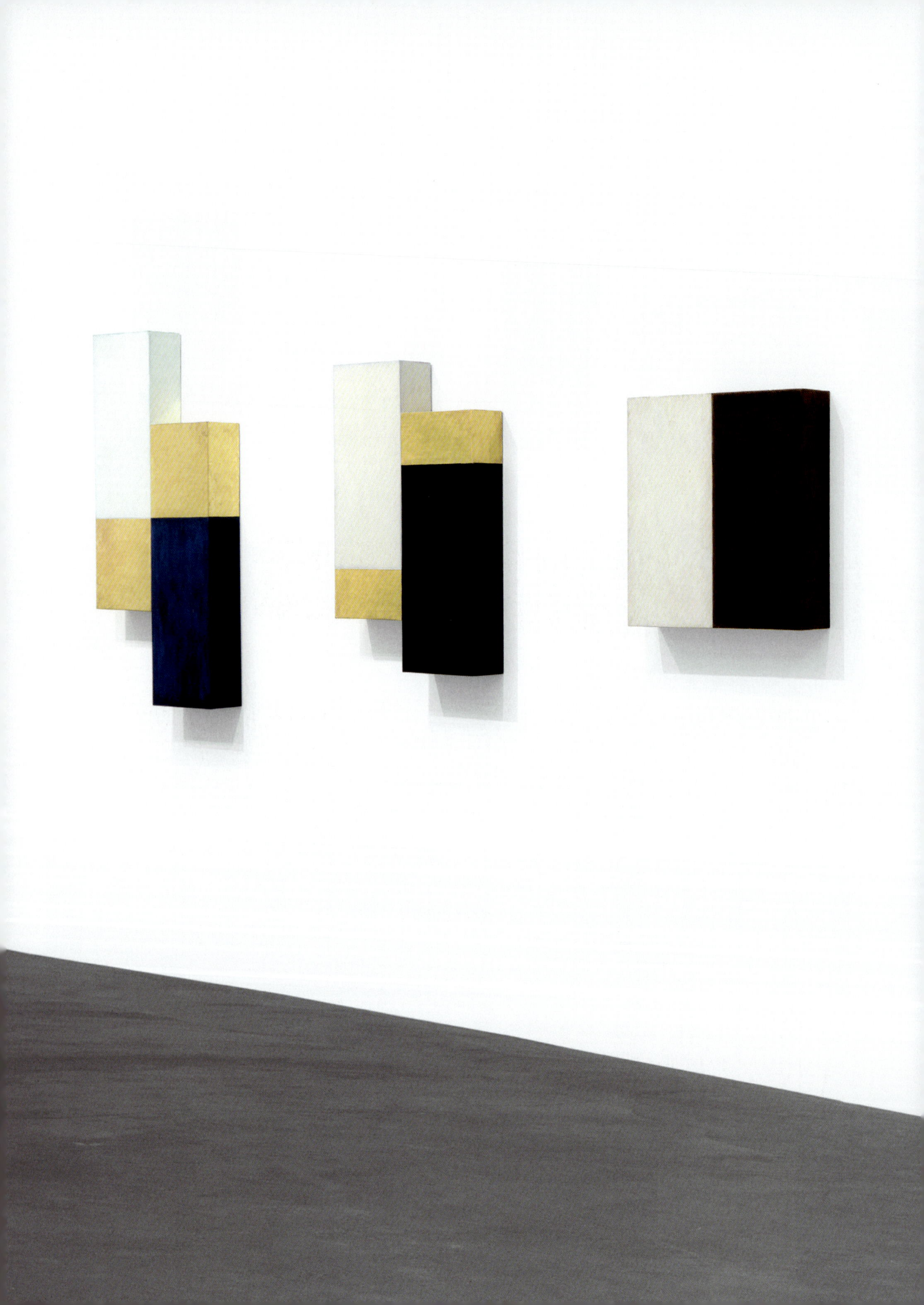

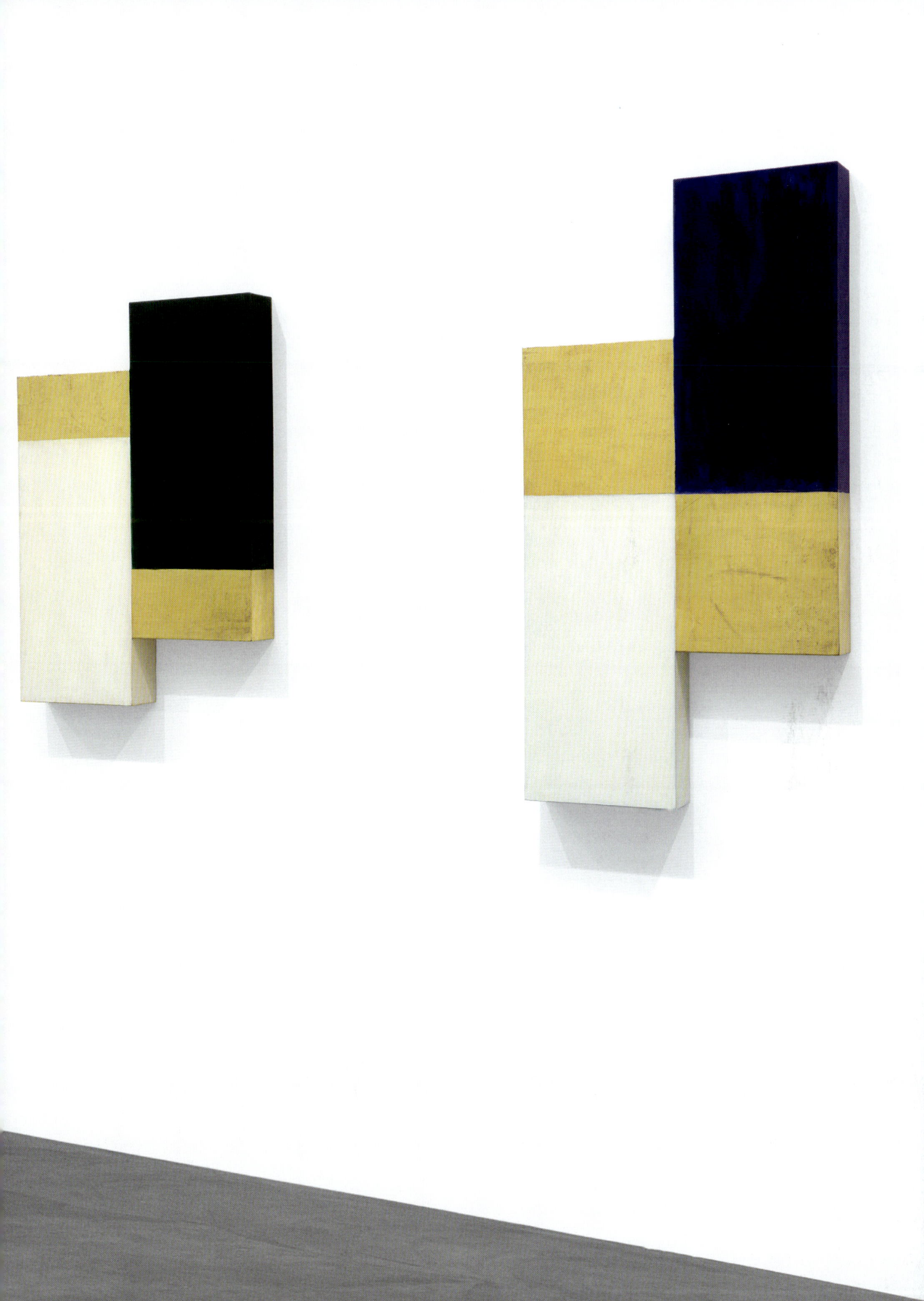

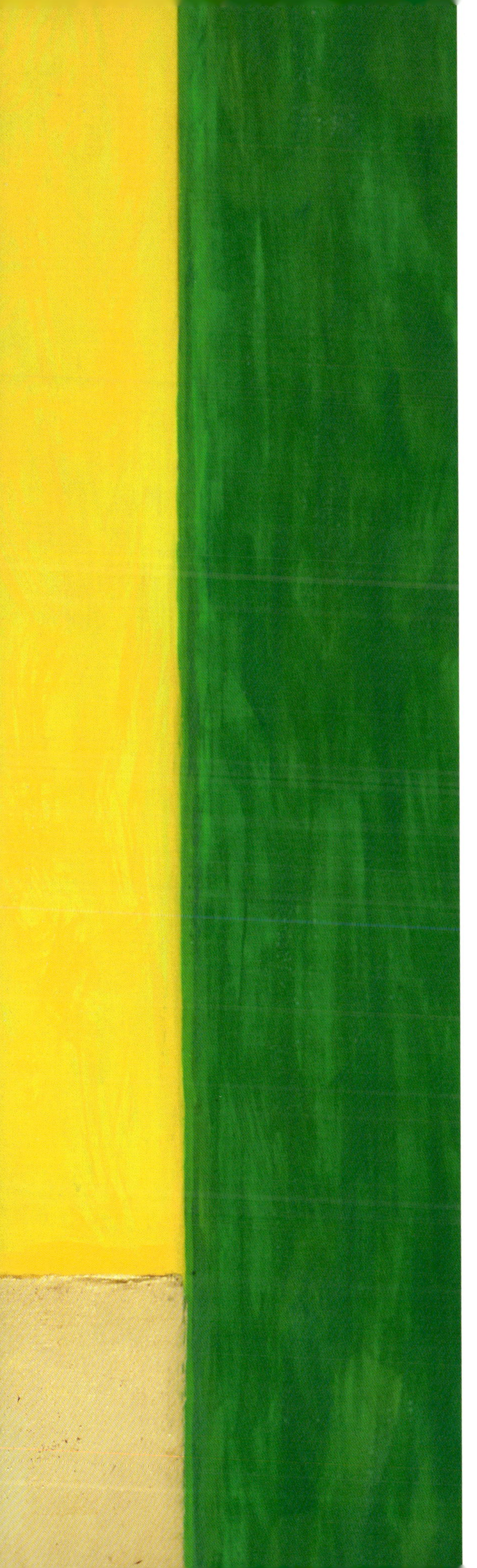

HANGING SERIES

In the later part of her career, Obering returned to formal concerns in the Drop series, substituting tacked pieces of acrylic on canvas for the materials to which she later became wed: tempera, gold leaf, gilding clay, and even stones taken from her studio in Lecce. Lush tempera rectangles wrap over and around Obering's gold leaf panels, cascading atop the front, as if suspended from the supports like drapery or flags. Modular in their execution, the Hanging series paintings produce rhythms across distinct panels through the oscillation and repetition of hue and geometry. Movement is promoted through the artist's suggestion to push beyond the pictorial plane, to the spaces between the panels: the walls themselves. The colors, materials, and proportions of this late series are indebted to Obering's vested interest in Italian frescoes, tiling, and Byzantine mosaics, which she distilled into Minimalist scapes in her decades-long artistic exploration.

KCB, BKC, CBK, 2003
Egg tempera and gold leaf
on gessoed panel
3 panels, 24×36 in. each
(61×91.4 cm each)

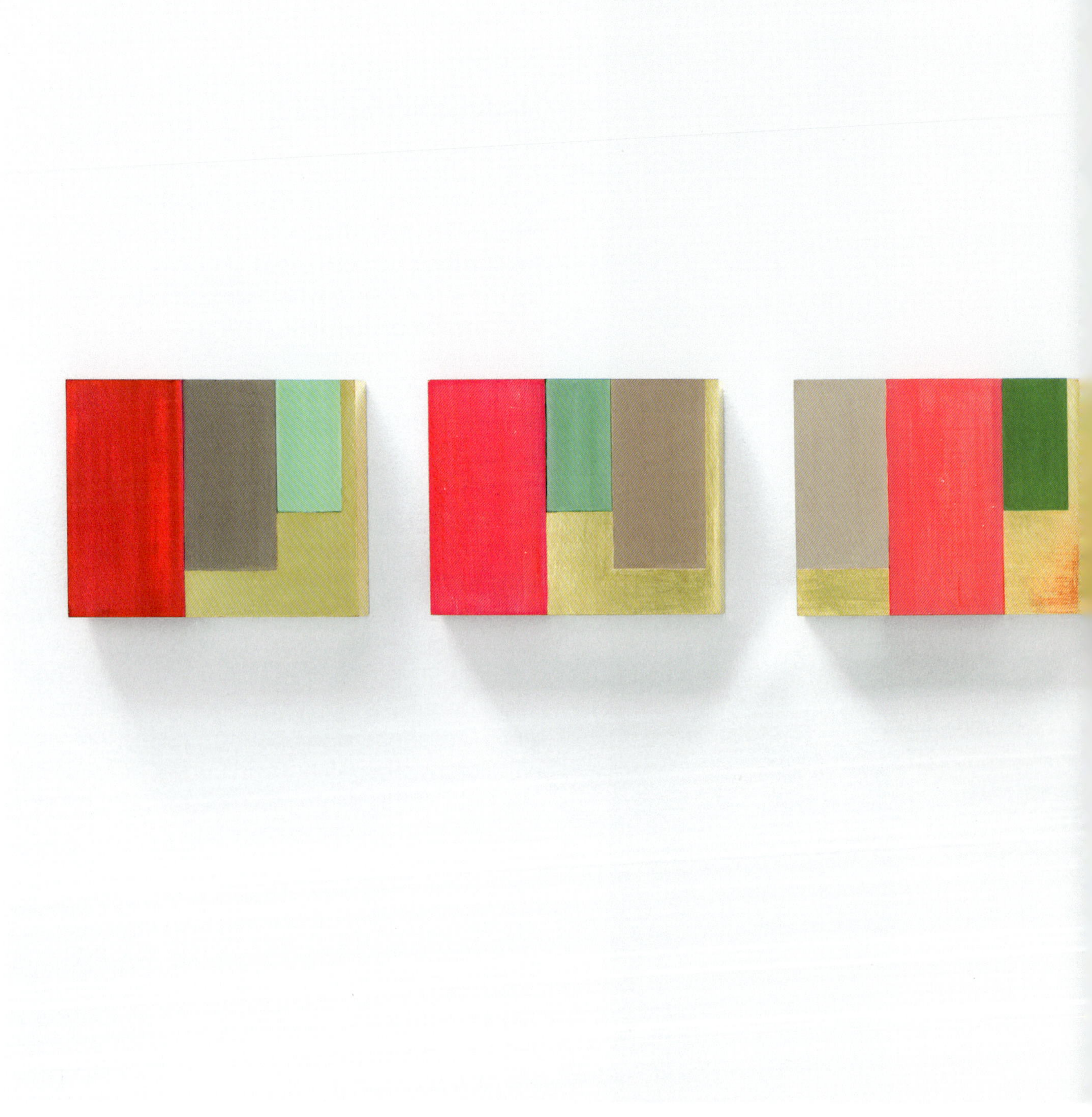

Story, 1999
Egg tempera and gold leaf
on gessoed panel
6 panels, 10×12 in. each
(25.4×30.5 cm each)

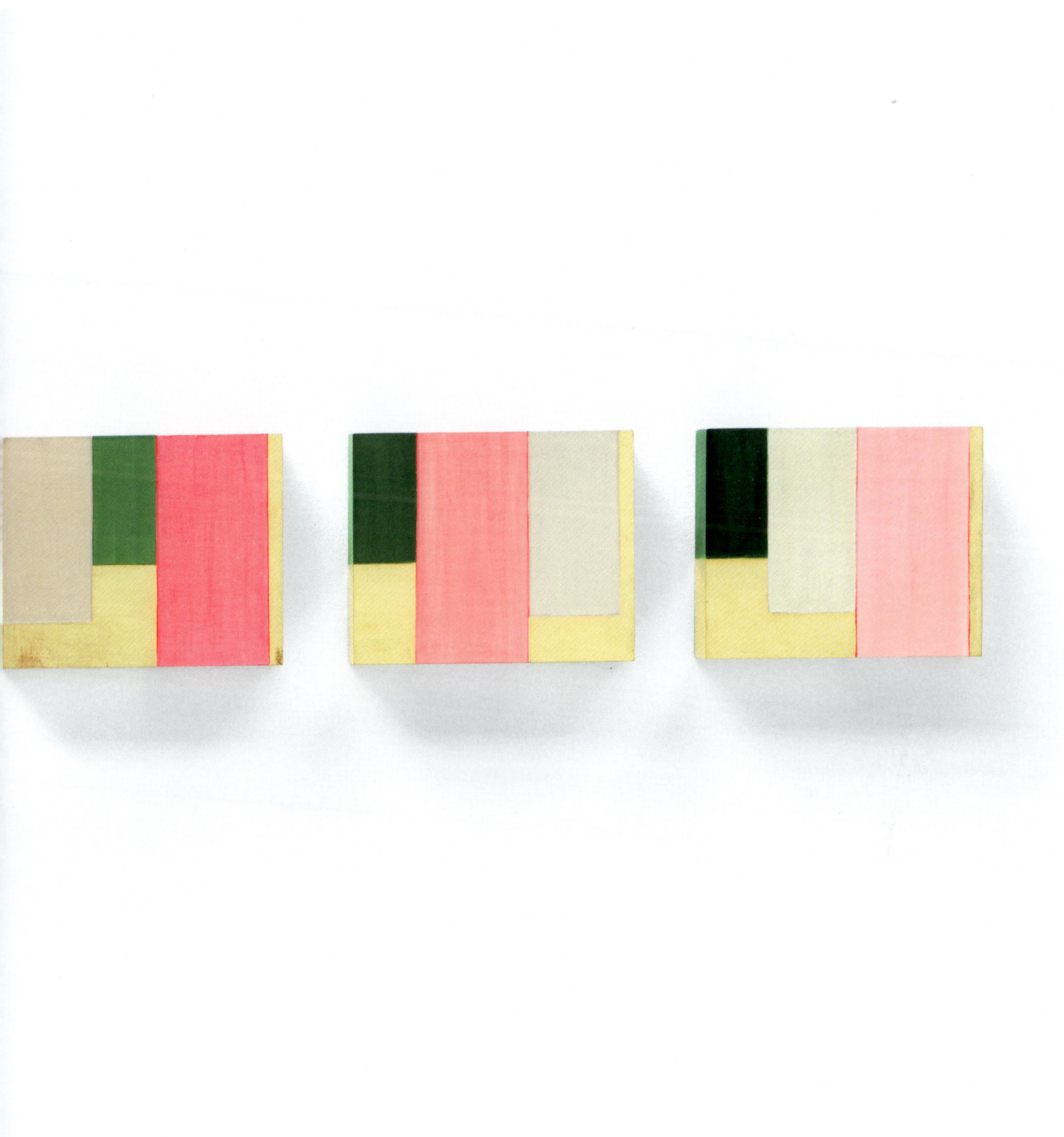

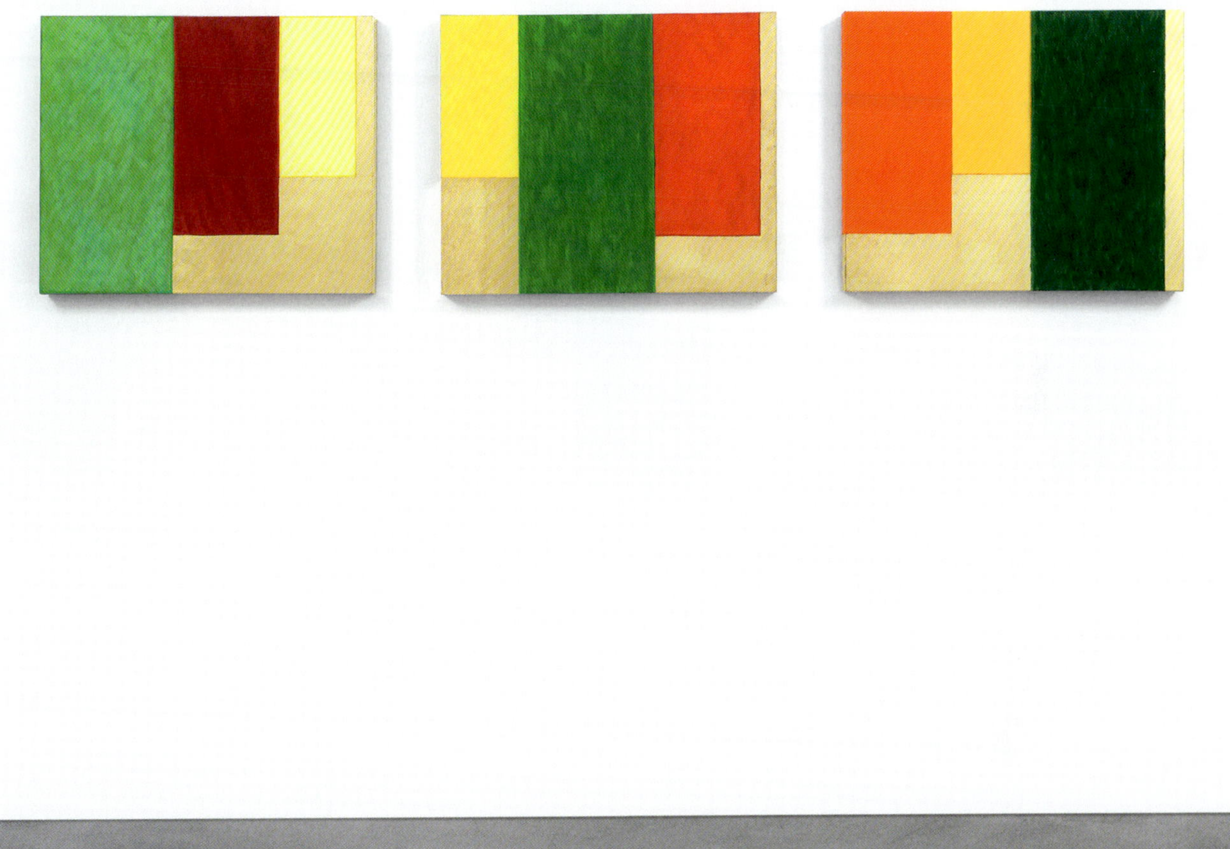

KCB, BKC, CBK, 2003
Egg tempera and gold leaf
on gessoed panel
3 panels, 24×36 in. each
(63.5×91.44 cm each)

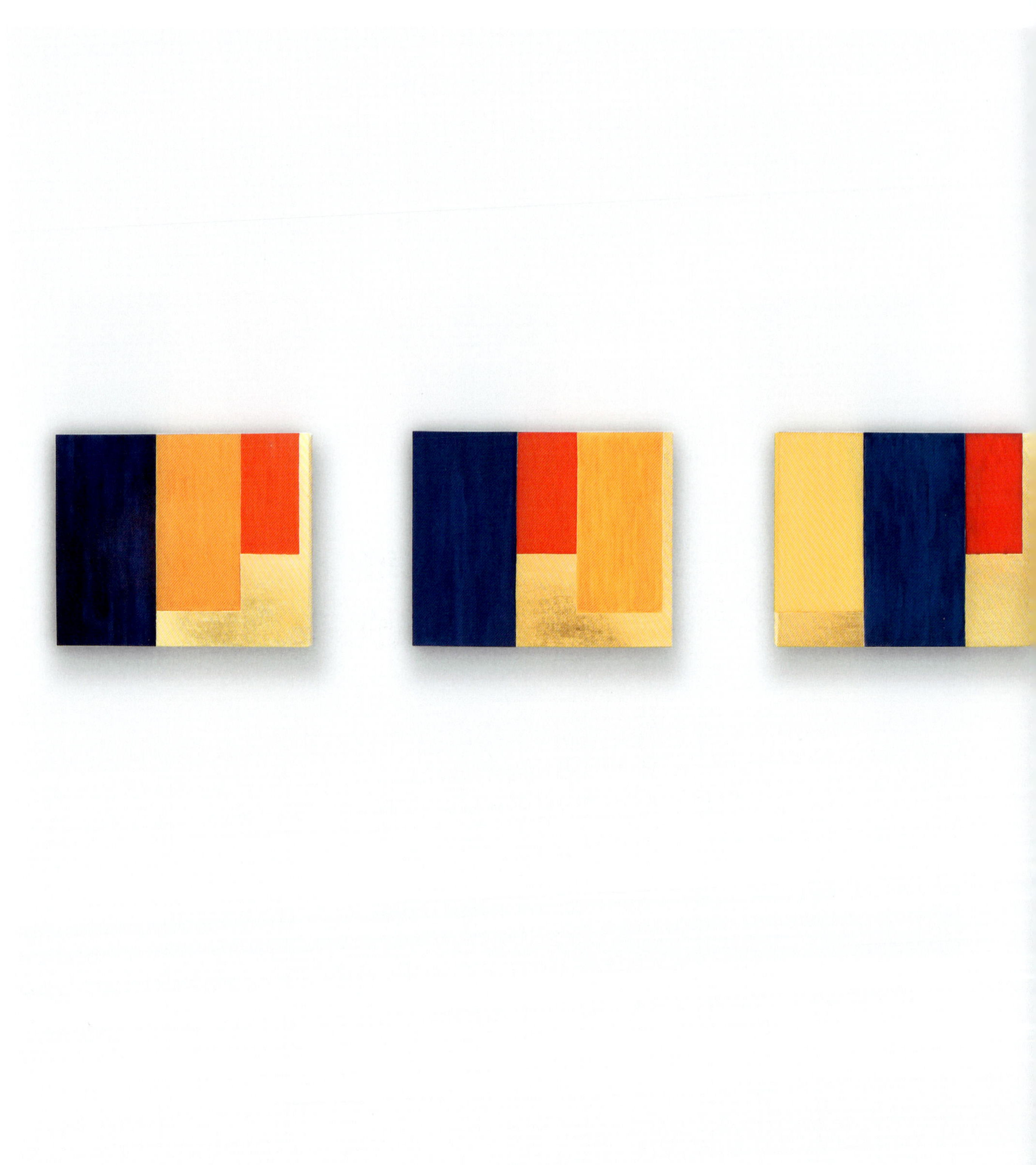

From Siena to San Sepolcro, 2003–04
Egg tempera and gold leaf
on gessoed panel
6 panels, 38½×48 in. each
(97.79×121.92 cm each)

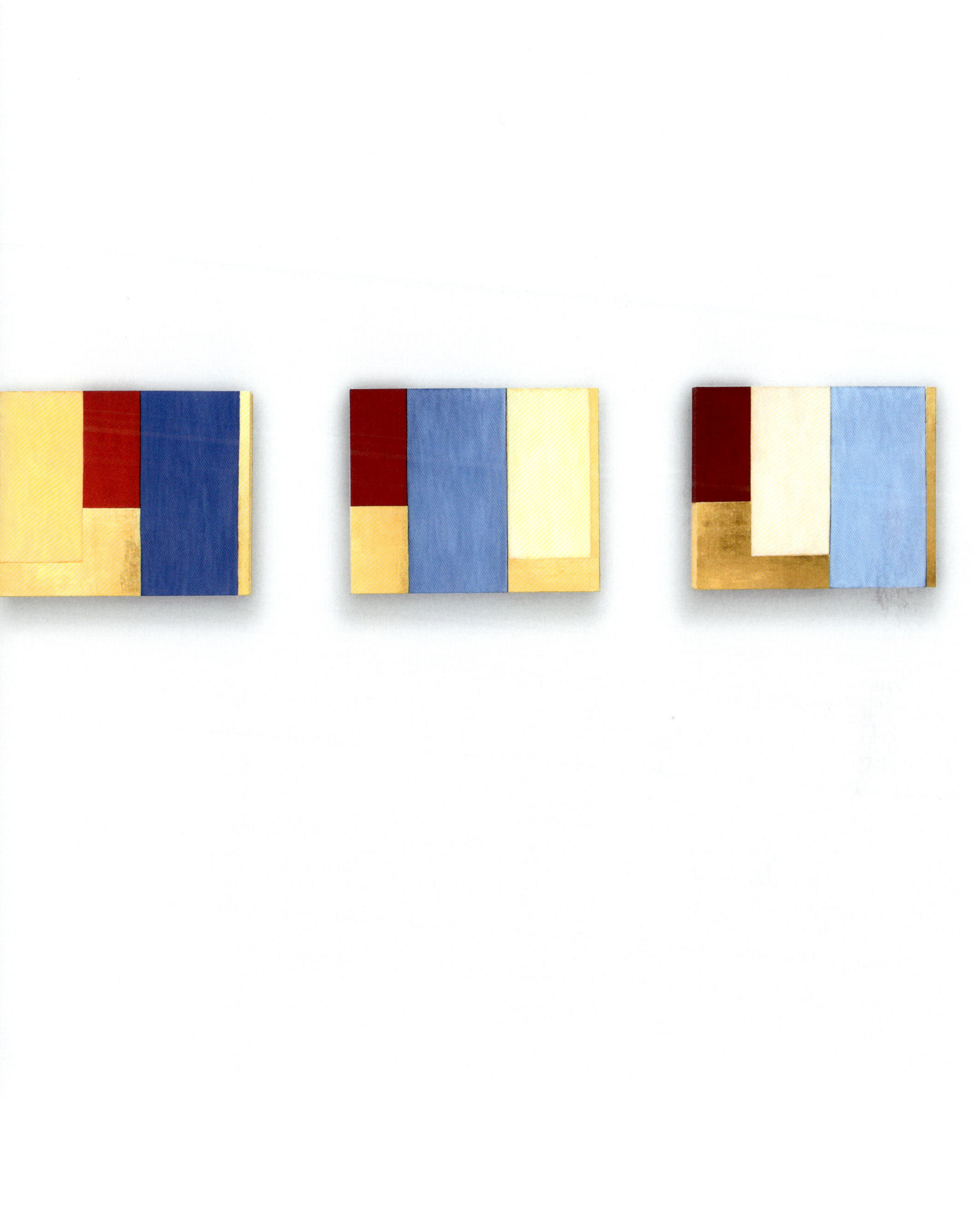

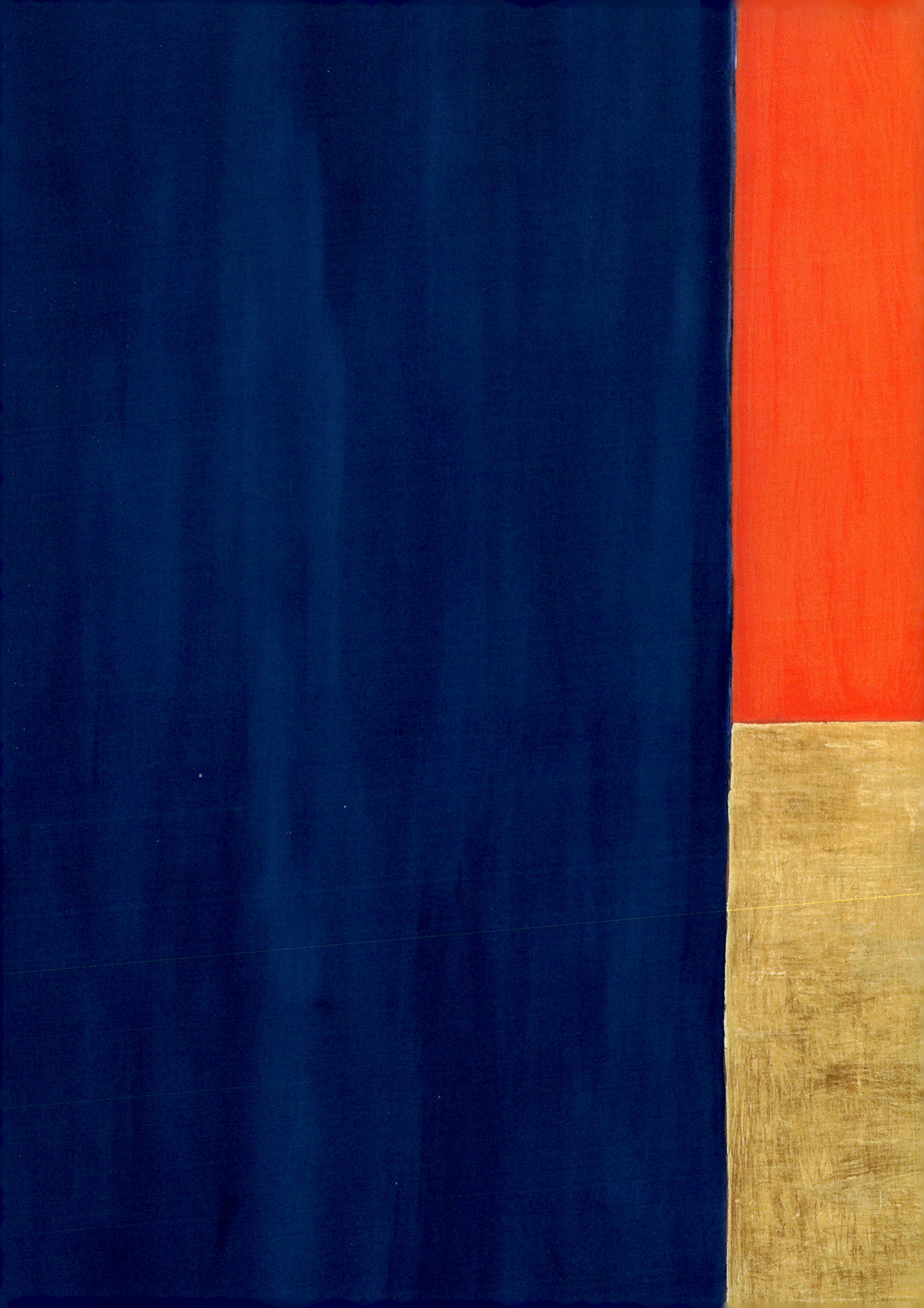

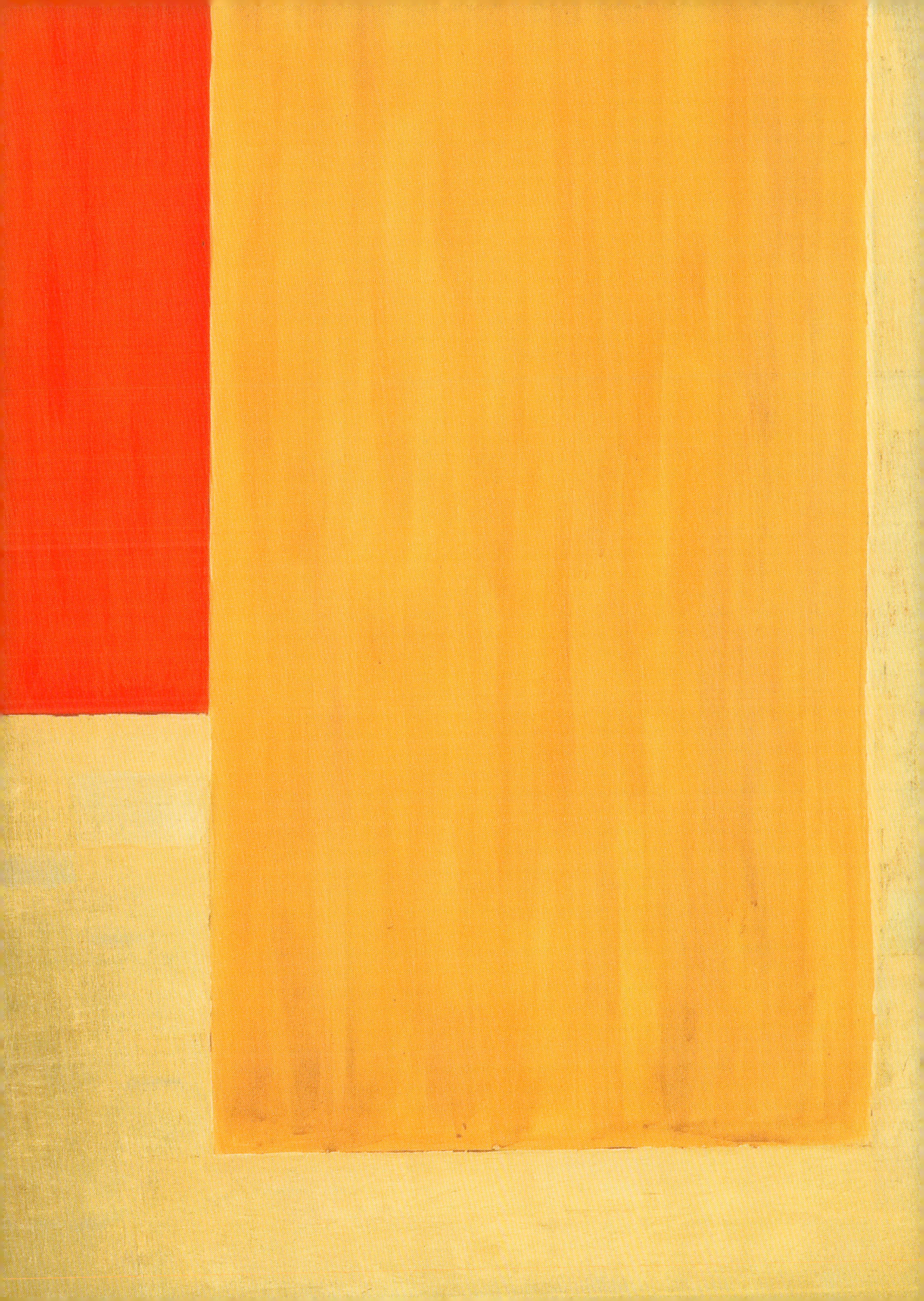

NOTEBOOKS

I think that the study of theoretical physics will give me some insight into what to paint. Trying desperately to get a better view of reality and what they are saying is that we can never see it. All of "matter" is symbolic and math is just describing the interactions of energies—all interconnected and held together by the glue of "that which is" and all the same. How can a painting be a symbol of that truth?

—Mary Obering, December 31, 1984

$\frac{1}{2}$ $12\frac{1}{2}''$ $17.5 \cdot 1.75 \cdot 1.6$ 1.75

$12\overline{)17.5}$ $4\overline{)7}$ $\times 20$ $\frac{4}{7.00}$

$\underline{12}$ $\frac{4}{30}$ 6.0 3 $1'9''$

$\underline{28}$ 20

$1' \times 2\frac{1}{2}''$ grey green

close

off white vermillion

$6 \times 3\frac{1}{2}''$
$\times 3'$
yellowish orangish
peachish etc.

grey green

close

vermillion
off white

black to brown $1'3\frac{1}{2}'' \times 2\frac{1}{2}'$

beige

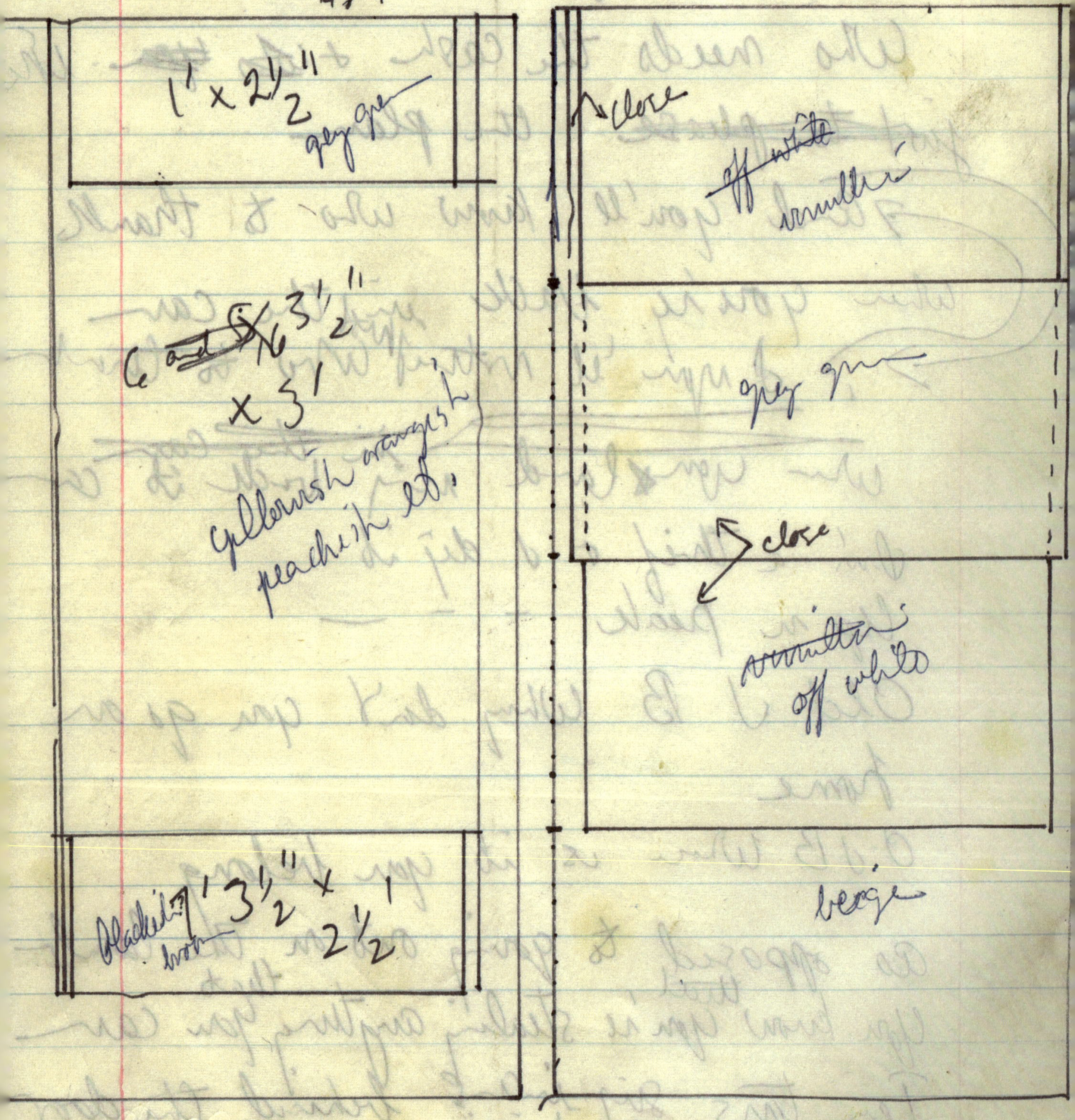

I AT and I dig it

9 ong it

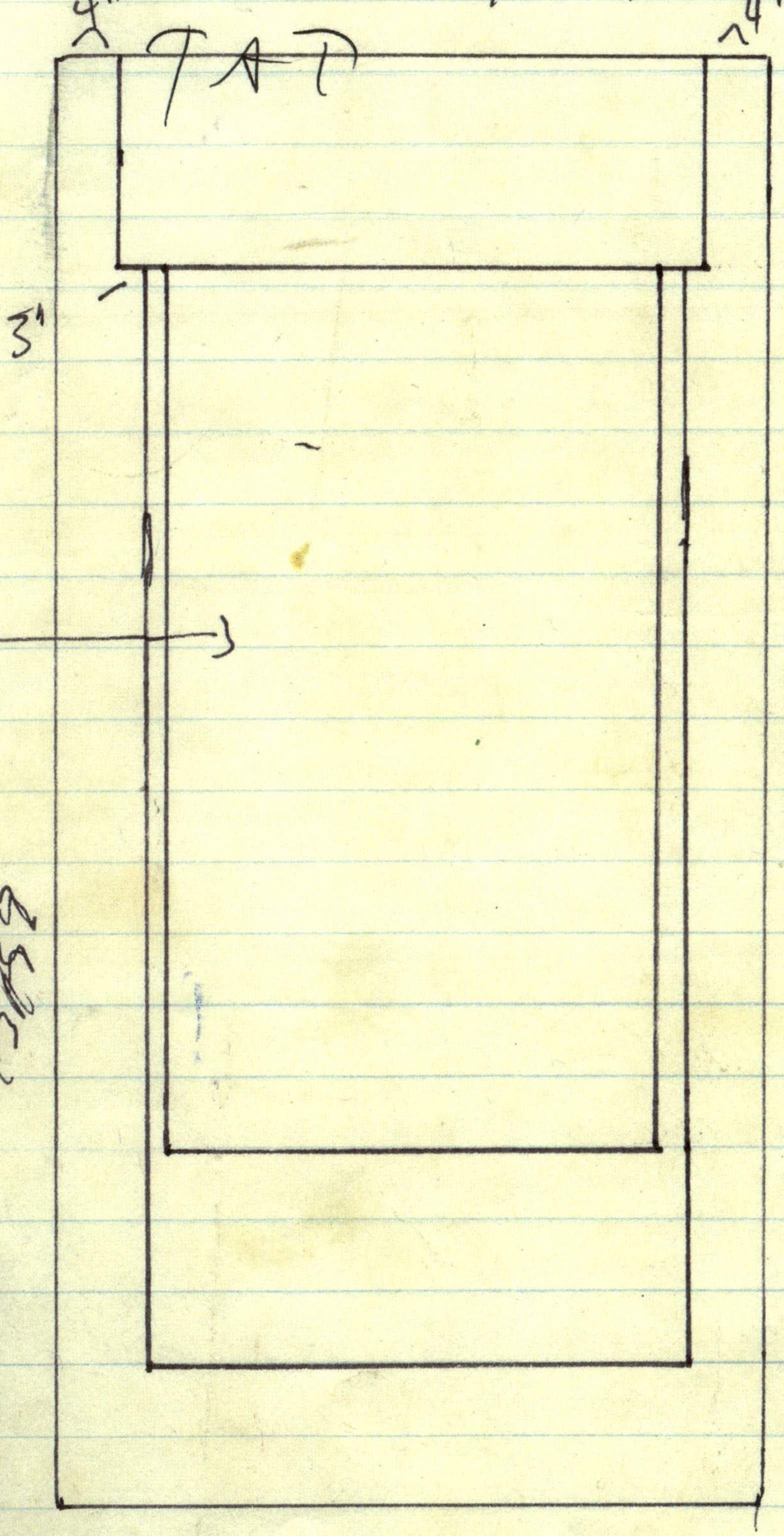

‟ ‟ ‟   4"   ^4"

I AT

3"

5'3" ———)
x 2'5"

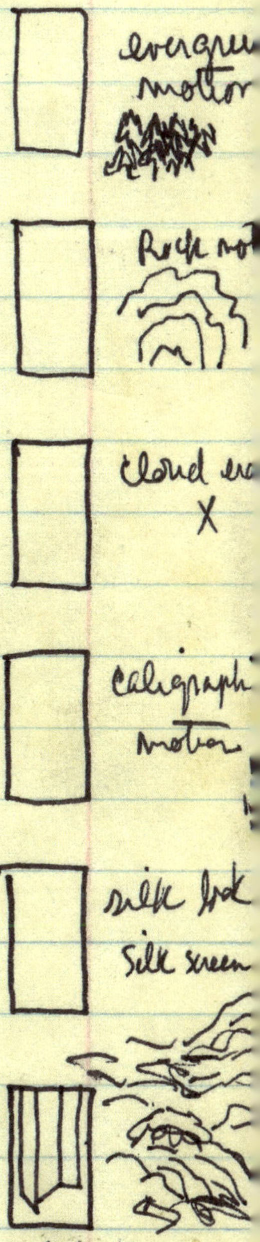

evergreen
mottoe

Rock mot...

cloud er
X

caligraph
mottoe

silk look
silk screen

wood cut look —

Colors, 1 beige (ocreist
2 palest pink
3 dull dk. turq.
4 dull grey grn
5 white

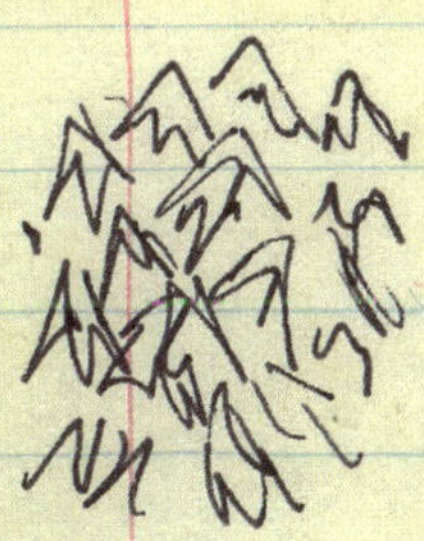

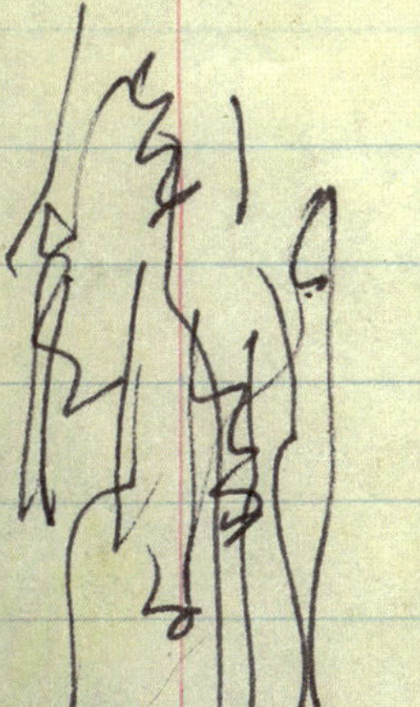

1 pink beige
2 grey
3 grey/grey grn
4 deep grn to black

1 black
2 yellow off white   7 combine
3 orange pink lt.
4 beige

1 beige
2 pale grey grn
3 vermilion
4 off white = dk. brown   or dull g...

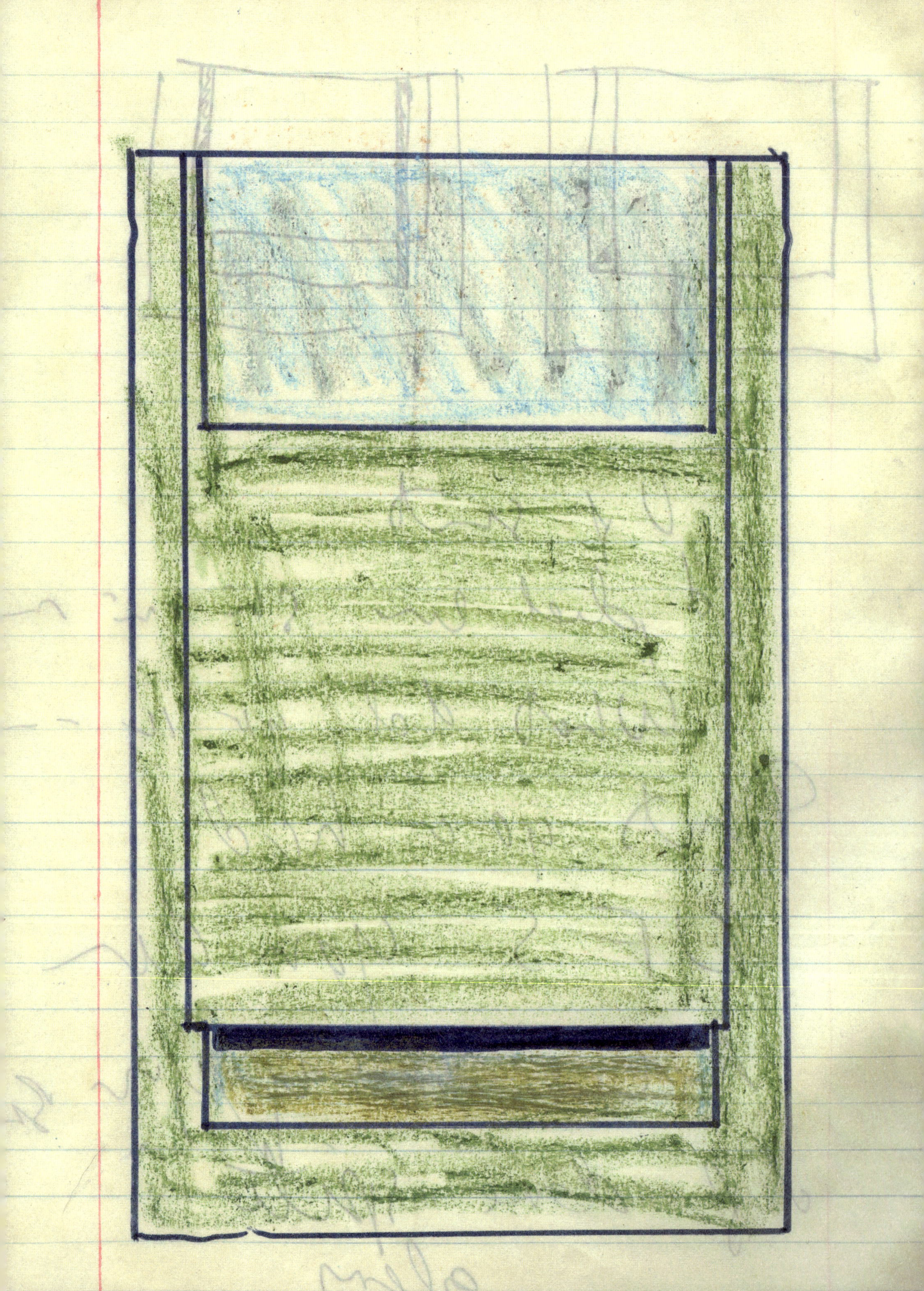

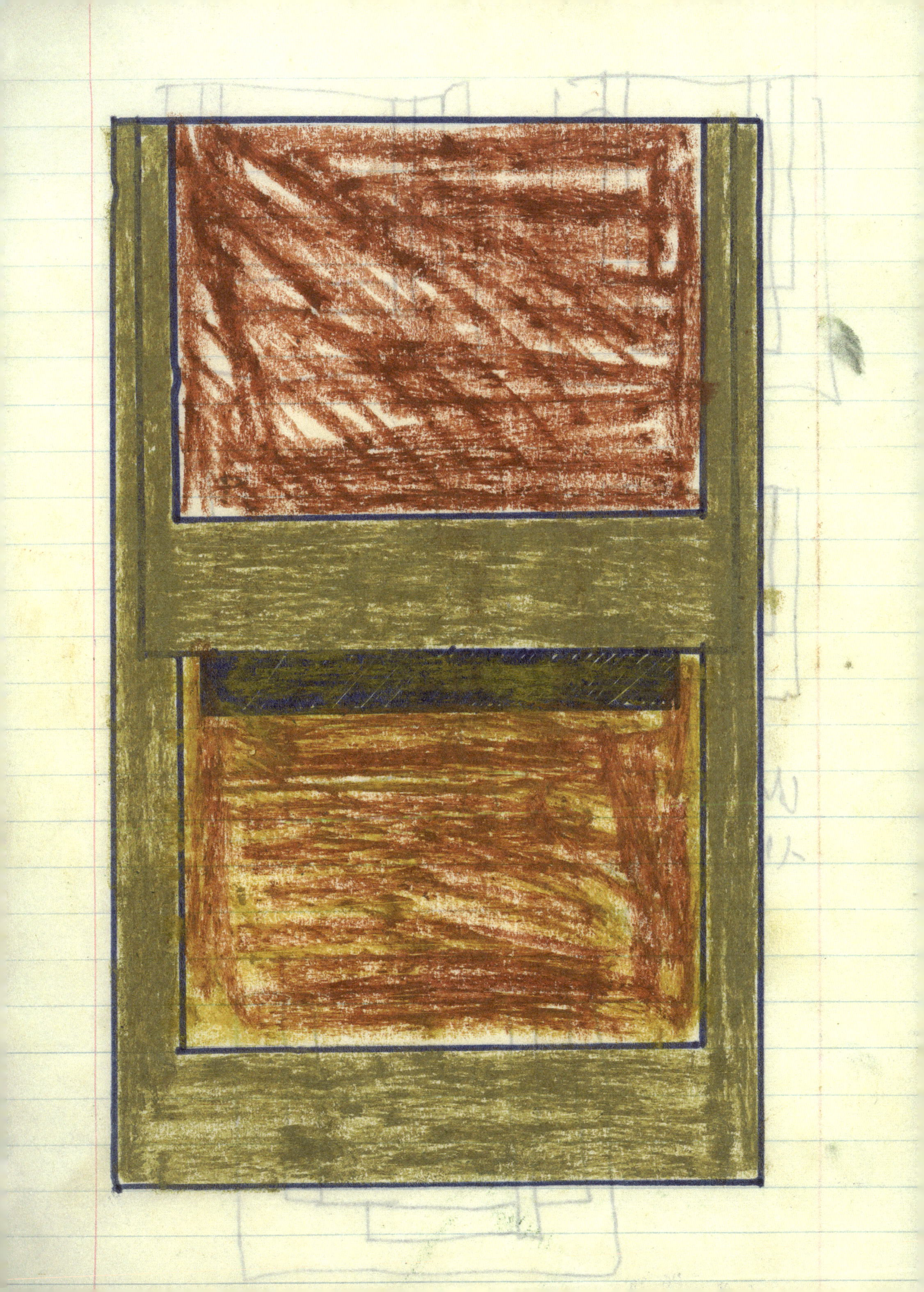

Arch-i-types

Problems ① Color

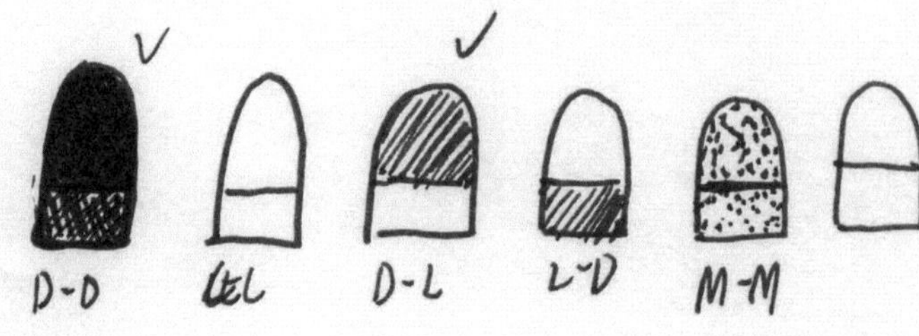

② #
1, 2, 3, 4, 5

③ Hts. of Lenyth

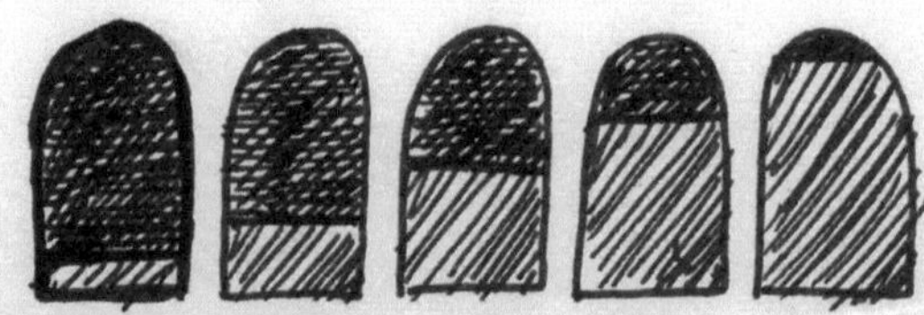

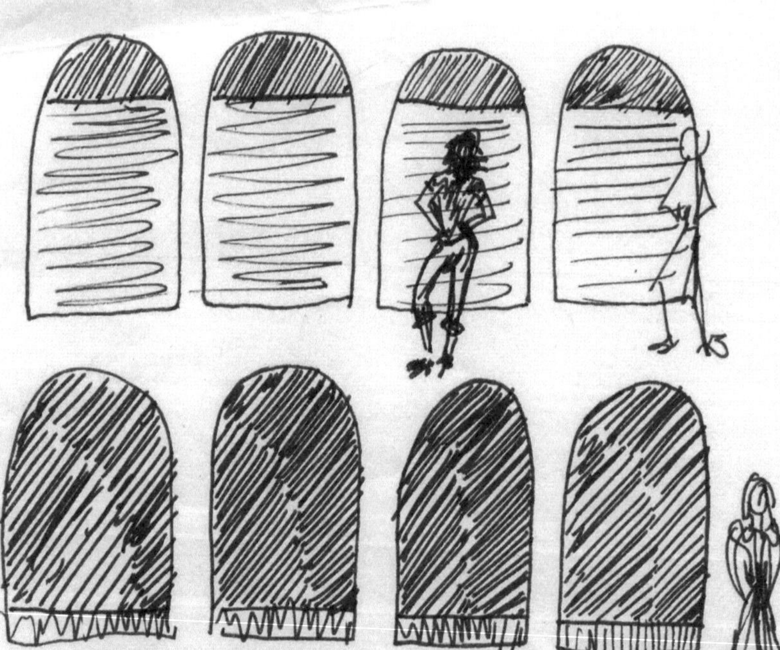

Other Possibilities

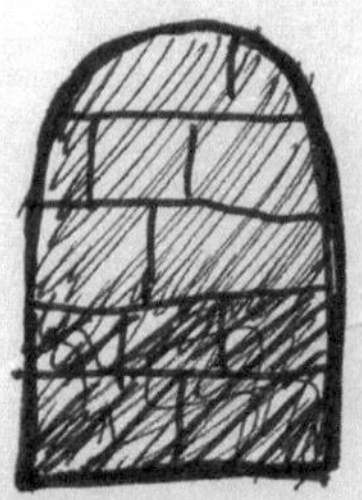 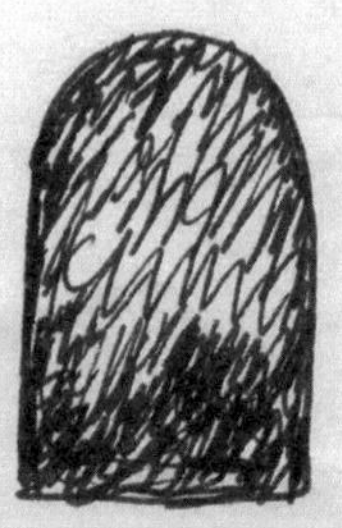 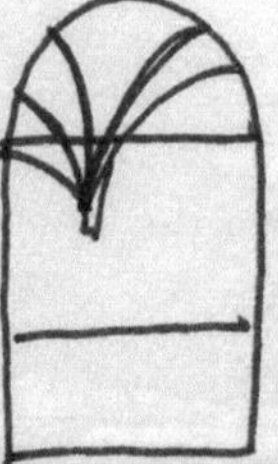 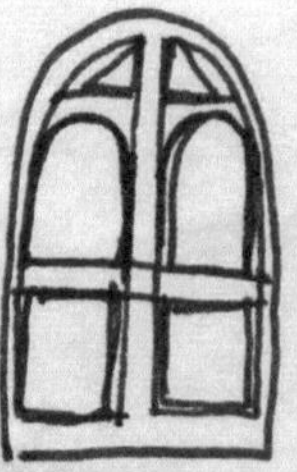 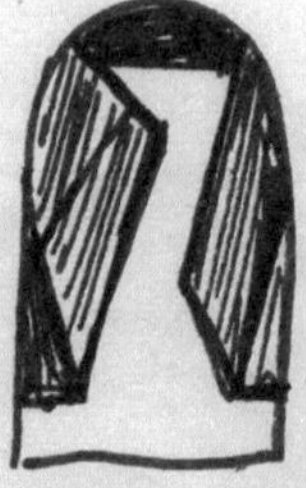 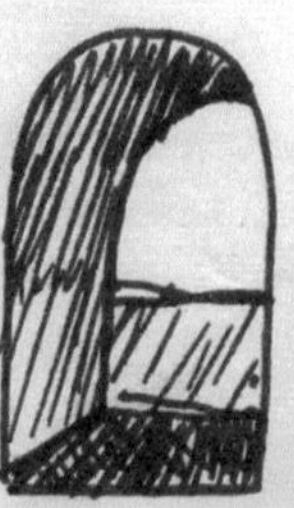 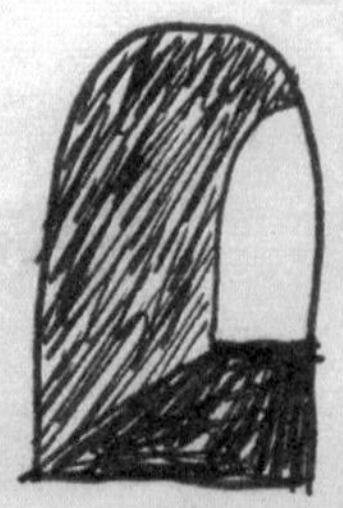

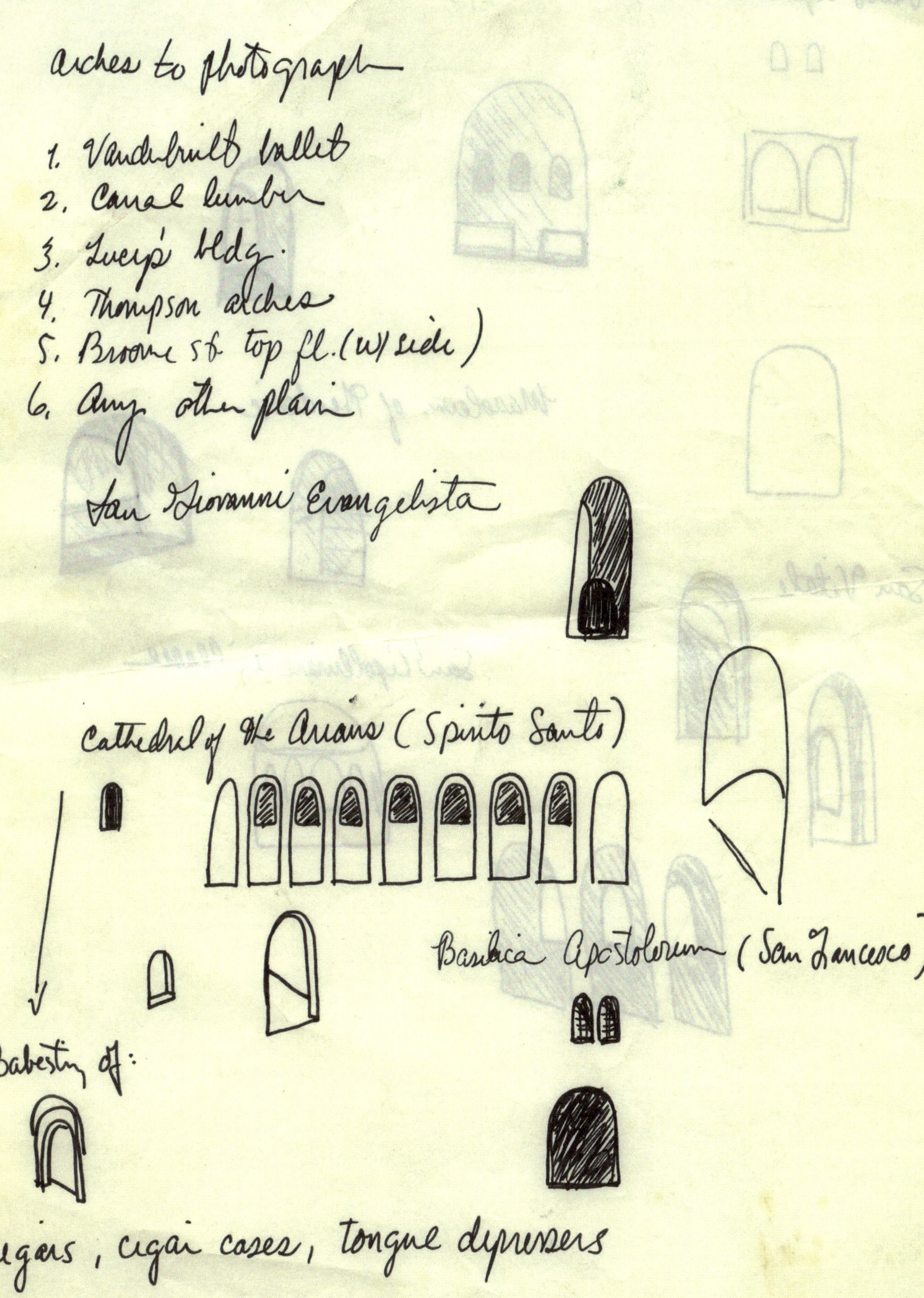

arches to photograph—

1. Vanderbuilt ballet
2. Canal lumber
3. Lueys bldg.
4. Thompson arches
5. Broome st top fl. (w/ side)
6. Any other plain

San Giovanni Evangelista

Cathedral of the Arians (Spirito Santo)

Basilica Apostolorum (San Francesco)

Baptistry of:

cigars, cigar cases, tongue depressers

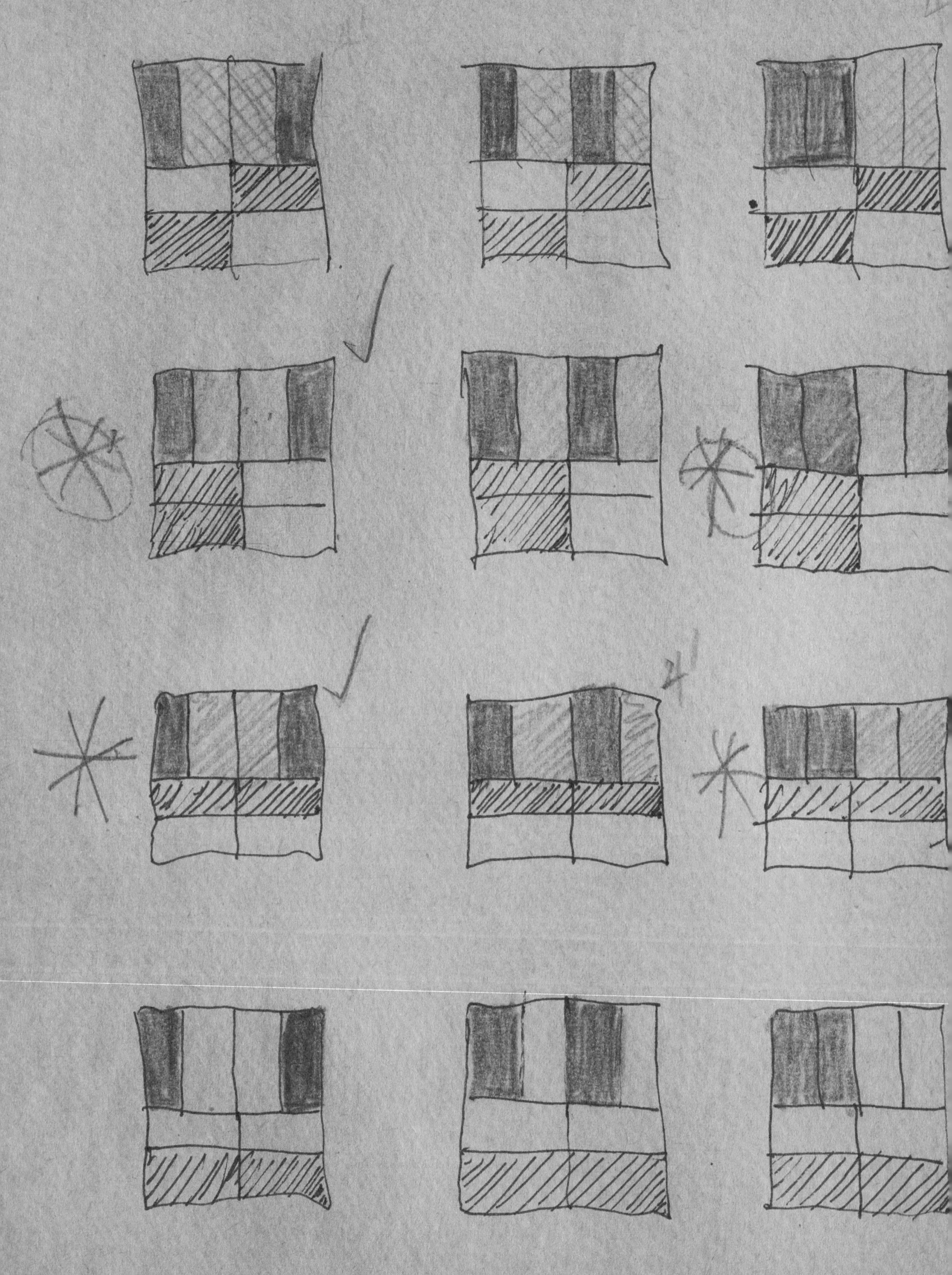

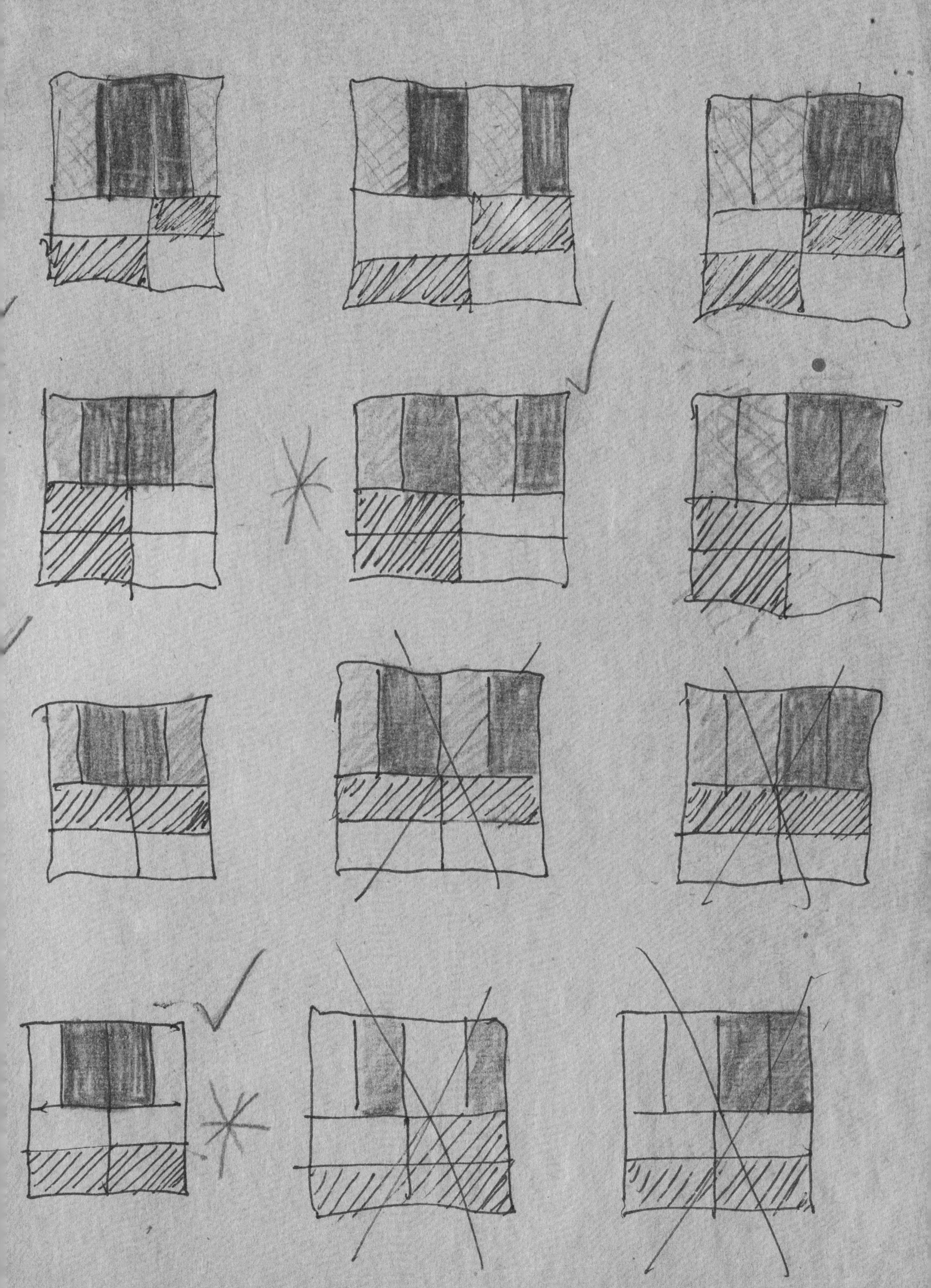

INSTALLATION IMAGES

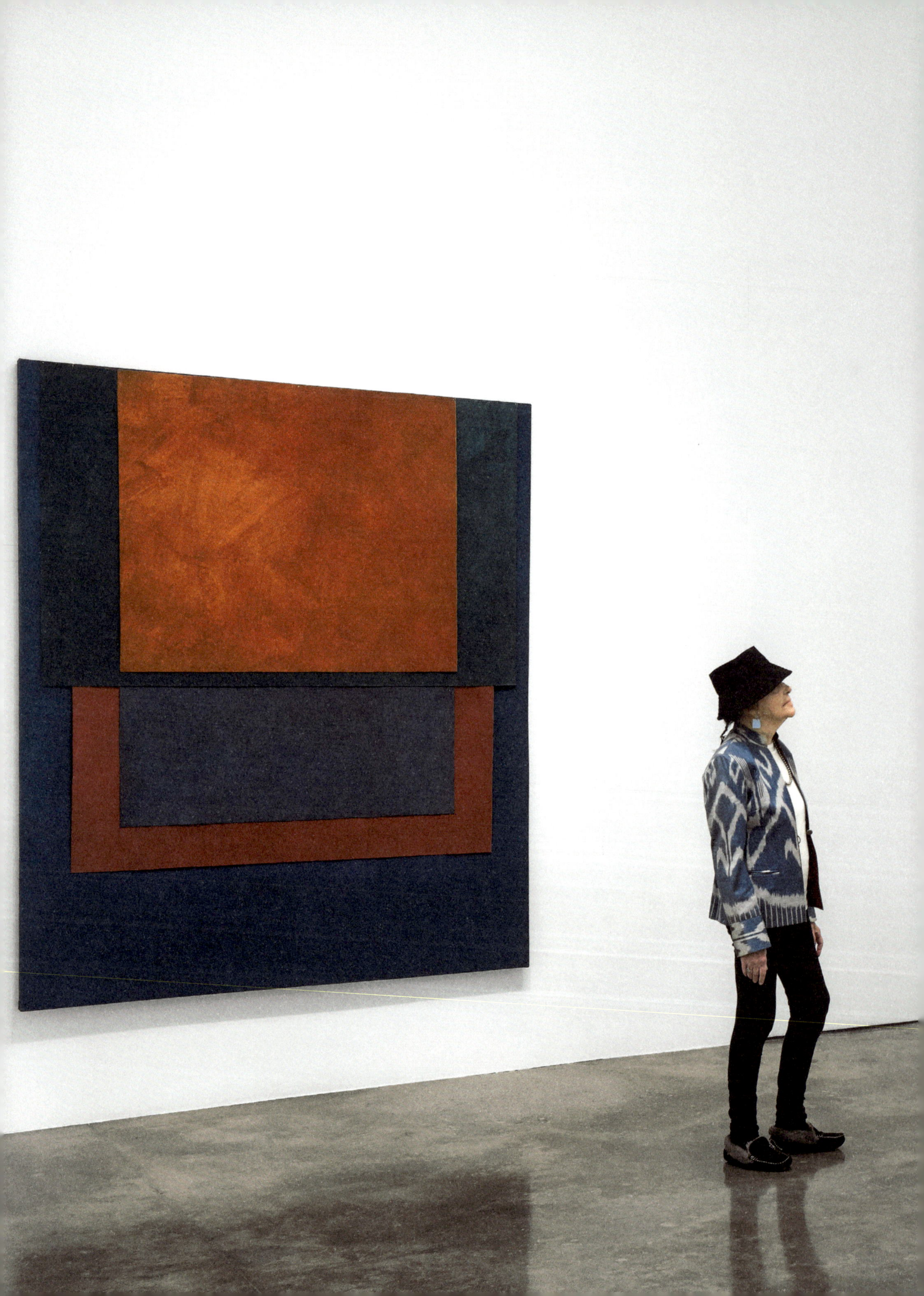

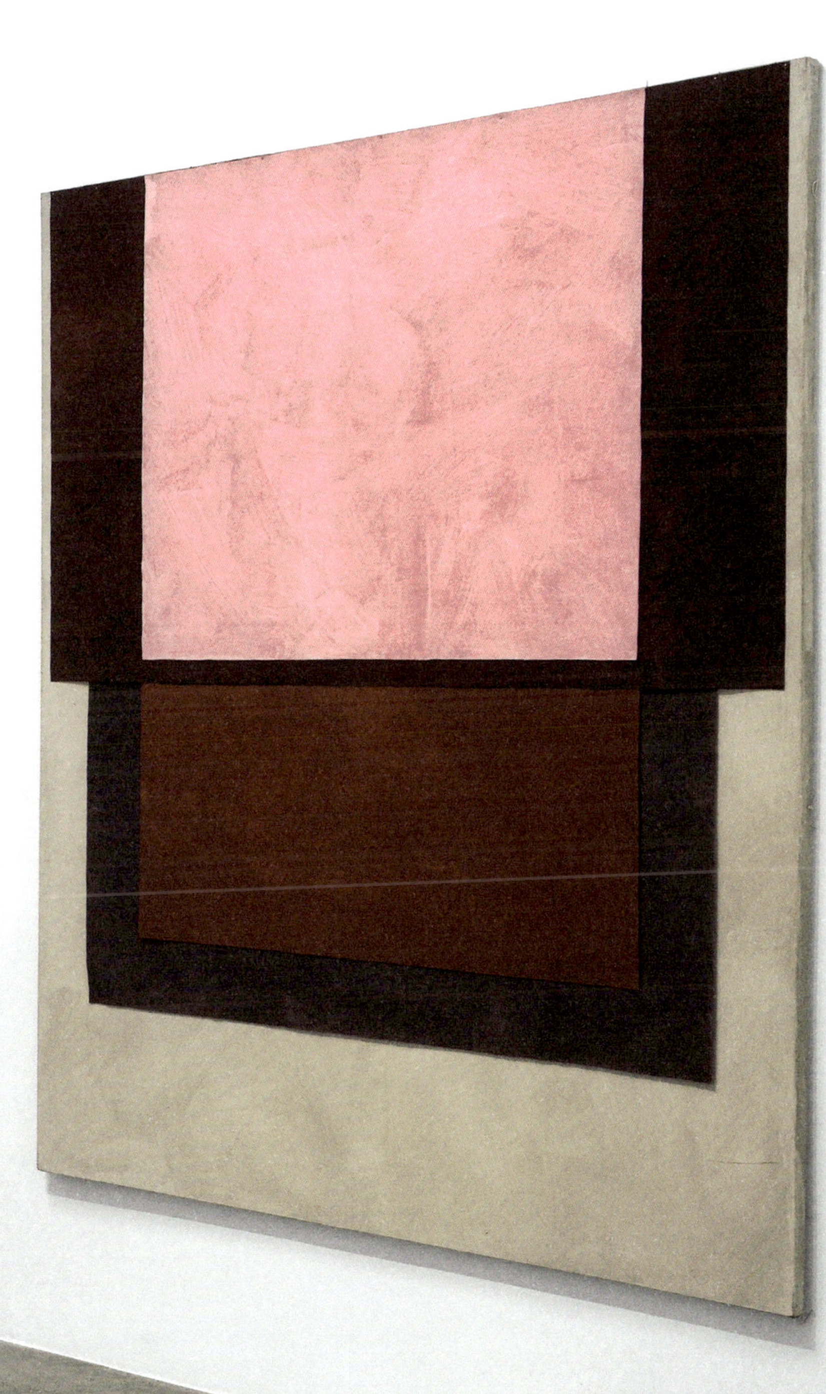

Mary Obering with her
1975 works at Kayne
Griffin Gallery, 2018

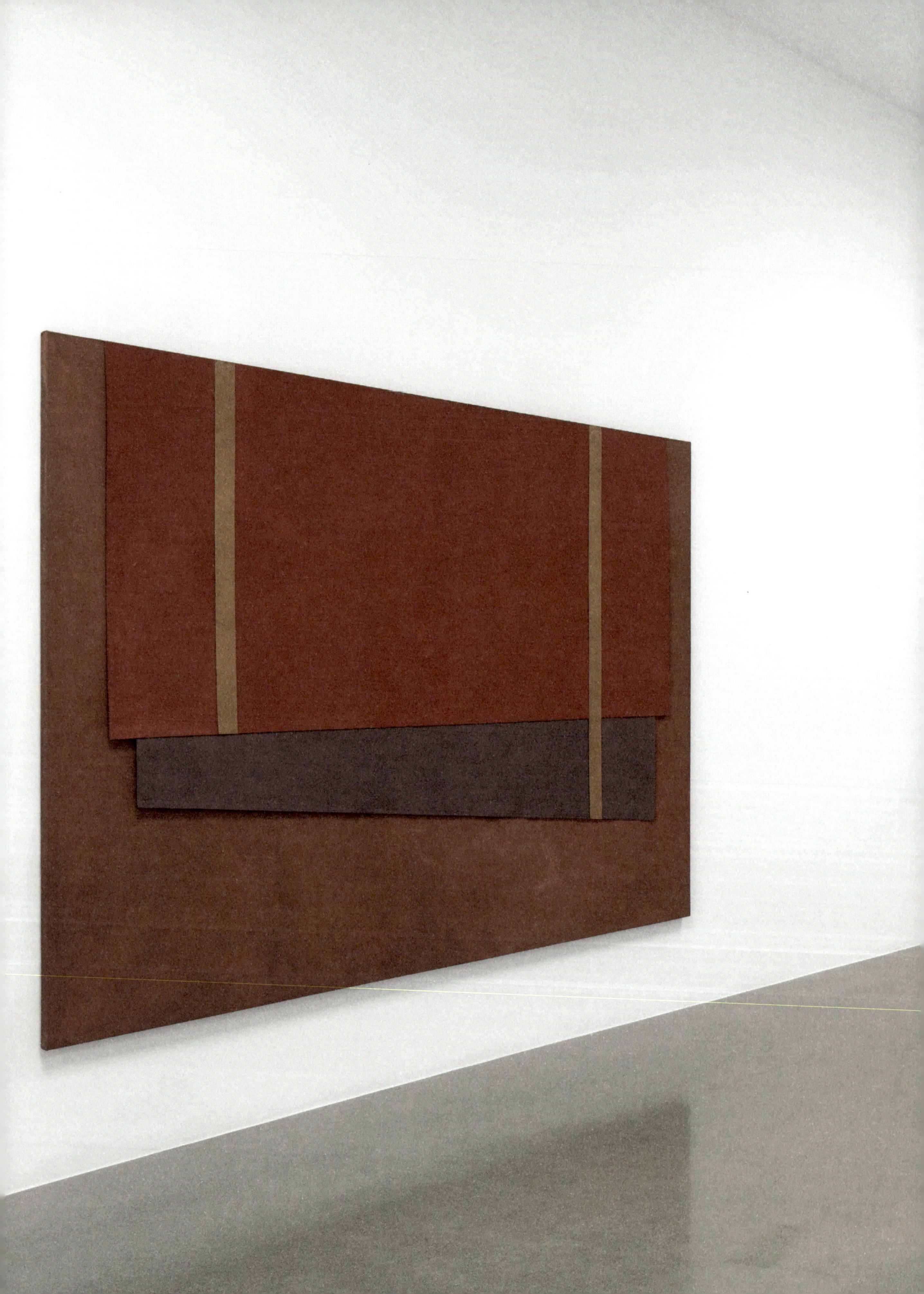

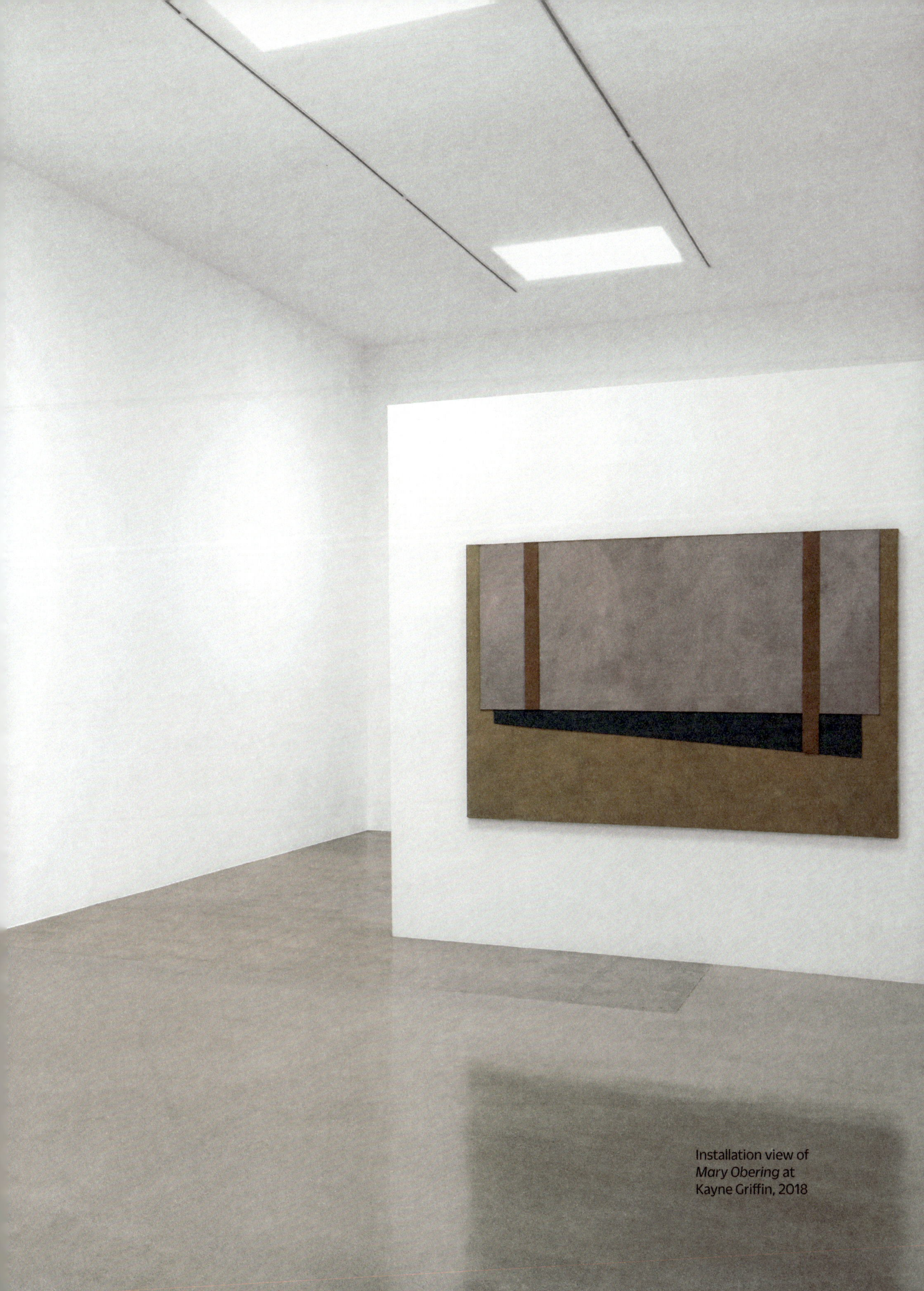

Installation view of
Mary Obering at
Kayne Griffin, 2018

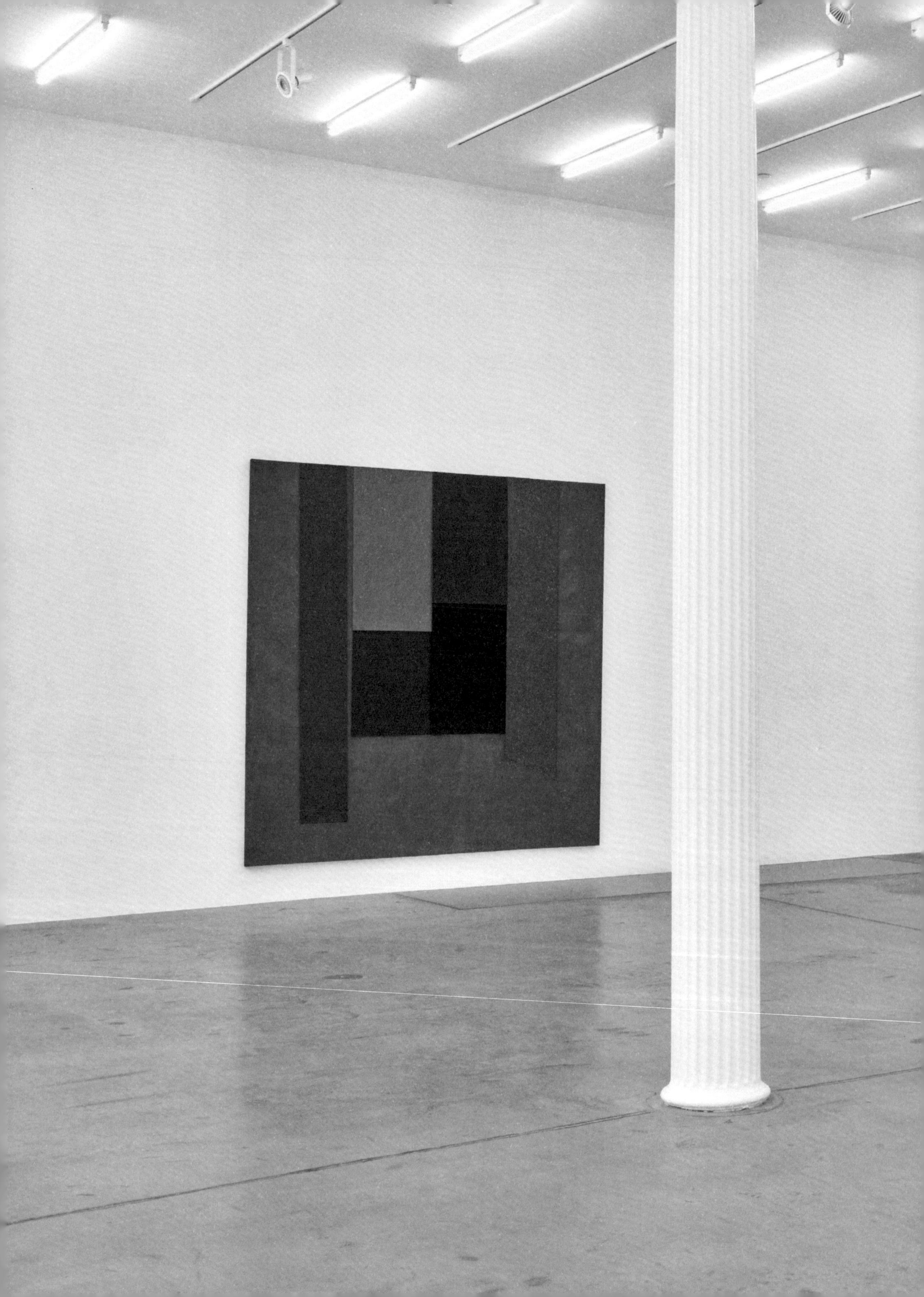

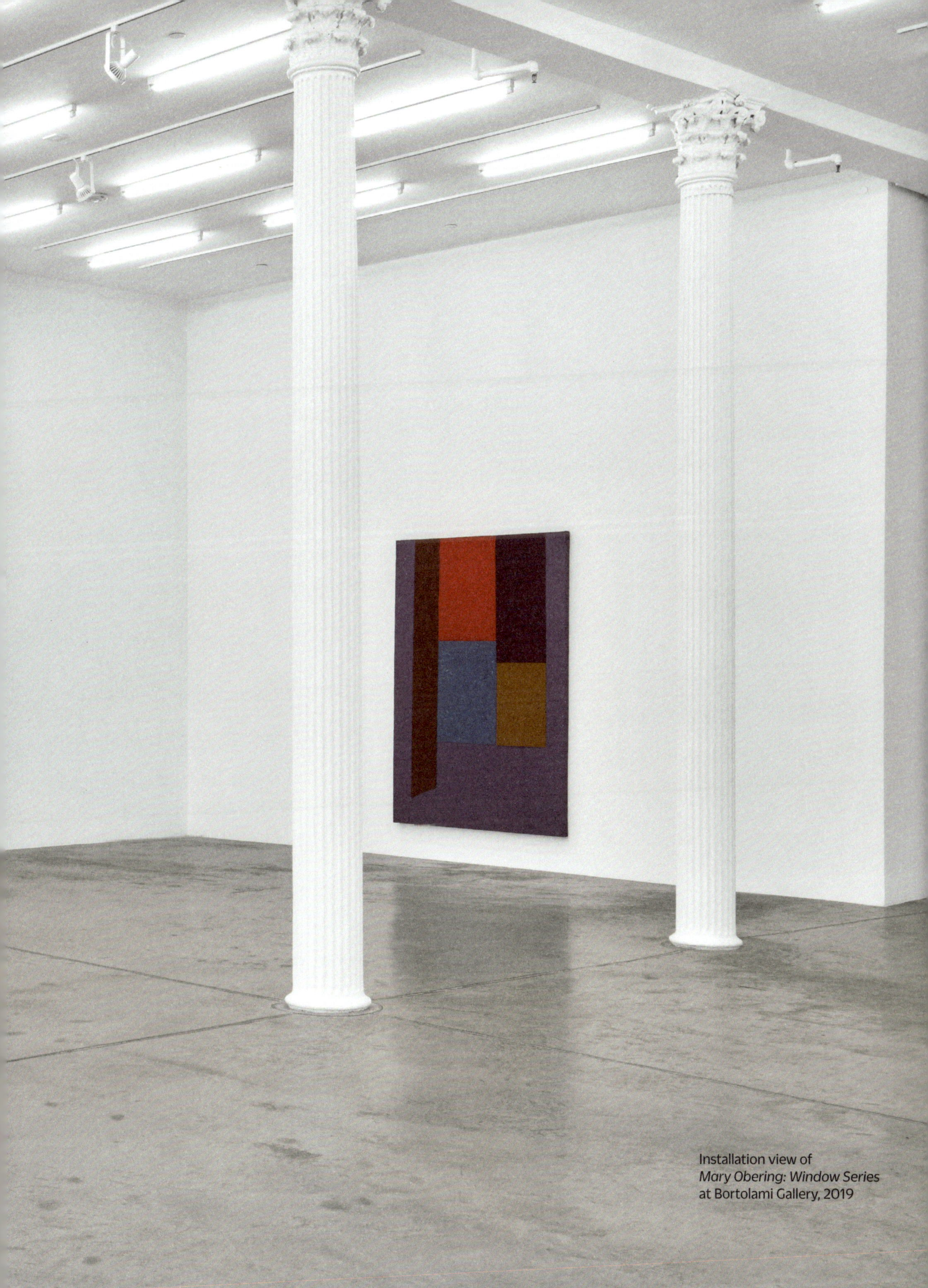

Installation view of
Mary Obering: Window Series
at Bortolami Gallery, 2019

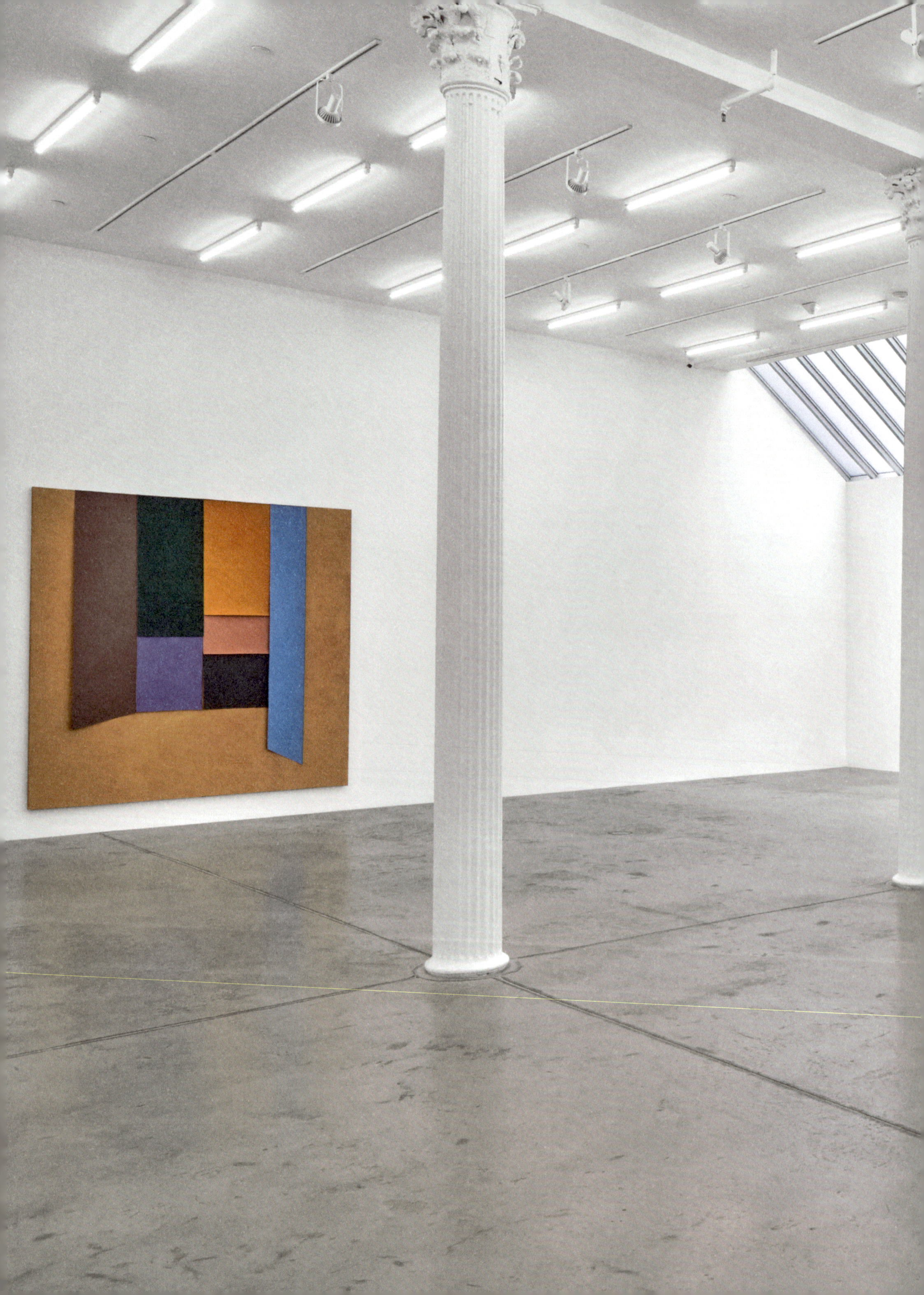

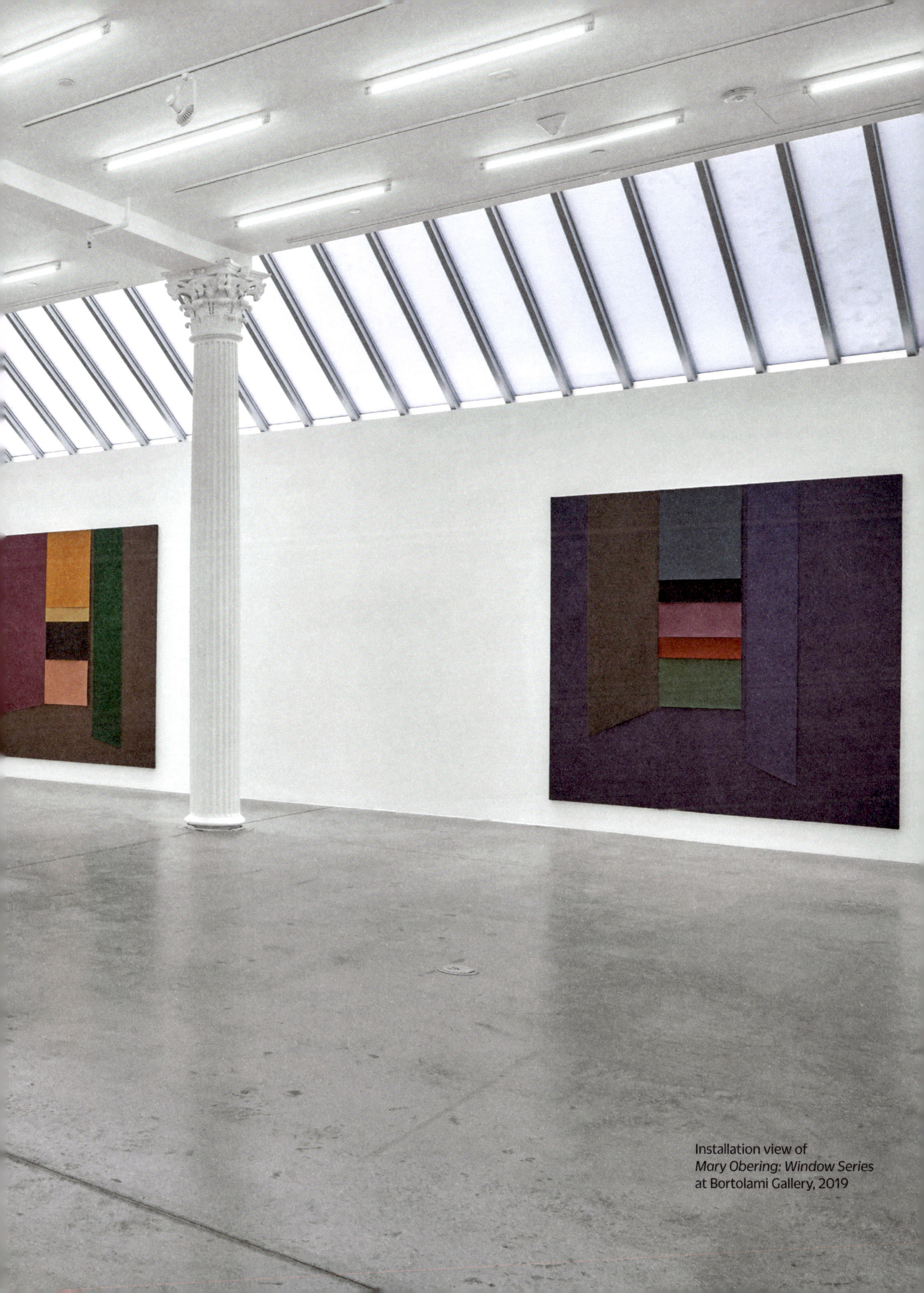

Installation view of
Mary Obering: Window Series
at Bortolami Gallery, 2019

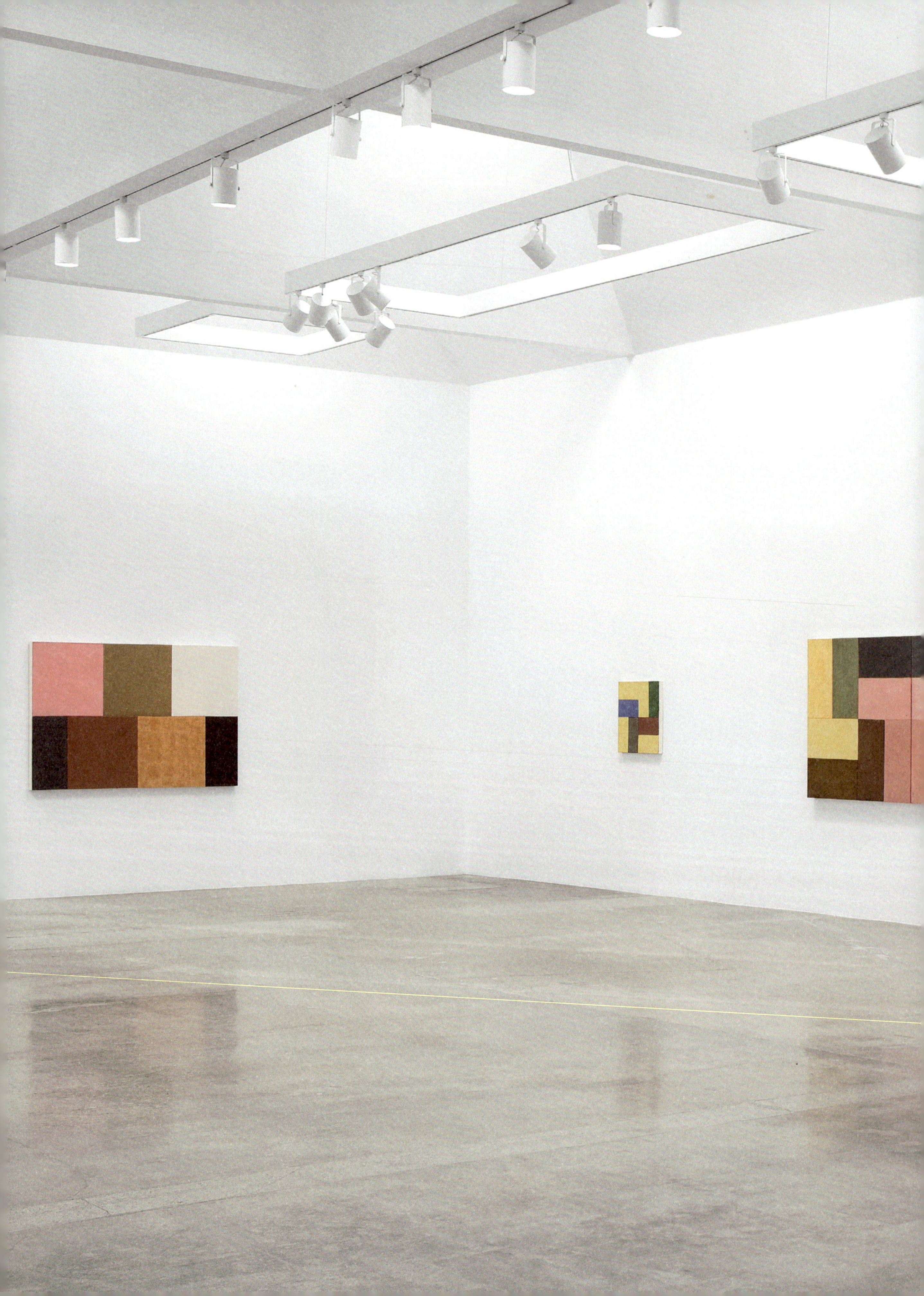

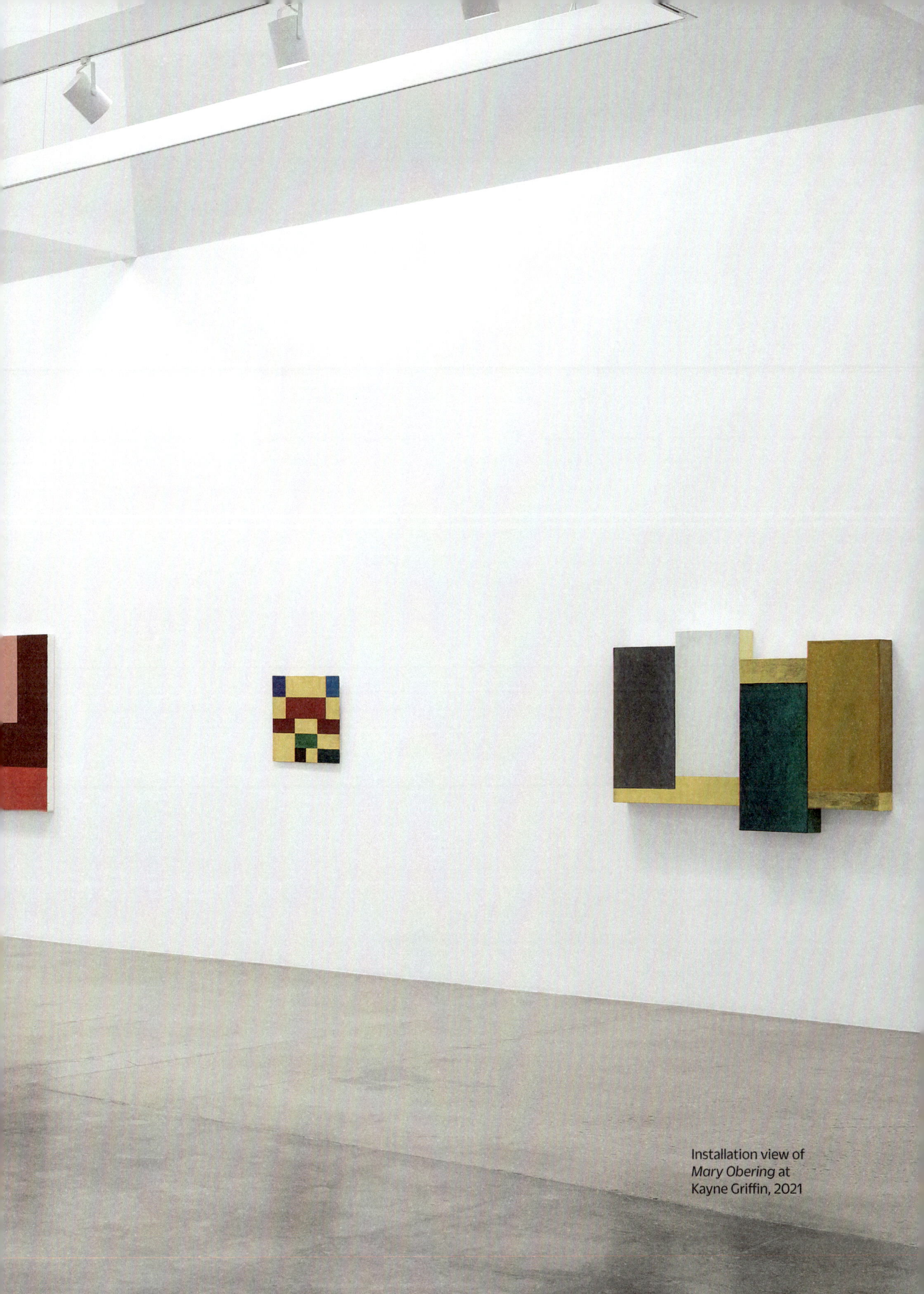

Installation view of
Mary Obering at
Kayne Griffin, 2021

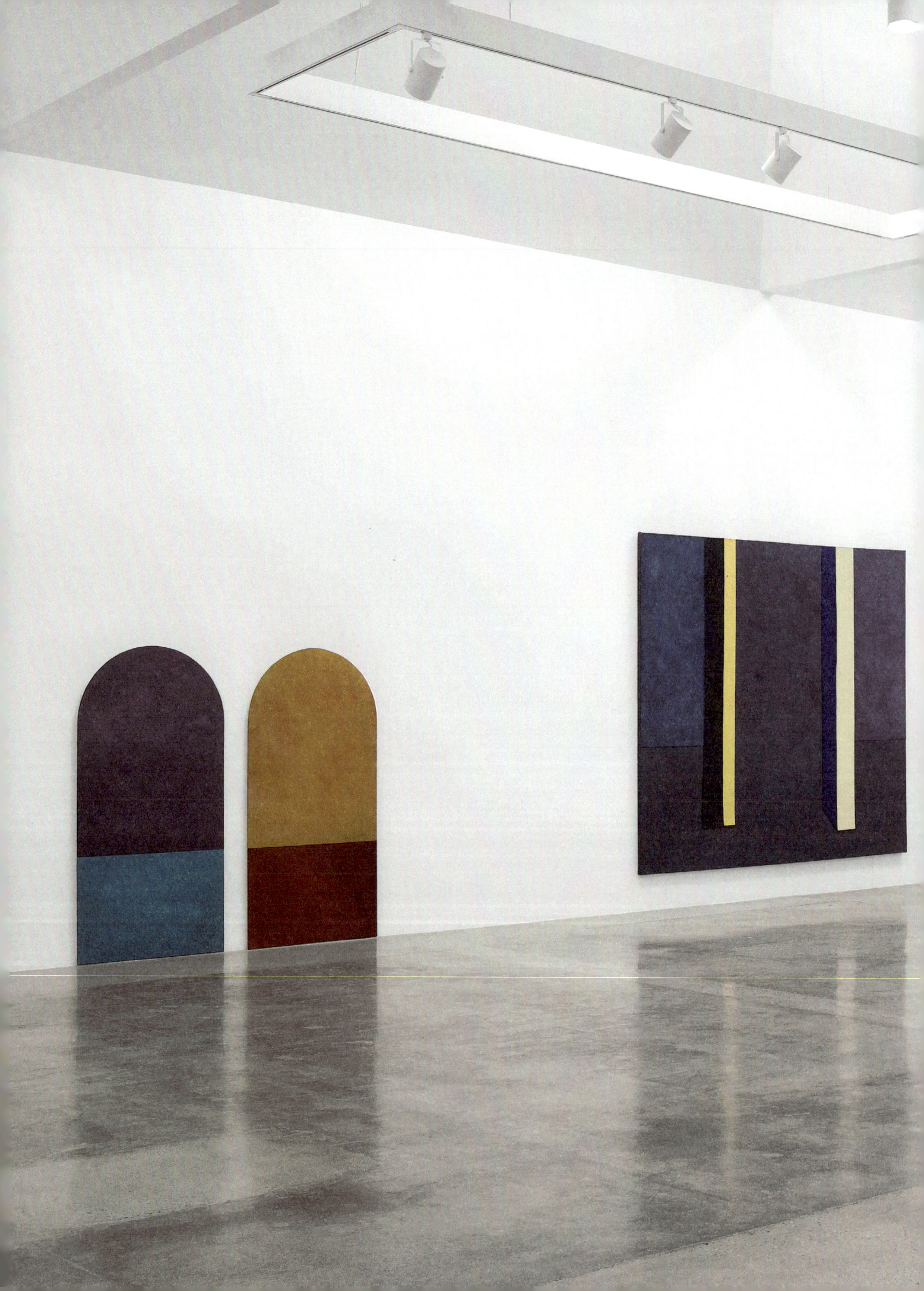

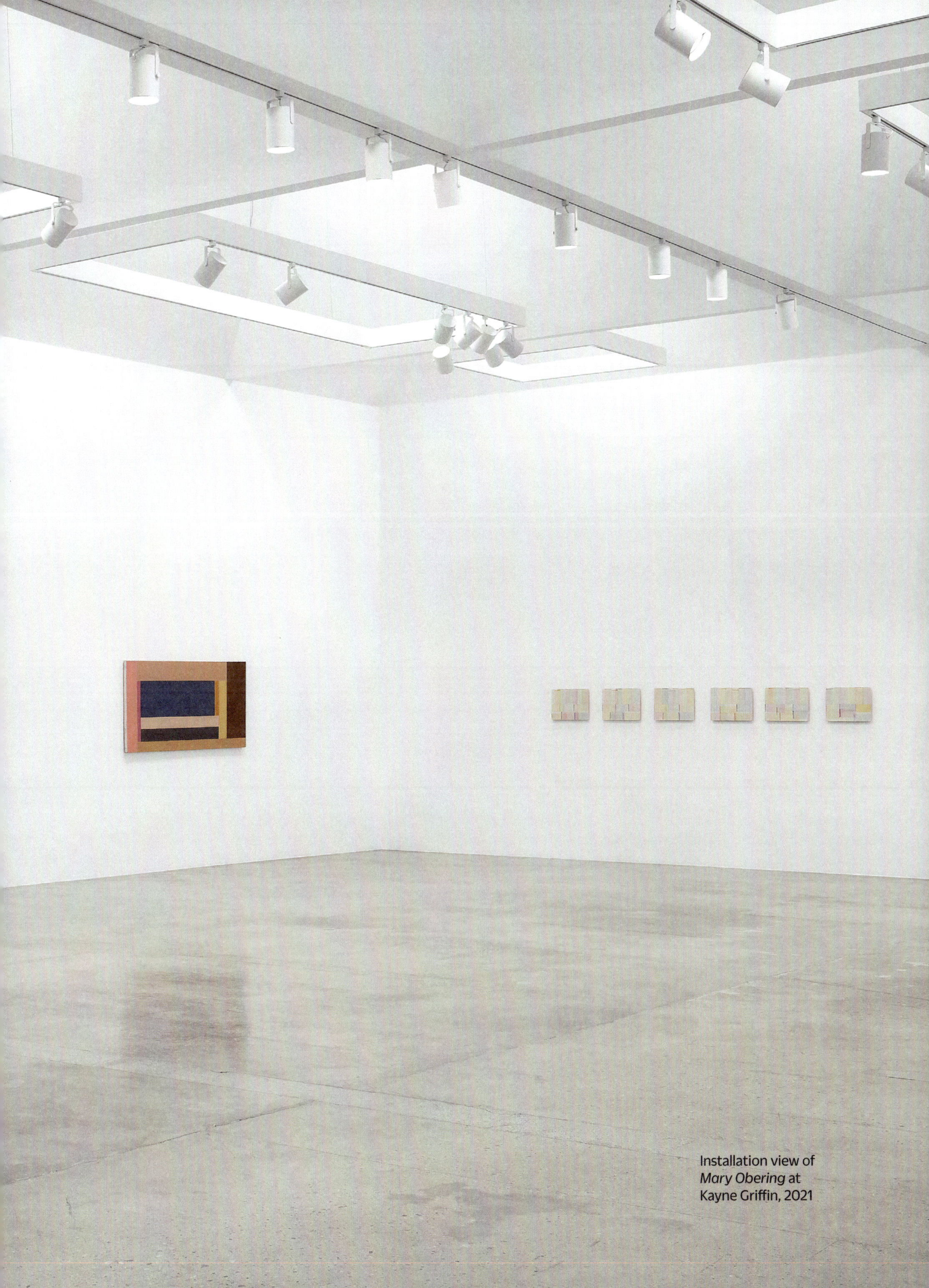

Installation view of
Mary Obering at
Kayne Griffin, 2021

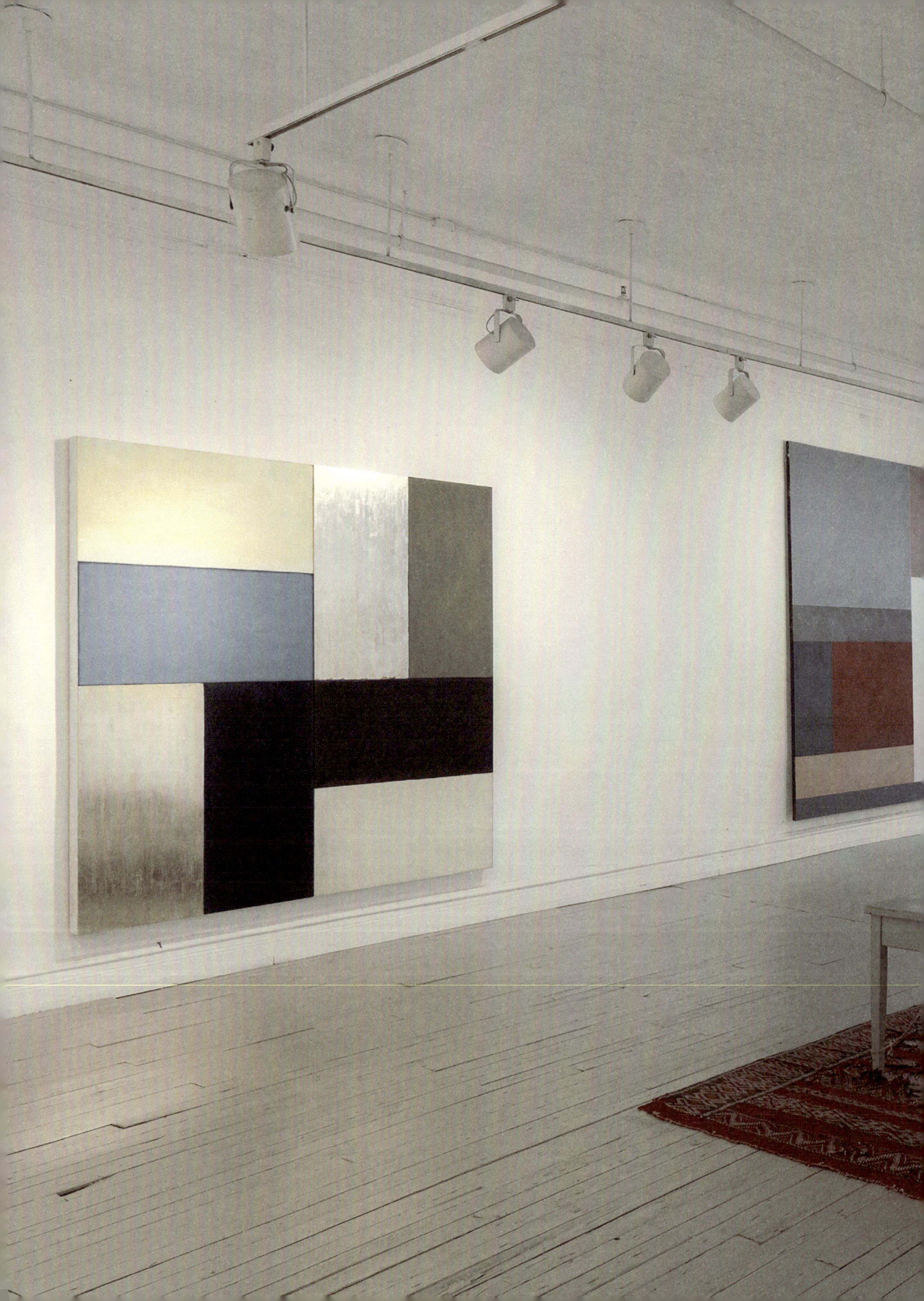

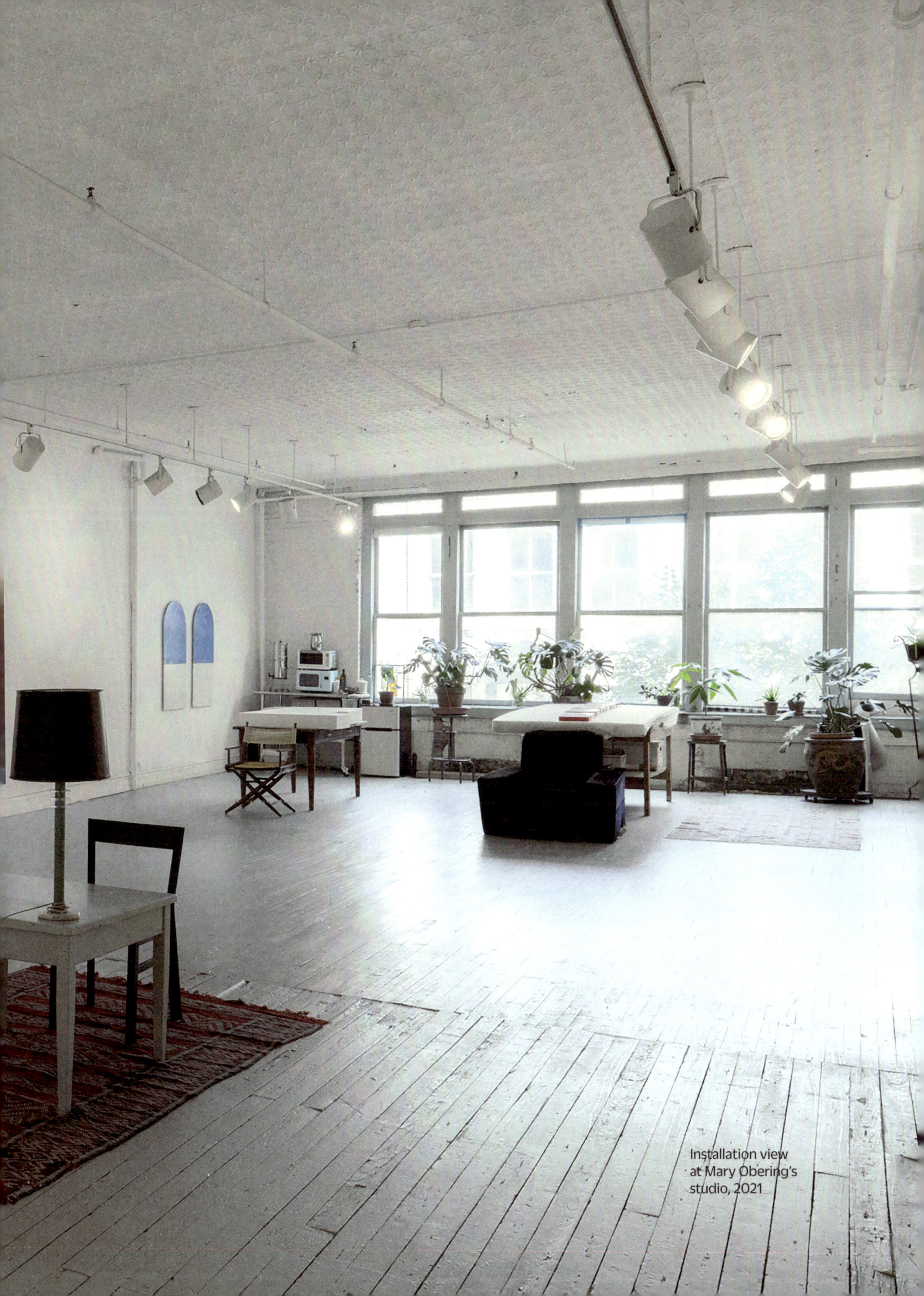

Installation view
at Mary Obering's
studio, 2021

MARY OBERING

Born 1937 Shreveport, LA
Lives and works in New York, NY

EDUCATION

1971 MFA, University of Denver, CO
1959 Graduate Study, Experimental Psychology, Radcliffe College at Harvard University, Cambridge, MA
1958 B.A. Psychology, Hollins College, Roanoke, VA

EXHIBITIONS

1968 Denver Jewish Community Center Gallery, Denver
Denver Art Museum, Denver
1969 Denver Art Museum, Denver

1970 University of Denver, Denver
1971 University of Colorado, Boulder
Great Western United Galleries, Denver (solo)
University of Denver Galleries, Denver (solo)
1972 *Andre, Holt, James, Miller,* Obering, John Weber Gallery, February, New York
Andre, Haacke, Holt, James, Miller, Obering, John Weber Gallery, November, New York
1973 *McArthur Binion, Jonathan Borofsky, Mary Obering,* Artists Space, New York (solo)
Aldrich Museum of Contemporary Art, Ridgefield, CT
1974 *New Work by Women Artists,* Civic Center Museum, Philadelphia
1975 Whitney Biennial, Whitney Museum of American Art, New York
Aldrich Museum of Contemporary Art, Ridgefield, CT
Soho Center for the Visual Arts, New York (solo)

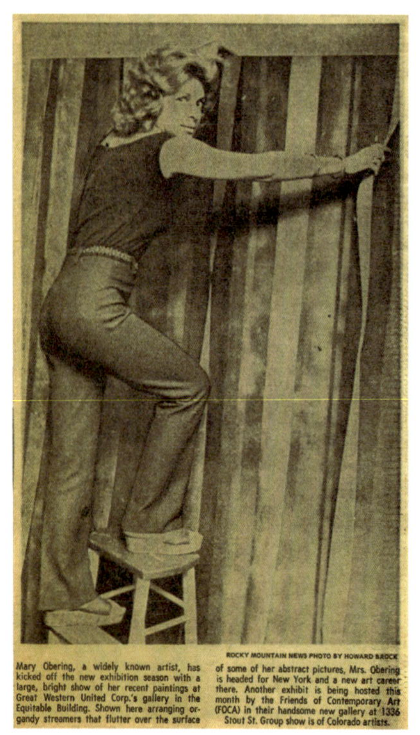

Rocky Mountain News, 1968

Artists Space, 1973

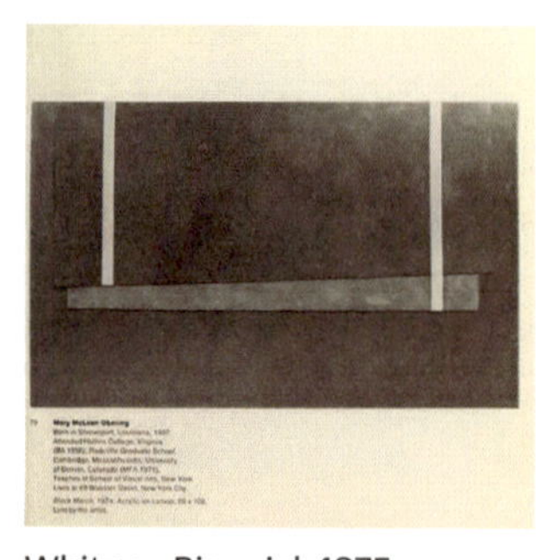

Whitney Biennial, 1975

1976 Hudson River Museum, Yonkers, New York
1977 $100 Gallery, New York
      Aldrich Museum of Contemporary Art, Ridgefield, CT
1978 Julian Pretto Gallery, New York
      Creative Artists Public Service Program, New York
1979 Julian Pretto Gallery, New York
1980 Sebastian Moore Gallery, Denver
      Interart Gallery, New York (solo)
1981 Julian Pretto Gallery, Weehawken, NJ
      Ben Shahn Museum, Wayne, NJ (solo)
1982 Steven Cardin Gallery, New York
      A.I.R. Gallery, New York
      C.D.S. Gallery, New York
1983 Julian Pretto Gallery, San Jose, Costa Rica (solo)
      Christminster Gallery, New York
      A.I.R. Gallery, New York
1984 C.D.S. Gallery, New York
      Gloria Luria Gallery, Bar Harbor Island, FL
      Christminster Fine Art, New York
1985 *American Abstraction: Four Currents*, Louis Meisel Gallery, New York
      Galeria de Arte Contemporaneo, San Jose, Costa Rica
1986 Julian Pretto Gallery, San Jose, Costa Rica (solo)
      American Abstract Artists Association, New York
      War Resisters League at 101 Spring Street Gallery, New York
1987 Julian Pretto Gallery, New York (solo)
      John Weber Gallery, New York

Condesco/Lawler Gallery, New York
City Gallery, (Department of Cultural Affairs), New York
1988 Annina Nosei Gallery, New York (solo)
      Julian Pretto Gallery, New York (solo)
      Museo de Arte Costarricense, San Jose, Costa Rica (solo)
      Group Show, Annina Nosei Gallery, New York
      Genovese Gallery, Boston
      Anne Plumb Gallery, New York
      Ruth Seigel Gallery, New York
1989 Plus-Kern Gallery, Brussels (solo)
      Annina Nosei Gallery, New York (solo)
      Julian Pretto Gallery, New York (solo)
      Ben Shahn Museum, Wayne, NJ
      C.D.S. Gallery, New York
      American Abstract Artists Association, 55 Mercer Street Gallery, New York
      Julian Pretto Gallery, New York
1990 Jan Turner Gallery, Los Angeles (solo)
      Julian Pretto Gallery, New York (solo)
      Bayley Museum, Charlottesville, VA
      Fashion Institute of Technology, New York
      New York Academy of Art, New York
      Edwin A. Ulrich Museum of Art, Wichita, KS
      Jan Turner Gallery, Los Angeles
      War Resisters League Benefit Exhibition, New York
      Julian Pretto Gallery, New York

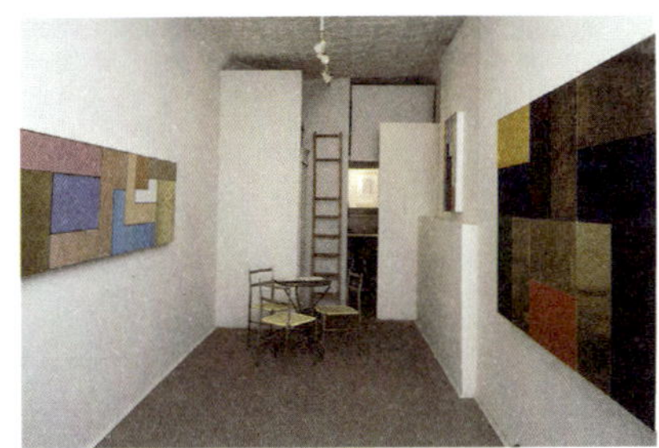

Julian Pretto, 1982

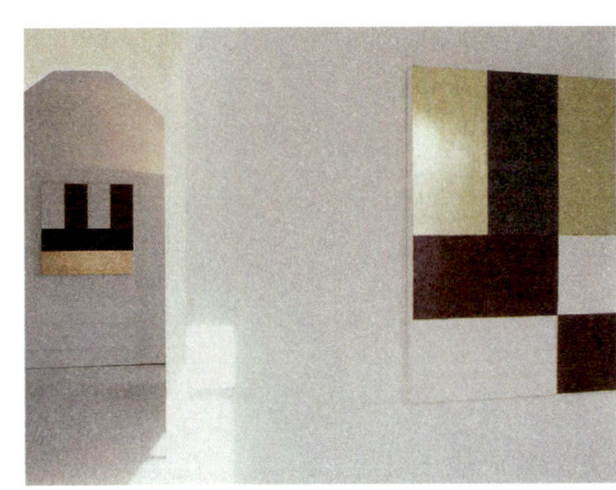

Julian Pretto, 1989

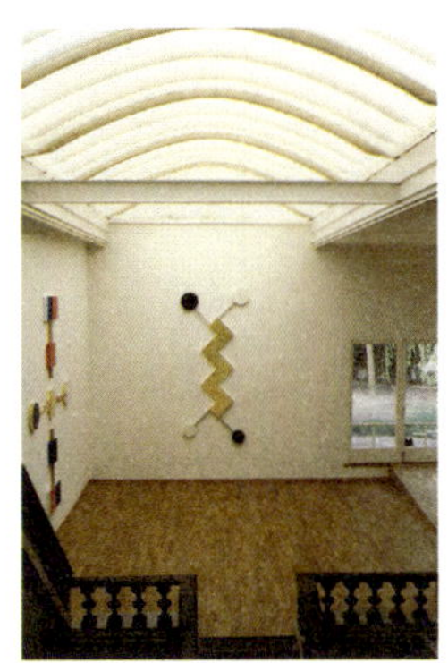

Plus-Kern, 1989

1991   Plus-Kern Gallery, Brussels (solo)
Julian Pretto Gallery, New York
(solo)
Julian Pretto Gallery, New York
1992   Jan Turner Gallery, Los Angeles
(solo)
The Artist's Mark, Wadsworth
Atheneum, Hartford, CT
American Abstract Artists, Ulrich
Museum of Art, Wichita, KS
Plus-Kern Gallery, Brussels
Julian Pretto Gallery, New York
1993   Julian Pretto Gallery, New York
(solo)
Pretto Gallery, New York
Wadsworth Atheneum, Hartford,
CT
Plus-Kern Gallery, Brussels
Natkin-Berta Gallery, Paris
1994   Jan Turner Gallery, Los Angeles
(solo)
Galerie Hugo Minnen, Antwerp
(solo)
Littlejohn/Sternau Gallery, New
York
Nelson Atkins Museum of Art,
Kansas City, MO
Association Culturale Hyphos,
Lecce, Italy
Noyes Museum, Oceanville, NJ
Vero Beach Museum, Vero Beach,
FL
1995   Littlejohn/Sternau Gallery, New
York (solo)
Museum of Fine Arts, Boston

CDS Gallery, New York
Littlejohn Contemporary, New York
1996   Primo Piano, Rome (solo)
Robin Rule Modern and
Contemporary Art, Denver (solo)
Wadsworth Atheneum, Hartford,
CT
James Howe Fine Arts Gallery, Kean
College, Union, NJ
Littlejohn Contemporary, New York
1997   Hugo Minnen Gallery, Antwerp
(solo)
Robin Rule Modern and
Contemporary Art, Denver
1998   White Creek Gallery, Salem, New
York
1999   Robin Rule Modern and
Contemporary Art, Denver (solo)
Exit Art, New York
2000   The Marfa Hotel, Marfa, TX (solo)
*Transparent, Translucent, Opaque:
Carl Andre, Melissa Kretschmer,
Mary Obering,* Galerie Frank, Paris
2001   Gallery 668, Greenwich, New York
(solo)
Ninni Esposito Arte
Contemporanea, Bari, Italy (solo)
Hunter College Art Gallery, New
York
2002   Museum of Contemporary Art
Denver, Denver
Swope Art Museum, Terre Haute,
IN
2003   Rule Modern and Contemporary
Art, Denver

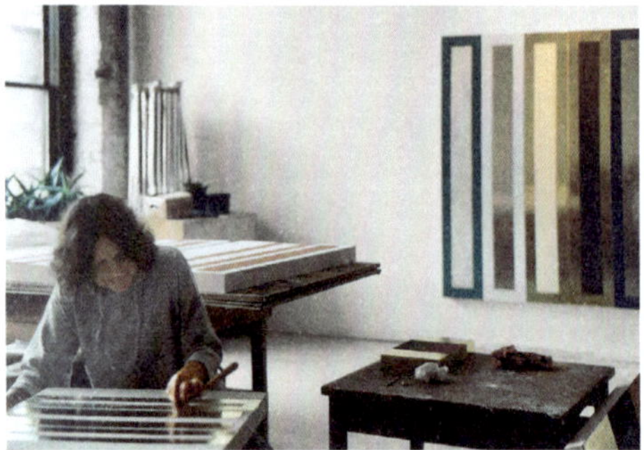

Mary Obering in her studio

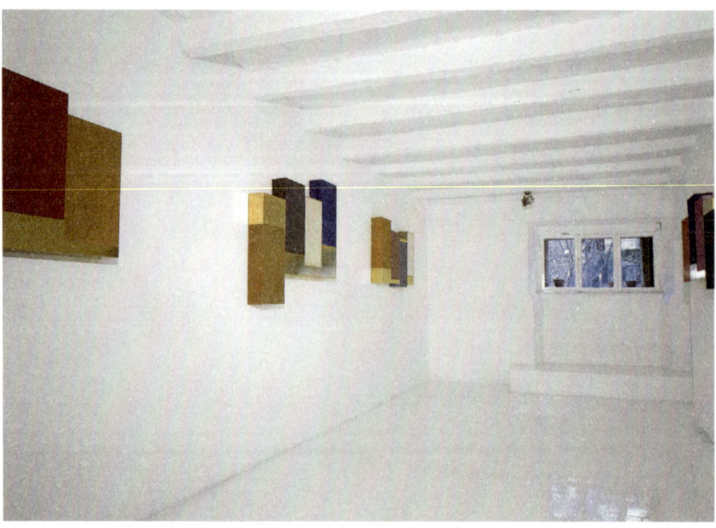

Primo Piano, 1996

2004   Gallery 668, Greenwich, NY (solo)
Mayo Center for Humanities in
Medicine, Scottsdale, AZ (solo)
Recent Paintings: Mary Obering,
Rule Modern and Contemporary
Art, Denver (solo)
2005   Gallery 668, Greenwich, New York
CDS Gallery, New York
2006   *Mary Obering,* Studio G7, Bologna,
Italy (solo)
*Carl Andre, Melissa Kretschmer,
Mary Obering, Doug Ohlson,*
Galleria Alfonso Artiaco, Naples
2007   Ninni Esposito Arte Conteporanea,
Bari, Italy (solo)
Paula Barr Chelsea, New York
2008   The Painting Center, New York
O.K. Harris, New York
2012   *Mary Obering,* Barbara Mathes
Gallery, New York (solo)
2013   *Works of the Jenney Archive,*
Gagosian Gallery, New York
Julian Pretto Gallery, Minus Space,
New York
2016   *Retrospettiva: Candeloro,
D'Agostino, Erben, Green, Tremlett,
Obering,* Studio G7,
Bologna, Italy
2017   *Mary Obering: Selected Works
1983-1987,* Marisa Newman
Projects, New York (solo)
Loretta Howard Gallery, New York
c.nichols Project, Los Angeles
2018   *Mary Obering,* Kayne Griffin
Corcoran, Los Angeles (solo)

2018   *Heads Roll,* Curated by Paul
Morrison, Graves Gallery, Sheffield,
UK
2019   *Mary Obering: Window Series, 1973,*
Bortolami Gallery, New York (solo)
2019   *Tempera,* Crystal Bridges Museum
of American Art, Bentonville, AR
2020   *Figures on a Ground: Perspectives
on Minimal Art*: Fondation CAB,
Brussels
2021   *Mary Obering,* Kayne Griffin, Los
Angeles (solo)
Mary Obering, Gana Art, Seoul
(solo)
2022   *Mary Obering,* Bortolami Gallery,
New York (solo)

PUBLIC COLLECTIONS

Detroit Institute of Art
Fogg Museum, Harvard University
The Hecksher Museum of Art
The Museum of Fine Arts, Boston
The Metropolitan Museum of Art
The Museum of Modern Art
Perez Art Museum, Miami
University of Michigan Museum of Art
Yale University Art Gallery
Walker Art Center
Wellin Museum of Art
Whitney Museum of American Art

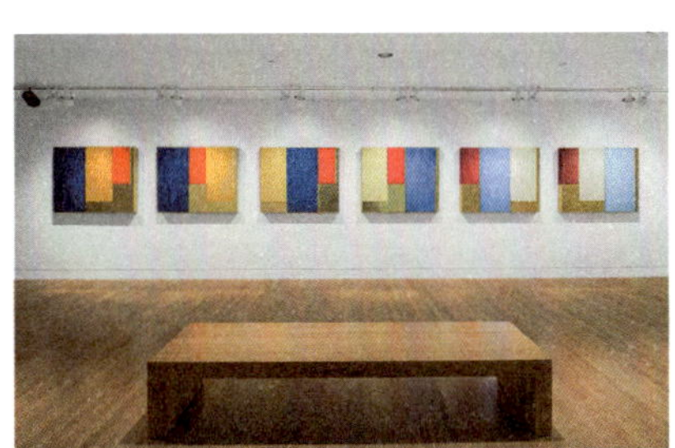

Crystal Bridges Museum, 2019

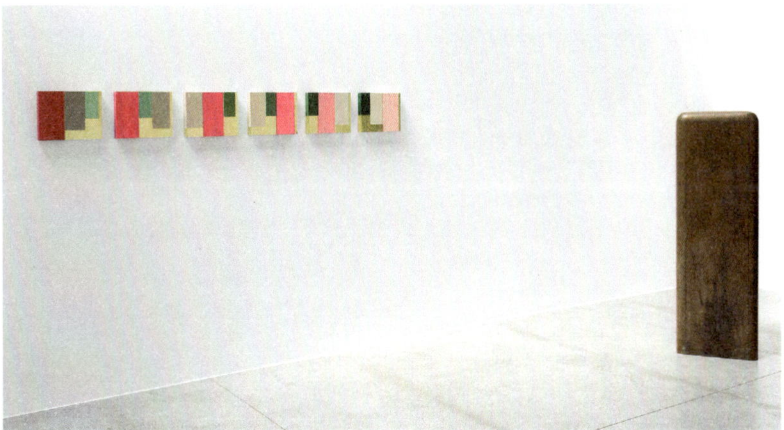

Art Fondation CAB, 2020

BIOGRAPHY

For the last fifty years, Mary Obering has painted geometric abstract compositions exploring the essence of color through the lens of reductivism.

In her early works from the 1970s, she explored color and space by creating monochrome fields of color in acrylic on canvas. She then cut the canvases into horizontal and vertical panels that she attached, one on top of the other, onto a large-scale monochrome field. This idea of layering, of creating space with minimal two-dimensional color field relationships, can be thought of in the broader context of painting in New York at the time, but also through the enduring influence of Josef Albers and his investigations of shape and color.

With the rise in New York in the 1970s of multimedia, performance, and the broadening influence of Conceptual art, painting seemed to be under siege. However, a group of New York painters, Obering among them, were radically returning to traditional methods of application. At this critical time in the history of painting, a shift in her technique occurred. Obering moved away from canvas and began to employ the old master process of egg tempera and gold leaf on gessoed panel. Her interest in these materials first developed when she experienced Renaissance paintings as a child on a trip to Italy—a place she would return to often. Additionally, the technical aspect of painting with these materials appealed to Obering's interest in scientific engagement, and she has subsequently employed these methods to explore scientific concepts such as particle physics and natural phenomena—a nod to her graduate studies at Harvard in the late 1950s.

Obering was born in 1937 in Shreveport, Louisiana. She received a BA in Experimental Psychology at Hollins College and her MA in Behavioral Science studying under B. F. Skinner at Harvard. In 1971, she received an MFA from the University of Denver. She has lived and worked in New York City since 1971. Obering's works have been included in exhibitions at 1975 Whitney Biennial, New York; the Museum of Fine Art, Boston; Artists Space, New York; the Wadsworth Atheneum, Hartford, Connecticut; the Denver Art Museum; and the Nelson-Atkins Museum, among others. Her works are in the permanent collections of major institutions, including the Whitney Museum of American Art, the Detroit Institute of Art, the Museum of Fine Arts, Boston, and the Wadsworth Atheneum.

CONTRIBUTORS

LYNN ZELEVANSKY is an art historian, curator, and writer living in New York. From 2009 to 2017, she was the Henry J. Heinz II Director of Carnegie Museum of Art. There she co-curated *Hélio Oiticica: To Organize Delirium* (2016–17) and *Paul Thek: Diver* (2010–11) and instituted a variety of new participatory and experimental programs. Previously, she was the Terri and Michael Smooke Curator and head of the contemporary art department at the Los Angeles County Museum of Art. Among the many exhibitions she organized or co-organized there were *Love Forever: Yayoi Kusama, 1958–68* (1998) and *Beyond Geometry: Experiments in Form, 1940s–1970s* (2004). Prior to arriving in Los Angeles in 1995, Zelevansky was a curatorial assistant in the Department of Painting and Sculpture at the Museum of Modern Art, New York, where she organized *Projects* shows for artists such as Gabriel Orozco (1993) and Cildo Meireles (1990), and curated *Sense and Sensibility: Women Artists and Minimalism in the Nineties* (1994). Zelevansky has published widely on modern and contemporary art.

MATTHEW L. LEVY is Associate Professor of Art History at Penn State Behrend. He is the author of *Abstract Painting and the Minimalist Critiques: Robert Mangold, David Novros, and Jo Baer in the 1960s* (Routledge, 2019). He is currently working on a book project about David Novros' murals and site-specific works.

ACKNOWLEDGMENTS

There are many people we would like to thank and appreciate for making this publication happen. A huge thank you goes to Mary's daughter, Amanda Obering, who was extremely helpful and encouraging throughout this process. We also owe plenty of thanks to Katherine Driscoll, who we relied on for research, fact checking, and more, and without whom this project would not have been possible. Our appreciation goes out to Philippe, gold conservator extraordinaire, who prepared Mary's work for photography. We would also like to extend our gratitude to Matthew Levy and Lynn Zelevansky for the beautiful words and the time put toward Mary's artwork. Finally, our gratitude goes to Bill Griffin, Maggie Kayne, Genevieve Day, John Zinonos, and Emma Skinner at Kayne Griffin, and Stefania Bortolami and Loreta Lamargese at Bortolami Gallery for the realization of this book, Mary Obering's first monograph.

Mary Obering
is published by Inventory Press,
Kayne Griffin, and Bortolami Gallery

Inventory Press
2305 Hyperion Avenue
Los Angeles, CA 90027
inventorypress.com

Kayne Griffin
1201 South La Brea Avenue
Los Angeles, CA 90019
310 586 6886
kaynegriffin.com

Bortolami Gallery
39 Walker Street
New York, NY 10013
212 727 2050
bortolamigallery.com

Editor
Eugenia Bell

Design
IN-FO.CO (Adam Michaels,
Marina Kitchen, Dani Grossman)

Color Separations
Echelon

Printed and Bound in Belgium
by die Keure

ISBN: 978-1-941753-49-1
LCCN: 2021948575

Distributed by
ARTBOOK | D.A.P.
75 Broad Street, Suite 630
New York, NY 10004
artbook.com